W9-BFR-259

The History of the Supreme Court
Part III

From the Warren Court to the Rehnquist Court

Professor Peter Irons

THE TEACHING COMPANY ®

PUBLISHED BY:

THE TEACHING COMPANY
4151 Lafayette Center Drive, Suite 100
Chantilly, Virginia 20151-1232
1-800-TEACH-12
Fax—703-378-3819
www.teach12.com

Copyright © The Teaching Company Limited Partnership, 2003

Printed in the United States of America

This book is in copyright. All rights reserved.

Without limiting the rights under copyright reserved above,
no part of this publication may be reproduced, stored in
or introduced into a retrieval system, or transmitted,
in any form, or by any means
(electronic, mechanical, photocopying, recording, or otherwise),
without the prior written permission of
The Teaching Company.

ISBN 1-56585-754-2

Peter Irons, Ph.D., J.D.

Professor of Political Science, University of California, San Diego

Peter Irons received his B.A. in sociology from Antioch College and an M.A. and Ph.D. in political science from Boston University. He earned a J.D. from Harvard Law School in 1978, where he served as senior editor of the *Harvard Civil Rights-Civil Liberties Law Review*.

Professor Irons is widely respected as an authority on the Supreme Court and constitutional litigation. He has taught at Boston College Law School, the University of Massachusetts, and the University of California, San Diego (UCSD), where he joined the political science faculty in 1982. At UCSD, he founded the Law and Society Program and the Earl Warren Bill of Rights Project, which he has directed since 1990, producing innovative curricular materials for high school and college courses. He has been a visiting professor at several law schools and universities and served as the Raoul Wallenberg Distinguished Visiting Professor of Human Rights at Rutgers University in 1988.

A prolific author, Professor Irons has written and edited 12 books, including *The New Deal Lawyers*; *Justice at War: The Story of the Japanese American Internment Cases*; *The Courage of Their Convictions: Sixteen Americans Who Fought Their Way to the Supreme Court*; *Brennan Vs. Rehnquist: The Battle for the Constitution*; and *A People's History of the Supreme Court*, on which this course is based. He also edited and narrated four sets of audiotapes of Supreme Court oral arguments in the *May It Please the Court* series, which is used in hundreds of colleges and law schools. His most recent book is *Jim Crow's Children: The Broken Promise of the Brown Decision*, published in 2002. His books have won an unprecedented five Silver Gavel awards from the American Bar Association for their contributions to "public understanding of the American legal system."

Professor Irons has lectured widely on the Supreme Court, including in the law schools at Harvard, Yale, Berkeley, and Stanford. He is also an active civil rights and liberties lawyer and belongs to several state and federal bars, including the Supreme Judicial Court of Massachusetts, the U.S. District Court for the Northern District of California, the U.S. Court of Appeals for the Ninth Circuit, and the United States Supreme Court. During the 1980s, he initiated the successful campaign to reverse the criminal convictions of Japanese Americans who resisted military curfew and evacuation orders during World War II. Professor Irons has served two terms on the national board of the American Civil Liberties Union.

Professor Irons has received Outstanding Teaching Awards from three of the UCSD colleges. He lives in San Diego, California, with his wife, Bonnie Fox, and their two daughters, Haley and Maya.

©2003 The Teaching Company Limited Partnership

Table of Contents

The History of the Supreme Court
Part III
From the Warren Court to the Rehnquist Court

iv   ©2003 The Teaching Company Limited Partnership

The History of the Supreme Court

Scope:

Over the years since its first session in 1790, the United States Supreme Court has risen from a body with little power and prestige to become the most powerful and prestigious judicial institution in the world. Its decisions have profoundly shaped not only American law but also our society, as the nation has grown dramatically in population, geographical expanse, racial and ethnic diversity, and technology.

This course on the Supreme Court in American history will trace the Court's development from its founding to the present, with a focus on the landmark cases that have reflected conflicts in American society. We will examine cases in such areas as federal and state power, economic regulation, slavery and segregation, political protest, religion, and such "privacy" issues as abortion and gay rights. Our discussion of each case will look at the parties on both sides, the justices who decided it, and the social and political context that affected the Court's ruling.

Over the course of 36 lectures, we will encounter dozens of people—most of them very ordinary Americans—whose cases wound up in the Supreme Court. Among these people are Dred Scott, Homer Plessy, Charles Schenck, Elsie Parrish, Joseph Schechter, Lillian Gobitis, Fred Korematsu, Carol Brown, Ernesto Miranda, Mary Beth Tinker, and Michael Hardwick. Different in age, race, gender, and religion, they all placed their names on landmark Supreme Court decisions. We will also encounter many of the 109 justices—all but two of them men and all but two white—who have sat on the Supreme Court bench over the past two centuries. They include such eminent and influential justices as John Marshall, Roger Taney, Oliver Wendell Holmes, Louis Brandeis, Charles Evans Hughes, Hugo Black, Felix Frankfurter, Earl Warren, and Thurgood Marshall.

These lectures are divided into three sections of 12 lectures each, corresponding to important periods in the Court's history. The first section covers the period from the American Revolution to the end of World War I. We begin with the framing of the Constitution and the Bill of Rights and look at the Court's structure and powers as it was shaped at the Constitutional Convention in 1787. We then examine the Court's first—and most ineffective—decade, during which its only significant decision was overturned by the Eleventh Amendment. During much of this first period, two chief justices with very different views, John Marshall and Roger Taney, dominated the Court, serving for 63 years between them. The landmark cases during this period include *Marbury v. Madison, McCulloch v. Maryland, Dred Scott v. Sandford*, and *Plessy v. Ferguson*, which dealt with such issues as judicial review, congressional power, slavery, and segregation.

Our second set of 12 lectures covers the period from the 1920s through the 1960s. The Court was led, during the 1920s, by Chief Justice William Howard Taft and followed his conservative, pro-business views in economic regulation cases. But the Court shifted course during the economic and social upheaval of the Great Depression. After striking down the twin pillars of President Franklin Roosevelt's New Deal program, the Court launched the "Constitutional Revolution" of 1937 by upholding state minimum-wage laws and federal labor regulation. The Court's adoption of the *strict scrutiny* test in 1938 paved the way for decisions that struck down local and state limitations on the rights of political, religious, and racial minorities. The major figure in this section is Earl Warren, who served as chief justice from 1953 until his retirement in 1969. These were momentous years in American history, marked by the Civil Rights movement, the campaign against Jim Crow schools, and conflict over the Vietnam War. The landmark cases during this period include *Brown v. Board of Education, Miranda v. Arizona*, and *Tinker v. Des Moines*. The Warren Court was "activist" in protecting and expanding civil rights and liberties, just as the Court between 1890 and 1937 was "activist" in protecting business from government regulation.

The final set of 12 lectures will deal with the Court under the leadership of Chief Justices Warren Burger and William Rehnquist, judicial conservatives who were both named by Republican presidents. Burger replaced Earl Warren in 1969 and retired in 1986, and Rehnquist became the first sitting justice to head the Court since Harlan Stone in 1941. Burger and Rehnquist both had "law and order" credentials, and both made clear their desire to reverse many of the Warren Court's "activist" decisions in criminal law and First Amendment rights. They were largely frustrated in this goal, because Justices William Brennan and Thurgood Marshall persuaded the Court's moderate justices to trim but not topple the Warren

  ©2003 The Teaching Company Limited Partnership

landmarks. During this period, the abortion ruling in *Roe v. Wade* provoked heated conflict, some of it violent, but Chief Justice Rehnquist fell one vote short in his campaign to reverse the *Roe* decision. Decisions on such issues as affirmative action, flag burning, and the presidential election in 2000 also divided the Court and sparked debate on the left and right. The course ends with a retrospective look at the Court's impact on American law and society over the past two centuries and its role as a model for judicial systems around the world.

Part II: From the Taft Court to the Warren Court

The lectures in this middle section of the course deal with the Supreme Court from the 1920s, under the leadership of Chief Justice William Howard Taft, through the 1960s, when the Court was led by Chief Justice Earl Warren. These were eventful years in American history, marked by the Great Depression of the 1930s, World War II, and the civil rights revolution that was led by the National Association for the Advancement of Colored People and its brilliant legal director, Thurgood Marshall. In these lectures, we will examine the Court's role in striking down the New Deal program of President Franklin Roosevelt and the "Constitutional Revolution" of 1937, in which the Court abruptly shifted course and upheld state and federal laws that set minimum wages and protected labor's right to organize unions. We will also look at the Court's adoption in 1938 of the *strict scrutiny* test, under which laws that abridged First Amendment rights and discriminated against racial and religious minorities were stripped of the *presumption of constitutionality*. Among the issues that came before the Court during this period were the internment of Japanese Americans during World War II, the government's prosecution of Communist Party leaders for their advocacy of revolution, and racial segregation in public schools. The lectures in this section examine such landmark cases as *Minersville School District v. Gobitis*, *Korematsu v. United States*, *Dennis v. United States*, and *Brown v. Board of Education*.

Lecture Twenty-Five
"We Beg Thy Blessings"

Scope:

The historical context of this lecture goes back to colonial days and to conflicts over religion, which led the Framers to provide, in the First Amendment, that "Congress shall make no law respecting an establishment of religion, or prohibiting the free exercise thereof." Not until the late 1930s, however, did the Supreme Court hold that state and local officials were bound by these provisions. This lecture looks at four major cases decided by the Court between 1947 and 1963 that dealt with government aid to religion and with prayer in public schools. The Court's opinions in the first two cases, *Everson* and *McCollum*, were written by Justice Hugo Black, and both affirmed the Court's commitment to governmental "neutrality" in religion, but these cases had different outcomes, which we will briefly analyze. The second pair of cases, *Engel* and *Schempp*, involved challenges to school prayer. We look at the Court's rulings in both cases, holding that classroom religious exercises violate the First Amendment. We conclude by looking at the long-term impact of these decisions, which the Court has reaffirmed but are still widely disobeyed in schools across the country.

Outline

I. This lecture discusses the Supreme Court's rulings in cases that involved the religion clauses of the First Amendment, between 1947 and 1963.

    A. The background of these cases reflects the religious diversity of the American people.

        1. More than six of out of seven people identify themselves as Christians.

        2. Protestants make up 56 percent of the population, and 27 percent belong to the Roman Catholic Church, with 62 million members.

        3. There are also several million Jews, Muslims, Hindus, Buddhists, and members of other non-Christian denominations.

        4. Some eight percent of the population has no religious affiliation.

B. These figures reflect divisions over religious belief and practices that create conflicts that often wind up in the Supreme Court.

II. During the colonial period, the Puritan settlers in Massachusetts and other colonies believed that church and state should both be governed by biblical principles.

    A. The first law code of Massachusetts was based on the Bible, with citations to Old Testament verses for authority.

    B. The Massachusetts colonists expelled those who questioned their religious orthodoxy.

        1. Roger Williams was banished to Rhode Island in 1636 for preaching that the state had no power to enforce religious edicts.

        2. Anne Hutchinson was also banished for holding religious meetings in her home.

    C. Advocates of separating church and state placed their views in the First Amendment, which provides: "Congress shall make no law respecting an establishment of religion, or prohibiting the free exercise thereof."

    D. The First Amendment applies only to acts of Congress, and the Supreme Court did not apply its provisions to the states until the 1920s.

    E. The Court's early decisions in religion cases involved the free exercise clause and the rights of religious minorities, such as the Jehovah's Witnesses.

III. The "establishment of religion" clause has presented the Court with a choice between two views.

    A. Thomas Jefferson said, in 1802, that the clause erected a "wall of separation" between church and state.

    B. Justice William Douglas said, in 1952, that the Court should "accommodate" the religious views of the people in public areas.

IV. The Court's first major establishment clause decision came in 1947, in the case of *Everson v. Ewing Township, New Jersey.*

©2003 The Teaching Company Limited Partnership

A. The state legislature provided that the school board could reimburse parents with children in religious schools for their bus transportation. The tax funds in Ewing Township were all paid to parents with children in Catholic schools.

B. This law was challenged by a parent named Arch Everson as violating the First Amendment.

C. The Court upheld the law by a five-to-four vote.

   1. Justice Hugo Black wrote for the majority, quoting Jefferson's words about the "wall of separation" between church and state.

   2. Black also said that "no tax in any amount" could be levied to support "any religious activities or institutions."

   3. However, he said that bus transportation did not aid the religious activities of the Catholic schools.

D. The dissenters cited the "religious test" by which tax funds were paid; they foresaw efforts to introduce religious observances into public schools.

V. In 1948, the Court struck down a program of religious education in public schools in *McCollum v. Champaign-Urbana School District of Illinois*.

A. In this case, Christian ministers and Jewish rabbis conducted religious classes in a "released time" program for students whose parents approved.

B. Justice Black also wrote for the majority in this case, holding that schools could not be used for "the dissemination of religious doctrines."

C. The sole dissenter, Justice Stanley Reed, said that the religion classes were part of the nation's history and did not violate the establishment clause.

VI. In 1962 and 1963, Chief Justice Warren upheld Sunday-closing laws in two cases.

A. In *McGowan v. Maryland*, he said that Sunday is "a day of rest for all citizens" and that the law's religious motivation was "irrelevant."

©2003 The Teaching Company Limited Partnership

B. In *Braunfeld v. Brown*, Warren said that Orthodox Jewish merchants who observed Saturday as their holy day could not challenge a Sunday-closing law.

VII. The Court faced the issue of school prayer in two landmark cases in 1962 and 1963.

    A. In 1962, the Court ruled that public schools in New York could not use a "non-denominational" prayer in classrooms.

        1. Justice Black again cited Jefferson's "wall of separation" in his majority opinion in *Engel v. Vitale*. He said that prayer established the "religious beliefs" of the lawmakers who approved its use.

        2. The sole dissenter, Justice Potter Stewart, said the Court's decision prevented students from sharing in "the spiritual heritage of our nation."

    B. The Court ruled in 1963 that Pennsylvania could not require the recitation of the Lord's Prayer and Bible verses in public schools.

        1. Justice Tom Clark wrote in *Abington Township School District v. Schempp* that "the state is firmly committed to a position of neutrality" in matters of religion.

        2. He said the Lord's Prayer and Bible readings showed the state's "official endorsement of Christian belief."

        3. Justice Stewart again dissented, saying the state should be able to "accommodate" the beliefs of the Christian majority in public school exercises.

    C. The *Engel* and *Schempp* decisions were widely criticized, and religious practices in public schools remain a source of division in American society.

Suggested Readings:

Peter Irons, *A People's History of the Supreme Court*, chapter 31 (1999).

Robert S. Alley, *Without a Prayer: Religious Expression in Public Schools* (1996).

Questions to Consider:

1. Do you think public schools should allow "released-time" programs for students to attend classes that are taught by ministers and rabbis, if attendance is voluntary?

2. Should schools be allowed to use Bible stories in teaching about moral values, if they also use the holy books of other religions, such as Islam and Buddhism?

©2003 The Teaching Company Limited Partnership

Lecture Twenty-Five—Transcript
"We Beg Thy Blessings"

In our previous lecture, we looked at the background and career of Earl Warren, who served as chief justice of the Supreme Court between 1953 and 1969. We devoted this lecture to Warren for several reasons. First, he was the most influential chief justice of the 20th century, rivaled only in the Court's entire history by John Marshall in the 19th century. Secondly, Warren presided over the Court during a critical period in American history. The Cold War with the Soviet Union, the Civil Rights movement of the 1950s and 60s, and the nation's involvement in the Vietnam War, all led to conflicts that produced landmark decisions. We looked at several of Warren's opinions, in the areas of criminal law, free speech, and racial equality, to examine his judicial philosophy in action. We saw that Warren most often balanced what he considered the community's interests against the rights of individuals, and that he avoided the "absolutist" positions of justices like Hugo Black and William O. Douglas.

One area in which Warren applied his balancing approach, with conflicting outcomes, was that of religion. Like most Americans, Warren was Christian, having been raised in the Lutheran church of his Scandinavian parents. But he considered his religious beliefs and practices a private matter. On the other hand, Warren presided at public ceremonies with religious elements. He administered the oath of office to Presidents Eisenhower, Kennedy, and Johnson, while they placed their hands on a Bible, adding the words, "So help me, God," to the oath in the Constitution. I've introduced this lecture with Chief Justice Warren, to make a point. He reflected the mainstream religious beliefs and practices that characterize our society.

More than six out of seven Americans identify themselves as Christians. Protestants make up some 56 percent of the population, and 27 percent belong to the Roman Catholic Church, the nation's largest single denomination, with 62 million members. But there are scores of Christian denominations, and dozens that are not Christian, including Jews, Muslims, Hindus, and Buddhists. The Census Bureau lists some 73 churches with at least 65,000 members, and there are hundreds of smaller religious groups. And some 8 percent of the population has no religious affiliation. These figures reflect divisions over religious belief and practices that often create conflicts that turn into lawsuits and wind up in the Supreme Court.

In this lecture, we're going to look at the Court's rulings in cases that involved the religion clauses of the First Amendment. We'll begin in the colonial period, before the Constitution and the Bill of Rights were adopted, and conclude with cases decided by the Warren Court in the 1950s and 60s. There is a powerful irony in the myth of colonial America as a haven for religious dissenters from the orthodoxy of the Church of England. Many colonists, in fact, were highly intolerant of those who challenged the new orthodoxy of the Puritans who settled in Massachusetts and other colonies. As their name implies, these colonists wanted to "purify" the church, of what they considered the corruption and "Romanism" of the English Church. The Puritans firmly believed that church and state should both be governed by Biblical principles. The first code of laws in Massachusetts, adopted in 1641, was explicitly based on the Bible, with citations to verses in the Old Testament next to each provision in the code.

Two episodes in Massachusetts illustrate the divisive effects of religious intolerance. The first was the expulsion of Roger Williams from the colony in 1636. Williams was a Puritan pastor, but he denounced from his pulpit the notion that civil authorities could enforce religious edicts. He challenged the colony's leaders with these words: "Let any man show me a commission given by the son of God to civil powers in the spiritual affairs of his Kingdom." For this heresy, the General Court of Massachusetts expelled Williams from the colony. He settled in nearby Rhode Island, which became a haven for religious dissenters. The next year, in 1637, the General Court also expelled Anne Hutchinson, the wife of a prominent colonist. Her offense was holding religious meetings in her home, where she preached the doctrine of "immediate revelation." This meant that God could speak directly to each person, and that salvation did not depend on earthly works, but on God's grace. This rejection of Puritan doctrine offended the colony's leaders, who also banished Anne Hutchinson to Rhode Island.

By the time of the American Revolution, advocates of religious toleration demanded the "disestablishment" of the churches that controlled most of the colonies. James Madison of Virginia took the lead in drafting the first state law that protected religious freedom.

 ©2003 The Teaching Company Limited Partnership

This law, adopted in 1785, provided that "no man shall be compelled to frequent or support any religious worship." It also stated, "all men shall be free to profess their opinions in matters of religion." Madison later incorporated these principles into the first two clauses of the First Amendment, which reads: "Congress shall make no law respecting an establishment of religion, or prohibiting the free exercise thereof."

It's important to note that the First Amendment applies only to acts of Congress, and not to those of the states. As we saw in an earlier lecture, the Supreme Court did not apply the First Amendment to the states until the 1920s, through its "incorporation" into the due process clause of the Fourteenth Amendment. We also saw that the Court's early decisions in religion cases involved members of the Jehovah's Witnesses, who challenged state laws under the free exercise clause of the First Amendment. Most of the Court's later rulings in free exercise cases also involved members of religious minorities, such as Orthodox Jews, the Amish, and Seventh Day Adventists. The religious practices of these groups often brought them into conflict with laws that made no allowance for their customs and beliefs.

In contrast, most of the Court's decisions in establishment clause cases have involved state laws that provided benefits to mainstream Christian denominations, or that promoted such practices as classroom prayers. As we'll see, the Supreme Court has been at the center of a long-standing debate over the meaning of the establishment clause. Does it erect, as Thomas Jefferson wrote in 1802, a "wall of separation" between church and state? Or does it require, as Justice William O. Douglas wrote in 1952, that the Court should "respect the religious nature of our people and accommodate the public service to their spiritual needs?" The cases we'll discuss in this lecture all reflect the divisions in our society that have provoked the judicial debate over the establishment clause.

The first case we'll discuss began in New Jersey. The state legislature had passed a law allowing local school districts to reimburse parents for the cost of sending their children to school on the public bus system. This law applied to both the public and private schools. In 1943, officials in Ewing Township had paid some $357 to the parents of children in the local Catholic schools. One of the township's residents, Arch Everson, filed a suit in state court seeking an injunction to block the payments to parents of parochial school students. Everson claimed that such a use of public funds violated the establishment clause, but the New Jersey Supreme Court upheld the program. Everson appealed this decision to the U.S. Supreme Court, which decided the case in February of 1947.

There are several interesting aspects to the Court's decision in *Everson v. Ewing Township*. The Court was sharply divided in this case, by a vote of five to four, but the lineup of justices was unusual. The Court's most liberal members were split down the middle. Justice Hugo Black wrote the majority opinion, which was joined by Justices William O. Douglas and Frank Murphy. The dissenters included Justices Felix Frankfurter, Wiley Rutledge, and Robert Jackson. On most First Amendment issues, these six justices were on the same side. But in the *Everson* case, they took opposing positions. It's also interesting that Justice Black's opinion looked to James Madison for authority. Black noted approvingly that Madison had argued, as Black put it, "that no person, either believer or non-believer, should be taxed to support a religious institution of any kind." Black also quoted Jefferson's words about the "wall of separation" between church and state.

With Madison and Jefferson as his guides, Black put his reading of the establishment clause in these words: "Neither a state nor the federal government can set up a church. Neither can pass laws which aid one religion, aid all religions, or prefer one religion over another. No tax in any amount, large or small, can be levied to support any religious activities or institutions, whatever they may be called, or whatever form they may adopt to teach or practice religion." Black also noted that Ewing Township's Catholic schools, as he wrote, "give their students, in addition to secular education, regular religious instruction conforming to the religious tenets and modes of worship of the Catholic faith."

Given these firm statements about the meaning of the establishment clause, and the facts of this case, it would seem almost inevitable that Black would side with Arch Everson. But he didn't. "We cannot say," Black wrote, "that the First Amendment prohibits New Jersey from spending tax-raised funds to pay the bus fares of parochial school pupils as part of a general program under which it pays the fares of pupils attending public schools." Black justified his ruling on public safety grounds. New Jersey did no more, in his view, than

©2003 The Teaching Company Limited Partnership

providing "a general program to help parents get their children, regardless of their religion, safely and expeditiously to and from their schools."

As I noted, the *Everson* case split the ranks of the Court's liberal members. The dissenters seemed puzzled by Black's opinion, which struck them as inconsistent in the principles he expressed and the outcome he reached. "It seems to me," Justice Robert Jackson wrote, "that the basic fallacy in the Court's reasoning, which accounts for its failure to apply the principles it avows, is in ignoring the essentially religious test by which beneficiaries of this expenditure are selected." Jackson noted that Ewing Township limited its reimbursement program to Catholic parochial schools. In his separate dissent, Justice Wiley Rutledge looked with alarm at the prospect of further efforts to breach the "wall of separation" between church and state. Rutledge foresaw pressures, as he wrote, "to introduce religious education and observances into the public schools."

That's exactly what happened in the next religion case the Court decided, just one year after its *Everson* ruling. This case involved a program in the public schools of Champaign, Illinois. Under this program, students were released from regular classes to receive religious instruction from ministers and rabbis, if their parents approved. The "released-time" program was sponsored by the Champaign Council on Religious Education, a private group that included Protestant, Catholic, and Jewish clergy. Vashti McCollum, whose children attended the Champaign public schools, challenged the program in state court as a violation of the establishment clause.

Once again, Justice Black wrote for the Court in *McCollum v. Champaign-Urbana Board of Education*. Once again, Black referred approvingly to Jefferson's words about the "wall of separation" between church and state, and he quoted at length from his *Everson* opinion. But he reached a different conclusion in the *McCollum* case. Black distinguished the two cases in these words: "Here not only are the state's tax-supported public school buildings used for the dissemination of religious doctrines. The state also affords sectarian groups an invaluable aid in that it helps to provide pupils for their religious classes through use of the state's compulsory public school machinery." In Black's view, aiding parents to get their children to school was different from aiding churches to give them religious instruction in the schools.

The liberal justices who had dissented in the *Everson* case welcomed Black's return to the fold. Justice Felix Frankfurter, a former law professor, couldn't resist lecturing Black in his concurring opinion. "Separation means separation, not something less," he wrote. "It is the Court's duty to enforce this principle in its full integrity." Only one justice dissented from the Court's ruling in the *McCollum* case. Stanley Reed had joined Black in the *Everson* case, and he saw no reason to change his position. He looked to history for support. "This Court cannot be too cautious in upsetting practices embedded in our society by many years of experience," Reed wrote. "The mere use of the school buildings by a non-sectarian group for religious education ought not to be condemned as an establishment of religion."

We saw in the *Everson* case that Justice Wiley Rutledge had foreseen efforts, as he wrote, "to introduce religious education and observances into the public schools." We're going to look now at two cases that involved religious observances in public schools, cases that provoked much greater public reaction than the *Everson* and *McCollum* decisions. Both cases reached the Court during the tenure of Chief Justice Earl Warren, and were decided in 1962 and 1963. As background to these cases, Warren had recently written opinions in two cases that challenged state laws that prohibited most retail businesses from opening on Sundays.

The Court upheld Sunday-closing laws from Maryland and Pennsylvania in 1961, and Warren found no violation of the establishment clause in either case. He conceded in *McGowan v. Maryland* that such laws, as he said, "were motivated by religious forces." But they also served the secular purpose of providing, as Warren wrote, "a uniform day of rest for all citizens. Sunday is a day apart from all others. The cause is irrelevant; the fact exists." Warren also denied a challenge to Pennsylvania's Sunday-closing law by Orthodox Jewish merchants, who closed their stores on Saturdays to observe the Jewish sabbath, and were forced by law to close on Sundays. Warren held in *Braunfeld v. Brown* that laws with a primarily secular purpose did not violate the Constitution, even when they imposed an indirect burden on religion.

The Sunday-closing cases provoked little public reaction, but the Court's rulings in two school prayer cases ignited a firestorm of criticism that has not yet cooled down. The first of these cases began in the town of New Hyde Park, in New York State. The town's

 ©2003 The Teaching Company Limited Partnership

schools began each day's classes with recitation of what was called the Regents' prayer. The state's board of regents, which governed the public schools, had adopted a prayer that read: "Almighty God, we acknowledge our dependence upon thee, and beg thy blessings upon us, our parents, our teachers, and our country." Schools were not required to use the prayer, but many communities made it part of their daily program. Steven Engel, whose children attended the New Hyde Park schools, headed a group of parents who challenged the religious practice. They filed a suit in state court against the school board president, William Vitale, and other town officials. State judges upheld the prayer as a "non-denominational" exercise, and the Supreme Court agreed to review this ruling.

As we saw, Justice Hugo Black had written for the Court in both the *Everson* and *McCollum* cases, back in the late 1940s. More than a decade later, in 1962, he again wrote for the Court in *Engel v. Vitale*. Once again, Black cited Jefferson's "wall of separation" for support. The walls of New Hyde Park's schools, in Black's view, were designed for classrooms, not for churches. "There can be no doubt," he wrote, "that New York's state prayer program officially establishes the religious beliefs embodied in the Regents' prayer." But Black was sensitive to those who felt the Court was insensitive to their religious beliefs. He wrote, "It has been argued that to prohibit state laws respecting an establishment of religious services in public schools is to indicate hostility toward religion or toward prayer. Nothing, of course, could be more wrong."

Black had these final words for the critics he anticipated: "It is neither sacrilegious nor antireligious to say that each separate government in this country should stay out of the business of writing or sanctioning official prayers, and leave that purely religious function to the people themselves and to those the people look to for religious guidance." Justice Potter Stewart was the sole dissenter in the *Engel* case. We'll look at his background in a later lecture, but Stewart was a classic middle-of-the-road justice, who valued tradition over doctrine. He based his *Engel* dissent on the free exercise clause, arguing that the Court's ruling would prevent students in New York's schools from praying in their classrooms. "To deny the wish of these school children to join in reciting this prayer," Stewart wrote, "is to deny them the opportunity of sharing in the spiritual heritage of our nation."

There were plenty of dissenters outside the Court. The *Engel* decision touched a live wire in American politics. Cardinal Francis Spellman of New York said he was "shocked and frightened" by the ruling. Evangelist Billy Graham was "shocked and disappointed." Seventy-five congressmen of both parties introduced bills to return prayer to classrooms through legislation or constitutional amendment. But many religious leaders praised the decision for returning religious devotions to the homes and churches of their members. President John Kennedy said the Court's ruling was "a welcome reminder to every American family that we can pray a good deal more at home, attend our churches with a good deal more fidelity, and make the true meaning of prayer much more important in the lives of our children."

But most Americans wanted their children to pray in school, as well as home and church, and the Court's next ruling on school prayer provoked more criticism. This case began in the high school attended by Roger and Donna Schempp in Abington Township, Pennsylvania, a suburb of Philadelphia. Classes began every morning with a reading of 10 verses from the Bible and recital of the Lord's Prayer. This ritual was required by state law, although children could be excused from the classroom at their parents' request. The Schempp family belonged to the Unitarian church, whose members reject the Christian trinity and are not bound by any creed. Edward Schempp filed suit on his children's behalf, arguing that forcing them to stand in the hallway while their classmates prayed would carry, as the suit read, "the imputation of bad conduct."

Supported by the American Civil Liberties Union, the Schempps won the first two rounds in federal court, and the school board appealed to the Supreme Court. The justices could easily have denied review in *Abington Township v. Schempp*, which differed from *Engel* only in the text of the classroom prayer. In my view, they wanted to tell the politicians who called for returning prayer to schools that the Court stood firm in the face of pressure. The Court heard oral arguments in the *Schempp* case in February of 1963. We're now going to hear excerpts of these arguments. The school board's lawyer, Philip Ward, takes the podium first. He points to the Bible as a source of morality.

> Ward: "See what we're doing. We're teaching morality without religion, cut adrift from theology. And that is proper

 ©2003 The Teaching Company Limited Partnership

for the people of Pennsylvania. We can bring to our children lessons of morality in their school days, as long as we're not bringing religion, not bringing theology. The people of Pennsylvania have wanted to do this, they have since the beginning wanted to bring these lessons in morality to the children. So what do they do? They pick a common source of morality, the Bible."

Ward admits the Bible is a religious book, but he defends its use in public schools.

Ward: "You can sum up our particular problem as this: Can you use, can you keep a tradition which has secular values? It does teach morality. It is noncompulsory; the child doesn't have to be there. But the only problem is, it involves part of the religious tradition of this country. It deals with a document that is of obvious religious origin, and, to many people, an obviously religious book."

Ward tries to separate the religious and secular elements of classroom devotions, reminding the justices of their rulings on the Sunday-closing laws.

Ward: "Must the government rip out that document, that tradition, simply because it involves a religious book? Must the government, any time, any tradition, in any way, reflects the fact that we are a religious people, must they rip out any tradition even, even if that tradition nobody has to abide by? The tradition isn't trying to teach anybody anything. The tradition isn't requiring a person to believe or disbelieve. The tradition has secular value; it has a purpose, like the Sunday-closing. It has a purpose, to teach morality to the children."

Henry Sawyer argues for the Schempp family. He disputes Ward's claims about the Bible as a secular document.

Sawyer: "You cannot separate the moral leaven from the religious leaven in the Bible. I think the two go absolutely together. And it teaches. They say it doesn't proselytize. It teaches, the book teaches from the opening chapter of Genesis to the last chapter of Revelations. It teaches, it teaches the way the world was created, and it teaches in a sectarian sense from the opening. From the very opening, it says, 'And lo, the spirit was upon the waters.' And in the King James version, and I'm sure the Douay version, that word is capitalized. It means the Holy Ghost. This is the beginning of a teaching of the concept of Trinity. It teaches."

Sawyer addresses the issue of religious tradition, taking issue with Philip Ward's argument.

Sawyer: "I think tradition is not to be scoffed at. But let me say this very candidly. I think it is the final arrogance to talk constantly about 'our religious tradition' in this country and equate it with this Bible. Sure, religious tradition. Whose religious tradition? It isn't any part of the religious tradition of a substantial number of Americans, of a great many, a great many things, and really some of the salient features of the King James version, or the Douay version, for that matter. And it's just to me a little bit easy, and I say arrogant, to keep talking about 'our religious tradition.' It suggests that the public schools, at least of Pennsylvania, are a kind of Protestant institution, to which others are cordially invited. And I think to some extent they have been, in our state."

On June 17 of 1963, the Supreme Court ruled in favor of Roger and Donna Schempp. Public schools could not use the Bible and prayer for classroom devotion. Justice Tom Clark, who, like Black, was a Southern Baptist, wrote the Court's opinion. "The place of religion in our society," he said, "is an exalted one. But religion's proper place," Clark added, "is in the home, the church, and the individual heart and mind." He restated the Court's earlier rulings in these words: "In the relationship between man and religion, the state is firmly committed to a position of neutrality."

Clark denied that Bible reading simply aided in teaching morality. He noted the "pervading religious character of the classroom ceremony and the state's official endorsement of Christian belief." But he also emphasized that "the Bible is worthy of study for its literary and historic quality" in classes that do not include religious exercises. Justice Potter Stewart had been the sole dissenter in the *Engel* case, and he dissented again in the *Schempp* case. He focused again on the First Amendment's free exercise clause. Stewart answered Clark in these words: "If schools are to be truly neutral in matters of religion, they must accommodate parents who desire to have their children's school day open with the reading of passages from the Bible."

The Court's reaffirmation of its stand on school prayer again provoked a heated public response. "We are a Christian nation, under God," one congressman said. "These decisions do not help us to be on God's side." And public opinion polls show consistent disagreement with the Court's rulings on this issue. Gallup polls in 1963 and again in 2000 both showed that 70 percent of the public supports prayer in public schools. This raises the question of whether the Court should bow to public opinion, or hold firm to its reading of the First Amendment.

The Court has faced the school prayer issue in many cases since 1963, and we'll discuss some of those decisions in a later lecture. But they reflect the fact that religion has long been, and still remains, a divisive issue in American society. The Court's role in balancing community sentiment and individual rights has never been easy. In our next lecture, we'll turn to another divisive issue, the rights of criminal defendants. We'll look at several landmark cases that forced the justices to balance the community's interest in public safety, with the Constitution's safeguards for those accused of criminal acts. The Court's rulings in these cases, as we'll see, have created controversy that lasts until now.

Lecture Twenty-Six
"You Have the Right to Remain Silent"

Scope:

The context of this lecture goes back to colonial days and the imposition of laws to define and punish criminal behavior. The Massachusetts Bay colony based its criminal laws on the Bible and provided capital punishment for religious crimes, such as idolatry, blasphemy, and witchcraft. The Constitution's Framers included in the Bill of Rights four amendments that protected the rights of criminal defendants in such areas as search and seizure, self-incrimination, the right to counsel, and the imposition of "cruel and unusual punishment." However, the Supreme Court did not begin applying these provisions to the states until the 1930s, and not until the Warren Court years did it fashion a national code of criminal procedure. We will examine several landmark decisions in this field, including *Mapp v. Ohio*, which dealt with search and seizure; *Gideon v. Wainwright*, which ruled that criminal defendants have the right to a lawyer at their trials; and *Miranda v. Arizona*, protecting the right against self-incrimination under police interrogation.

Outline

I. This lecture examines the Supreme Court's rulings, between 1942 and 1966, in cases that involve the criminal law provisions of the Constitution. As background, the Declaration of Independence denounced King George for obstructing "the administration of justice" and depriving the colonists of "trial by jury."

II. The Bill of Rights included several provisions that established a code of criminal procedure to protect the rights of criminal defendants.

    A. The Fourth Amendment protects the right to be secure "against unreasonable searches and seizures" and requires a warrant based on "probable cause" that describes "the place to be searched, and the person or things to be seized."

    B. The Fifth Amendment has several criminal law protections.

        1. It requires an indictment by a grand jury for criminal charges.

©2003 The Teaching Company Limited Partnership

2. It also protects defendants against being "twice put in jeopardy of life or limb."
3. It says no person "shall be compelled in any criminal case to be a witness against himself."
4. It provides that no person shall "be deprived of life, liberty, or property without due process of law."

C. The Sixth Amendment includes several protections for criminal defendants.
   1. It provides "the right to a speedy and public trial by an impartial jury."
   2. Criminal defendants must be "informed of the nature and cause of the accusation" against them.
   3. They also have the rights "to be confronted by the witnesses" against them; to have "compulsory process" to obtain witnesses in their defense; and to "have the assistance of counsel" for their defense.

D. The Eighth Amendment prohibits "excessive" bail and fines and the imposition of "cruel and unusual punishments."

III. The criminal law provisions of the Bill of Rights were intended to apply only in federal prosecutions.

A. Beginning in the 1920s, the Supreme Court "incorporated" provisions of the Bill of Rights into the Fourteenth Amendment in cases dealing with First Amendment rights and applied them to the states.

B. Questions remained about the "incorporation" of the criminal law provisions and their application to state prosecutions.

IV. Federal courts have long applied the search-and-seizure provision of the Fourth Amendment in federal cases through the *exclusionary rule* that bars the admission of illegally seized evidence.

A. In 1949, the Supreme Court ruled in *Wolf v. Colorado* that the exclusionary rule did not apply to the states.

B. In 1961, the Court overruled the *Wolf* decision in *Mapp v. Ohio*.
   1. This case involved a police search of Dollree Mapp's home in Cleveland, Ohio, looking for a criminal suspect. The police did not have a search warrant.

2. The officers did not find the suspect, but they seized allegedly obscene materials, and Mapp was convicted for possessing them.
3. The Court reversed her conviction, holding that applying the exclusionary rule to the states "makes very good sense" in subjecting states to the federal standard.

V. The Court also "incorporated" the right-to-counsel provision of the Sixth Amendment into the Fourteenth.

A. In 1942, the Court ruled in *Betts v. Brady*, by a vote of six to three, that indigent defendants in state cases did not have a right to counsel.
1. The majority said the denial of counsel in state cases did not result in "fundamental unfairness" to defendants.
2. The dissenters said criminal defendants should not be denied counsel "merely because of their poverty."

B. This ruling was reversed in 1963 by unanimous vote in *Gideon v. Wainwright*.
1. Clarence Gideon was convicted of burglary after the trial judge denied his request for court-appointed counsel.
2. The Court held that an indigent defendant "cannot be assured of a fair trial unless counsel is provided for him."

VI. The Court also applied the self-incrimination provision of the Fifth Amendment to the states.

A. In 1964, the Court ruled in *Escobedo v. Illinois* that criminal suspects who request a lawyer must be provided access to one.

B. The Court expanded this ruling in 1966 in the landmark case of *Miranda v. Arizona*.
1. Ernesto Miranda was arrested for the kidnapping and rape of a young woman.
2. He confessed after two hours of police questioning but was not informed of his rights to remain silent and to consult a lawyer.

C. The Court ruled by a five-to-four vote that Miranda's confession was not "the product of his free choice."
1. Chief Justice Earl Warren's opinion in *Miranda* required a detailed set of warnings that police must provide to

suspects, including the right to remain silent and to obtain a lawyer.

    2. Justice Byron White warned in dissent that the Court's ruling would return criminals to the streets.

D. In Miranda's case, he was convicted a second time without the excluded confession. Four years after his release from prison, he was stabbed to death in a fight in a Phoenix bar. When the police arrested the assailants, they were read their Miranda rights.

E. In subsequent cases, the Court has trimmed the *Miranda* ruling but has never overruled it.

Suggested Readings:

Peter Irons, *A People's History of the Supreme Court*, chapter 31 (1999).

Liva Baker, *Miranda: Crime, Law, and Politics* (1983).

Questions to Consider:

1. Should juries be allowed to consider evidence of criminal acts that is obtained by police officers without "probable cause" to seize it?

2. Do you think lawyers should be present whenever police question a suspect who is held in custody?

Lecture Twenty-Six—Transcript
"You Have the Right to Remain Silent"

In our previous lecture, we looked at the Supreme Court's rulings in cases that involved the "establishment of religion" clause of the First Amendment. As we saw, the justices have been divided in cases that challenged the provision of government aid or support for religious institutions and practices. In the 1940s, the Court ·upheld a New Jersey law that provided reimbursement to parents for the transportation of students to Catholic parochial schools, but the Court also struck down a program in Illinois that allowed ministers and rabbis to offer religious instruction in public schools. Justice Hugo Black wrote for the Court in both of these cases, and he drew a distinction between direct and indirect governmental aid to religion. Black also stressed in both cases that the state, as he put it, must be "neutral" in matters of religion.

But religious belief and practices are matters on which few people are truly "neutral." The question of prayer in public schools shows that most Americans have taken sides on this divisive issue. And the vast majority has disagreed with the Court's rulings that classroom prayer and Bible reading violate the establishment clause. In this lecture, we'll discuss another issue on which many people disagree with the Court's decisions. Over the past half-century, the Court has decided more than a thousand cases in the field of criminal law. Very seldom are the justices concerned about the guilt or innocence of criminal defendants. These are normally questions for juries and trial judges to decide. But the Court *is* concerned with the fairness of the process under which people are charged and tried for criminal acts. The Court bases its rulings in these cases on the provisions of the Bill of Rights, which established a federal code of criminal procedure.

We're going to look at cases that involve three of the first ten amendments to the Constitution. As background to these cases, it's worth noting that the men who voted for the Declaration of Independence in 1776 were motivated in part by outrage at the British government's disregard of its own criminal laws. Among the "repeated injuries and usurpations" of King George, they said, were those of obstructing "the administration of justice" and "depriving us, in many cases, of the benefit of trial by jury." To remedy these injuries, and to protect the rights of American citizens, the men who drafted and adopted the Bill of Rights included several provisions that are worth quoting here. The Fourth Amendment reads: "The right of the people to be secure in their persons, houses, papers, and effects, against unreasonable searches and seizures, shall not be violated, and no warrants shall issue, but upon probable cause, supported by oath or affirmation, and particularly describing the place to be searched, and the person or things to be seized."

The criminal law provisions of the Fifth Amendment are these: "No person shall be held to answer for a capital, or otherwise infamous crime, unless on a presentment or indictment of a grand jury, nor shall any person be subject for the same offense to be twice put in jeopardy of life or limb, nor shall be compelled in any criminal case to be a witness against himself, nor be deprived of life, liberty, or property, without due process of law." The Sixth Amendment provides: "In all criminal prosecutions, the accused shall enjoy the right to a speedy and public trial by an impartial jury, to be informed of the nature and cause of the accusation, to be confronted with the witnesses against him, to have compulsory process for obtaining witnesses in his favor, and to have the assistance of counsel for his defense."

As I said, these provisions of the Bill of Rights established a fairly detailed code of criminal procedure. They were designed to protect those who are accused of crime, beginning with police investigations, and continuing through arrest, charging, trial, and sentencing. The basic principle behind them is fairness to the defendant. The men who drafted the Declaration of Independence knew that a "mock trial," as they put it, was not a trial at all, but an act of injustice, and those who drafted the Constitution stated in its preamble their desire to "establish justice" for the people of the United States. Putting these principles into practice, of course, is not always easy or popular, especially when the public is outraged by a vicious crime, or swayed by prejudice against a criminal defendant. Those defendants are often poor, uneducated, and members of racial and ethnic minorities.

We're going to focus our discussion of the Supreme Court's rulings in these areas, which involve three phases of the criminal process: search and seizure, the right to counsel, and self-incrimination. We'll look at six cases the Court decided between 1942 and 1966. Before we look at these cases, it's worth noting that they all began in state courts. That's true of most of the Supreme Court's rulings on criminal law, and this raises an issue that needs some preliminary discussion. In most criminal cases, the Supreme Court defers to the verdicts and sentences of state courts. That's the basic principle of federalism, under which the states are responsible for enforcing their own criminal laws. The justices will reverse those judgments only when they find a clear violation of the federal Constitution.

But this raises another question. Under what circumstances should the Supreme Court rule that state courts have violated the Constitution? We've seen in previous lectures that the Court has "incorporated" the provisions of the First Amendment into the due process clause of the Fourteenth Amendment, and has applied them to the states. Should the Court also apply the criminal law provisions of the Bill of Rights to the states? As we'll see, the Court has been sharply divided on this question. We'll look now at several cases that illustrate the judicial debate over the "incorporation" issue in criminal law.

The first case involved the Fourth Amendment's prohibition of "unreasonable" searches and seizures. Federal courts have long applied what's called the *exclusionary rule* to ban the admission of evidence in federal trials that was illegally obtained by the police. Whether that rule should apply to the states came before the Supreme Court in the case of *Wolf v. Colorado*, which was decided in 1949. Interestingly, the majority opinion of Justice Felix Frankfurter said nothing about the facts in this case. But the state court opinion noted that a physician, Dr. Wolf, had been convicted of performing an illegal abortion. The evidence against him was based on records that had been taken by the police from his office, without a search warrant.

Wolf's lawyer asked the judge to suppress the evidence, as a violation of the Fourth Amendment, but the judge rejected his motion. Upholding that decision, Frankfurter wrote that the exclusionary rule was fashioned by judges and was not required by the Fourteenth Amendment. In other words, the Fourth Amendment's ban on illegally seized evidence did not apply to the states. Justice Frank Murphy, one of three dissenters in the *Wolf* case, argued that Frankfurter's opinion, as he put it, "will do inestimable harm to the cause of fair police methods in our cities and states. For the Court now allows what is indeed shabby business: lawlessness by officers of the law."

Twelve years later, in 1961, the Court adopted Murphy's dissent and overruled the *Wolf* ruling in *Mapp v. Ohio*. This case involved a warrantless police search of Dollree Mapp's home in Cleveland, breaking down her door to search for a fugitive. Interestingly, the person they were seeking was suspected of bombing the house of an alleged numbers racketeer, Don King, who later became a prominent boxing promoter. The police did not find the suspect, but they did find allegedly obscene material in Mapp's basement. After a state judge denied her lawyer's motion to suppress the evidence, Mapp was convicted of possessing obscenity and sentenced to prison.

Justice Tom Clark, who was normally a hard-liner in criminal cases, wrote for the Court in the *Mapp* case, striking down her conviction. Clark stated, "Our holding that the exclusionary rule is an essential part of both the Fourth and Fourteenth Amendments makes very good sense. There is no war between the Constitution and common sense." Clark pointed out the problem of having two sets of legal rules, in these words: "Presently, a federal prosecutor may make no use of evidence illegally seized, but a state's attorney across the street may, although he supposedly is operating under the provisions of the same amendment. Thus, the state, by admitting evidence illegally seized, serves to encourage disobedience to the federal Constitution which it is bound to uphold."

Justice Frankfurter dissented in the *Mapp* case from the overruling of his *Wolf* opinion. He remained committed to his notion of federalism. "I do not believe," Frankfurter wrote, "that the Fourteenth Amendment empowers this Court to mould state remedies effectuating the right to freedom from arbitrary intrusion by the police to suit its own notions of how things should be done." But in 1961, the Court's majority was committed to another notion of federalism, under which the states were required to apply the provisions of the Bill of Rights in their courts. As we saw in earlier lectures, Chief Justice John Marshall imposed the Court's power over the states in cases that involved the commerce clause of the Constitution. More than a century later, the Court followed Marshall's notion of judicial nationalism in fashioning a uniform national system of criminal law.

We're going to look now at two cases that raised another basic question of fairness to criminal defendants. Most of us would be shocked if we were placed on trial for a serious crime, but were told by the judge that we couldn't have a lawyer to defend us. Some of us might tell the judge, "Your honor, the Sixth Amendment to the Constitution says, 'In all criminal prosecutions, the accused shall have the assistance of counsel for his defense.'" And the judge might say, "I'm sorry. The Sixth Amendment applies only to federal trials, and this is a state court. Are you ready to proceed?" Most of us would agree that going to trial without a lawyer wouldn't be fair. But, for many years the Supreme Court said that denying counsel to defendants in state courts who couldn't afford a lawyer did not violate the Constitution.

As we saw, the exclusionary rule for illegally obtained evidence stemmed from judicial interpretation of the search-and-seizure clause in the Fourth Amendment. In other words, this was a judge-made rule. But the situation is different in the "right to counsel" cases. The wording of the Sixth Amendment is clear, and doesn't involve a judge-made rule. But, as we've seen, the Court has been divided over incorporating the Bill of Rights into the due process clause of the Fourteenth Amendment, and applying its protections to the states. In the past, the Court has limited the incorporation doctrine to what it calls "fundamental rights." But which provisions of the Bill of Rights are so fundamental that denying them to criminal defendants in state courts would violate the Constitution?

That was the question before the Court in *Betts v. Brady*, which was decided in 1942. A man named Smith Betts was charged in Maryland with robbery. At his arraignment, Betts told the judge he was too poor to hire a lawyer, and asked the judge to appoint one to represent him. The judge replied that lawyers were appointed for indigent defendants only in rape and murder cases, so Betts acted as his own lawyer. He cross-examined the state's witnesses, and called his own witnesses, to establish an alibi. Betts didn't do a bad job, but the judge found him guilty, and imposed a prison sentence of eight years. While Betts was in prison, he filed a *habeas corpus* petition in state court, naming the prison warden as the defendant. Betts argued that denying him the right to counsel violated the Fourteenth Amendment. The state judges ruled against him, but the Supreme Court agreed to review his case.

 ©2003 The Teaching Company Limited Partnership

The justices were divided in *Betts v. Brady*. Justice Owen Roberts wrote for a majority of six. The due process clause of the Fourteenth Amendment, he noted, "does not incorporate the specific guarantees found in the Sixth Amendment." Provisions in the Bill of Rights would be applied to the states, Roberts added, only if their denial resulted in "fundamental unfairness" or was "shocking to the universal sense of fairness." Roberts looked to state practices for guidance. He found 26 states that didn't require the appointment of lawyers for indigent defendants, and 18 that did. "In the great majority of states," he concluded, "it has been the considered judgment of the people, their representatives, and their courts, that appointment of counsel is not a fundamental right, essential to a fair trial."

It's worth noting that Roberts based his conclusion on counting the states. Deciding what constitutes a fundamental right became an arithmetic problem. Justice Hugo Black wrote for the three dissenters. He noted that every criminal defendant enters the courtroom with a presumption of innocence. "A practice cannot be reconciled with fundamental ideas of fairness," Black wrote, "which subjects innocent men to increased dangers of conviction merely because of their poverty. Whether a man is innocent cannot be determined from a trial in which, as here, denial of counsel has made it impossible to conclude, with a satisfactory degree of certainty, that the defendant's case was adequately presented." We saw that the Court later overruled the *Wolf* case, and adopted Justice Murphy's dissenting position on the exclusionary rule. Twenty-one years after their *Betts* ruling, in 1963, the justices revisited the right to counsel issue in a case that was virtually a carbon copy.

The case of *Gideon v. Wainwright* has become widely known, partly because of a book and a movie about the case, both called *Gideon's Trumpet*. Anthony Lewis, who covered the Supreme Court for the *New York Times*, wrote the book, and Henry Fonda played the role of Clarence Earl Gideon in the film. Gideon was charged with burglarizing a poolroom in Panama City, Florida. The burglar left with several packs of cigarettes, and change from a soda machine that was pried open. Like Smith Betts had done, Gideon told the judge at his arraignment that he couldn't afford a lawyer. He then said, "The United States Supreme Court says I am entitled to be represented by counsel." The judge replied, "Mr. Gideon, I am sorry, but I cannot appoint counsel to represent you in this case. Under the laws of Florida, the only time the court can appoint counsel is when the defendant is charged with a capital offense." Gideon defended himself at his trial.

As the Supreme Court later said, "Gideon conducted his defense about as well as could be expected from a layman." The state produced no witnesses who saw Gideon enter or leave the poolroom, but one state witness said he had seen Gideon near the building, and later saw him with a lot of change. The jury found him guilty, and the judge sentenced him to a five-year prison term. Gideon read law books in the prison library, and sent a *habeas corpus* petition to the Florida Supreme Court, which ruled against him. Gideon then sent a handwritten petition to the U.S. Supreme Court, which agreed to review the case. The justices also provided Gideon with a lawyer. Not just any lawyer, but one of the most experienced and respected lawyers in the country.

Abe Fortas had founded a prestigious Washington law firm, and had argued many cases before the Supreme Court, most of them for wealthy clients and corporations. Fortas joined the Court himself in 1965, and we'll discuss his background and record in our next lecture. His argument in the *Gideon* case rested on the unfairness of matching an experienced prosecutor against an untrained layman. Fortas asked the justices to look at his client. "I do believe that in some of this Court's decisions," he said, "there has been a tendency to forget what happens to these poor, miserable, indigent people, when they are arrested and brought into jail and questioned, and later on they are brought in these strange and awesome circumstances before a court and there, Clarence Earl Gideon, defend yourself."

Twenty-one years after he dissented in the *Betts* case, Justice Hugo Black had the satisfaction of writing an opinion that overturned that ruling. The Court unanimously held that Clarence Gideon had a right to a lawyer. "Reason and reflection," Black wrote, "require us to recognize that in our adversary system of justice, any person haled into court, who is too poor to hire a lawyer, cannot be assured a fair trial unless counsel is provided for him." The justices sent the *Gideon* case back to the Florida courts for a new trial. This time, Gideon had an experienced defense lawyer to represent him, and the jury found him not guilty.

 ©2003 The Teaching Company Limited Partnership

The Court ruled in the *Gideon* case that all criminal defendants have the right to a lawyer at their trials. But what about a criminal suspect who has been detained and is being questioned by the police? Does that suspect have the right to consult a lawyer in the station house? The Supreme Court addressed this issue in 1964, a year after the *Gideon* ruling. The justices agreed to review the conviction of Danny Escobedo, who had been arrested in Chicago for murdering his brother-in-law. Escobedo refused to answer any questions, and demanded to consult his lawyer, who had come to the police station but had been refused access to his client. After 14 hours of interrogation, Escobedo confessed to the killing. He explained that he was protecting his sister from abuse by her husband. But a jury found Escobedo guilty of murder, and he received a 20-year prison sentence.

The Supreme Court reversed the conviction by the narrow margin of five to four. Justice Arthur Goldberg, who had joined the Court in 1962, wrote for the majority. He admitted, "any lawyer worth his salt will tell the suspect in no uncertain terms to make no statement to police under any circumstances." But the prospect of obtaining fewer confessions, if criminal suspects consulted a lawyer, did not faze Goldberg. "If the exercise of constitutional rights will thwart the effectiveness of a system of law enforcement," he wrote, "then there is something very wrong with that system."

The four dissenters in *Escobedo v. Illinois* felt it was wrong to hinder the police in questioning suspects. Justice Byron White, who also joined the Court in 1962, had been a federal law enforcement official. He deplored, as he wrote, "the goal which the Court seemingly has in mind, to bar from evidence all admissions obtained from an individual suspected of crime, whether involuntarily made or not." Justice White may have exaggerated the majority's goal in the *Escobedo* ruling. But the Warren Court *was* determined to protect criminal suspects from making statements to police that would incriminate them, without first being informed of their rights to remain silent, and to consult a lawyer.

We're going to conclude this lecture with the famous case of *Miranda v. Arizona*, which the Court decided in 1966. This case began with the kidnapping and rape of a young woman in Phoenix, Arizona. Ten days after this crime, the police took Ernesto Miranda to the station house for questioning. He had been linked to the crime by a witness's description of a car in which the victim was seen. After two hours of questioning, Miranda made an oral confession, and then signed a written statement. The confessions were admitted at his trial, and the victim made a positive identification of Miranda as her assailant. After he was sentenced to a 20-year prison term, lawyers from the American Civil Liberties Union sought a new trial for Miranda, arguing that his confession had been coerced by the police. The Arizona courts denied these motions, but the U.S. Supreme Court agreed to review the case.

We're going to listen now to excerpts of the oral arguments in *Miranda v. Arizona*. John Flynn argues for Miranda. He faces a question from Justice Potter Stewart, who asks whether Miranda should have been informed of his rights to remain silent, and to consult a lawyer, before the interrogation started.

> Flynn: "I think that the man at that time has the right to exercise, if he knows, and under the present state of the law in Arizona, if he's rich enough, and if he's educated enough, to assert his Fifth Amendment right, and if he recognizes that he has a Fifth Amendment right, to request counsel. But I simply say that at that stage of the proceeding, under the facts and circumstances in Miranda, of a man of limited education, of a man who certainly is mentally abnormal, who is certainly an indigent, that when that adversary process came into being, that the police, at the very least, had an obligation to extend to this man not only his clear Fifth Amendment right, but to afford him the right of counsel."

Gary Nelson argues for the state of Arizona. He asks the justices to avoid the "extreme" position of giving suspects access to counsel during an interrogation.

> Nelson: "If the extreme position is adopted that says he has to either have counsel at this stage, or intelligently waive counsel, that a serious problem in the enforcement of our criminal law will occur. First of all, let us make one thing certain. We need no empirical data as to one factor: what counsel will do if he is actually introduced. I am talking now about counsel for defendant. At least among lawyers there can be no doubt as to what counsel for the defendant is to do. He is to represent him 100 percent, win, lose, or draw, guilty

or innocent. That's our system. When counsel is introduced at interrogation, interrogation ceases."

When the Court decided the *Miranda* case in 1966, five justices agreed with John Flynn's position, and four with Gary Nelson's. Chief Justice Earl Warren wrote for the majority, striking down Miranda's conviction. Warren was himself a former prosecutor, and his opinion drew on police manuals for questioning suspects. He quoted from one manual, advising officers that the key to getting a confession was "being alone with the person under interrogation." Warren then looked at Miranda's treatment in the Phoenix police station. In his words, Miranda "was thrust into an unfamiliar atmosphere and run through menacing police interrogation procedures. This atmosphere carries its own badge of intimidation."

Warren noted that Miranda was a man with little education and serious mental problems. Given these facts, Warren concluded, "No statement obtained from the defendant can truly be the product of his free choice." To ensure that confessions were voluntary, the chief justice rewrote the police manual. A person in custody, he said, "must be warned prior to questioning that he has the right to remain silent, that anything he says can be used against him in a court of law, that he has the right to the presence of an attorney, and that if he cannot afford an attorney one will be appointed for him prior to any questioning if he so desires." These are what we now call "Miranda warnings," and we've all seen television shows in which the police read suspects these warnings from a card.

The four dissenters in the *Miranda* case accused the majority of handcuffing the police. Justice White repeated the warnings from his *Escobedo* dissent. "Under this new version of the Fifth Amendment," he wrote, "a good many criminal defendants will either not be tried at all or will be acquitted if the state's evidence, minus the confession, is put to the test of litigation." White predicted, "The Court's rule will return a killer, a rapist, or other criminal to the streets, to repeat his crime whenever it pleases him." But that's not what happened in the *Miranda* case. Ernesto Miranda was tried a second time, convicted without his confession, and sent back to state prison, with another 20-year sentence.

It's worth noting that judicial rulings that exclude illegally seized evidence, or confessions that are obtained without giving suspects their Miranda warnings, rarely result in defendants walking out of the courtroom, thumbing their noses at the judge. In most of these cases, the defendants are tried a second time, and most often convicted, like Ernesto Miranda. Justice White, himself, later joined most police officials in supporting the *Miranda* decision, as a protection against charges the police had pressured criminal suspects into confessions. Before we conclude, there's an ironic footnote to this story. Miranda was released on parole from prison in 1972. Four years later, he got into a fight in a Phoenix bar and was stabbed to death. When the police arrested his assailants, they were read their Miranda rights.

We've seen in this lecture that Chief Justice Warren presided over a Court that greatly expanded the rights of criminal defendants. But the Warren Court's rulings provoked criticism and debate that has continued over the past four decades. Efforts to overturn the *Mapp* and *Miranda* decisions have failed, but the Court has trimmed these holdings in more recent cases. For example, the Court ruled in 2002 that police can ask passengers on interstate buses to search their clothing and luggage, without informing them of their right to refuse. And the Court has allowed confessions that police obtain by lying to suspects about what they know. Many people support rulings like these, as legitimate efforts to fight crime. Others feel the real casualty in the war on crime is the Bill of Rights. But this whole debate began with the Warren Court's rulings on criminal law. In our next lecture, we'll discuss the Warren Court's decisions in other areas of law, rulings that also expanded constitutional rights and provoked more controversy.

Lecture Twenty-Seven
The Warren Court Reshapes the Constitution

Scope:

In this lecture, we examine several of the landmark decisions of the Warren Court during the 1960s, the decade of its greatest influence. We first look at the justices who served under Earl Warren during this period: William Brennan, Potter Stewart, Byron White, Arthur Goldberg, Abe Fortas, and Thurgood Marshall. Justice Brennan, in particular, had a profound influence on the Court, not only during Warren's tenure as chief justice, but also during the following decades, when he protected the legacy of the Warren Court from reversal by the conservative justices who were named by Presidents Nixon, Ford, Reagan, and Bush. We will examine several cases in which the Warren Court expanded the protections of the Bill of Rights. These cases include *Baker v. Carr* and *Reynolds v. Sims*, which established the principle of one person, one vote in state and federal legislative apportionment; *Heart of Atlanta Motel v. United States*, upholding the "public accommodations" provisions of the 1964 Civil Rights Act; and *Tinker v. Des Moines*, in which the Court upheld the right of public school students to protest the Vietnam War by wearing black armbands to classes.

Outline

I. This lecture concludes our discussion of the Warren Court and examines several of its rulings in cases that provoked controversy and debate.

    A. We first look at the justices who served under Chief Justice Warren, between his appointment in 1953 and his retirement in 1969.

    B. We then discuss cases in the areas of legislative representation, civil rights enforcement, and free speech.

II. During the first five years of Warren's tenure, four justices left the Court through death or retirement.

    A. Justice Robert Jackson died in 1954 and was replaced by John Marshall Harlan. He was a judicial conservative, but he supported First Amendment rights in many cases.

B. Justice Sherman Minton retired in October 1956, one month before the presidential election.

    1. President Eisenhower named William Brennan of New Jersey, who sat on his state's supreme court. He was a Democrat and a Catholic, and the president wanted to appeal to these groups before the election.

    2. Brennan's judicial philosophy was based on protecting the "dignity and well-being" of all Americans, a principle that he absorbed from the "social gospel" of the Catholic Church.

    3. Brennan served for 34 years before he retired in 1990. He became the intellectual leader of the Warren Court and used his political skills and personal charm to persuade moderate justices to join liberal opinions.

    4. Eisenhower later said that placing Warren and Brennan on the Court had been his two biggest mistakes.

C. Justice Stanley Reed retired in 1957, and Eisenhower replaced him with Charles Whittaker of Missouri, a former corporate lawyer and federal appellate judge.

    1. Whittaker developed a writer's block and produced very few opinions.

    2. He retired as "disabled" in 1962 and was ranked a failure by legal scholars.

D. Justice Harold Burton retired in 1958, and Eisenhower's final nominee was Potter Stewart of Ohio.

    1. Stewart had backed Eisenhower for the 1952 presidential nomination and was placed on the federal appellate bench in reward.

    2. On the Court, Stewart was a moderate who backed civil rights but was conservative in religion and criminal cases.

III. President John Kennedy was elected in 1960 and placed two justices on the Court.

  A. Kennedy replaced Justice Whittaker with Byron White of Colorado.

    1. White was a former professional football star who served with Kennedy in World War II.

    2. He became deputy attorney general in 1961, enforcing federal civil rights laws.

3. On the Court, White had a liberal record in civil rights cases but was conservative on criminal law and abortion, which he consistently opposed.

B. Justice Felix Frankfurter retired in 1962, and Kennedy replaced him with Arthur Goldberg, the general counsel of the steelworkers' union.
1. Goldberg served only three years and was a consistent liberal.
2. He left the Court in 1965 to become United Nations ambassador.

IV. President Lyndon Johnson succeeded Kennedy in 1963 and placed two justices on the Court.

A. He replaced Goldberg with Abe Fortas, who had given Johnson legal and political advice for many years.
1. Fortas founded a prominent Washington law firm and argued the *Gideon* case before the Court.
2. Fortas served for three years and left the Court under a cloud of scandal for his financial dealings.

B. Justice Tom Clark retired in 1967, and Johnson replaced him with Thurgood Marshall.
1. We have examined Marshall's long career as NAACP general counsel and his role in the school segregation cases in the 1950s.
2. He had served as a federal appellate judge and U.S. solicitor general.
3. Marshall retired in 1991 and was a consistent liberal ally of Justice Brennan.

C. The justices named by Kennedy and Johnson, along with Chief Justice Warren and Justice Brennan, made up a solid liberal majority in most cases.

V. The Warren Court reshaped American law in several crucial areas.

A. In two decisions in 1962 and 1964, the Court ordered state legislative reapportionment on a basis of one person, one vote.
1. Chief Justice Warren said, in *Reynolds v. Sims*, "legislators represent people, not trees or acres."

2. These decisions benefited minority voters in big cities and Republicans in suburban districts.

B. In 1964, Congress passed a civil rights law that banned racial discrimination in places of public accommodation, such as restaurants and hotels.

    1. The Court upheld this law in *Heart of Atlanta Motel v. United States*.

    2. The justices said Congress could legislate against the "moral and social wrong" of race discrimination.

C. In 1969, the Court struck down a ban on wearing black armbands by students in Des Moines, Iowa.

    1. Mary Tinker and other students wore the armbands to protest the Vietnam War and challenged their suspensions by school officials.

    2. The Court said public schools are not "enclaves of totalitarianism" and that students and teachers have First Amendment rights.

    3. Justice Hugo Black dissented, saying the decision would produce a "revolutionary era of permissiveness" in schools.

Suggested Readings:

Bernard Schwartz, *Super Chief: Earl Warren and His Supreme Court* (1983).

John W. Johnson, *The Struggle for Student Rights: Tinker v. Des Moines and the 1960s* (1997).

Questions to Consider:

1. Do you think it violates the Constitution to draw state and congressional legislative districts to ensure the election of racial and ethnic minorities?

2. Should a high school student be allowed to wear a shirt or jacket with the Confederate battle flag on it? What about a Black Power slogan?

Lecture Twenty-Seven—Transcript
The Warren Court Reshapes the Constitution

In our previous lecture, we looked at the Supreme Court's landmark rulings in the area of criminal law. We saw that the Bill of Rights includes four amendments that were designed to protect the rights of criminal defendants. These amendments provide a code of criminal procedure, beginning with the investigation of crime, through arrest, trial, and sentencing. We examined cases that dealt with search and seizure, the right to counsel, and protections against self-incrimination. Under the leadership of Chief Justice Earl Warren, the Court expanded the rights of defendants, and applied the criminal law provisions of the Bill of Rights to the states. These rulings, particularly the famous *Miranda* case in 1966, provoked controversy and debate that continues today.

In this lecture, we're going to conclude our discussion of the Warren Court, and look at other cases that also provoked controversy and debate. We'll begin with brief sketches of the justices who served with Chief Justice Warren, particularly those who joined the Court between his appointment in 1953 and his retirement in 1969. We'll then discuss several of the Warren Court's landmark rulings in the areas of political representation, civil rights enforcement, and free speech. This lecture will also set the stage for our discussion in following lectures of the Court under Warren's successor, Chief Justice Warren Burger.

We've already been introduced to the eight justices who sat on the Court, when Earl Warren took his seat in 1953. Five of those justices had been named by President Franklin D. Roosevelt: Hugo Black, Stanley Reed, Felix Frankfurter, William O. Douglas, and Robert Jackson. These were the "New Deal" justices, who were all then in their 40s and early 50s when they joined the Court. President Harry Truman had picked the other three justices: Harold Burton, Tom Clark, and Sherman Minton. The Court had aged since Roosevelt had carried out his pledge to add "new blood" to the bench. Warren himself was 62 when he became chief justice, which was the average age of the other eight justices as well.

These were not the "Nine Old Men" of the 1930s, and the Court had none of the judicial reactionaries who had frustrated Roosevelt's New Deal programs. It's fair to say the Court in 1953 was neither liberal nor conservative. On some issues, such as civil rights, the justices stood together, most notably in the cases that struck down school segregation. On other issues, such as the prosecution of Communist Party leaders, the Court's majority took a restrictive position on First Amendment rights. I think it's accurate to characterize the Court as a moderate institution when Earl Warren became the chief justice.

During the first five years of Warren's tenure, four justices left the Court, through death and retirement. President Dwight Eisenhower, who was elected as a moderate Republican, filled all these empty seats on the bench. Justice Robert Jackson died in 1954, and was replaced by John Marshall Harlan. We've already met Harlan, who had been a Wall Street lawyer for 20 years before he joined the Court. Harlan took a generally conservative position on most issues, although he supported First Amendment rights in many cases. But Eisenhower's next appointment added a firmly liberal voice to the Court.

Justice Sherman Minton retired in October of 1956, just one month before the presidential election, in which Eisenhower sought a second term in the White House. The president surprised many people by naming William J. Brennan to replace Minton. Electoral politics played a role in this choice. Brennan was a highly respected judge on the New Jersey Supreme Court, and his legal abilities were beyond question. But he was also a Democrat and a Catholic from a northern state, and Eisenhower hoped to pick up votes from these groups in his reelection campaign. As it turned out, the president swamped his Democratic opponent, Adlai Stevenson, and hardly needed any votes that Brennan's nomination might swing in the election. There's an amusing story about Brennan's journey to the Supreme Court. Herbert Brownell, who was Eisenhower's attorney general, called Brennan one night and asked him to come to Washington the next morning. Brennan thought Brownell wanted his advice on court reform. This was an issue the two men had recently discussed at a judicial conference. Brownell later said that when he offered Brennan the Supreme Court position, "I never heard a man say yes so fast."

It's fair to say that Brennan had a greater impact on the Supreme Court than any other justice in the 20th century. His tenure spanned 34 years, from 1956 until his retirement in 1990. During these years,

Brennan wrote dozens of landmark opinions, which reflected his bedrock commitment to "human dignity" as a guiding principle. In one case, Brennan upheld the right of John Kelly, a disabled welfare recipient, to receive a hearing before officials cut off his benefits. Brennan put the broader issue in these words: "From its founding, the nation's basic commitment has been to foster the dignity and well-being of all persons within its borders." He absorbed this principle from his church and his family. Brennan learned the Catholic "social gospel" from his church's teachings. "Justice demands that the dignity of the human personality be respected," one encyclical stated. Brennan's father was an Irish immigrant who stoked furnaces in a brewery, and who fought for his fellow workers as a union leader.

On the Court, Brennan's personal warmth, his Irish charm, and his legal brilliance made him the leader of the liberal justices. He often persuaded the Court's moderate justices, and even conservatives, to join the majority in many closely divided cases. For almost three decades after Earl Warren left the Court, Brennan kept the legacy of the Warren Court alive, protecting many of its landmark decisions from reversal by judicial conservatives. Even his critics paid tribute to Brennan's unflagging devotion to the principles he espoused for so many years. But he didn't win over the president who named him to the Court. Someone later asked Eisenhower if he made any mistakes as president. "Yes, two," he replied. "And they are both sitting on the Supreme Court." Eisenhower was referring to Earl Warren and William Brennan, but his biggest mistake in picking justices came in his fourth nomination.

Stanley Reed's retirement in 1957 opened a seat that could be filled without political considerations. Eisenhower replaced Reed with Charles Whittaker, who had practiced corporate law in Kansas City for 30 years, and who came to the Court after three years on the federal appellate bench. Whittaker proved totally unfit for his new job. He developed a paralyzing writer's block and produced no opinions of any significance. Whittaker retired in 1962 as "disabled," and was rated by scholars as a judicial failure.

Eisenhower's fifth and final Supreme Court nomination went to another mid-western corporate lawyer who also served on the federal appellate bench. Justice Harold Burton retired in 1958, and was replaced by Potter Stewart of Ohio. Stewart had practiced law in

Cincinnati after graduating from Yale Law School. He was a friend and political ally of Senator Robert Taft, the Republican Party's conservative leader. But Stewart risked his political future by backing Eisenhower over Taft at the 1952 Republican convention. He was rewarded in 1954 with a federal appellate court position, and won respect for well-crafted opinions that stuck to the facts and bowed to precedent. During 23 years on the Supreme Court, Stewart wrote more than 600 opinions, but just one contains a memorable phrase. Writing in a case that reversed an obscenity conviction for showing a French "art" movie, Stewart put the difficulty of defining "hardcore" pornography in these words: "I know it when I see it, and the motion picture involved in this case is not that."

With the exception of William Brennan, the justices named by President Eisenhower did not shift the Court's moderate balance. In fact, Justices Harlan and Whittaker turned the Court slightly to the right. What we now call the Warren Court did not really emerge until Presidents John Kennedy and Lyndon Johnson added four new justices between 1962 and 1967. Kennedy and Johnson were both Democrats, and they were supported by their party's liberal coalition of black voters, Jews, and labor unions. So it's not surprising that their Supreme Court nominees had close ties with these groups. Kennedy got his first chance to reshape the Court when Justice Whittaker retired as disabled in 1962. He named Byron White of Colorado, who was probably the most physically able justice in the Court's history.

White earned both a Phi Beta Kappa key and All-American honors in football at the University of Colorado, where he gained the nickname "Whizzer" for his speed as a running back. He later juggled his studies at Yale Law School with games for the Detroit Lions, and he served as a PT-boat skipper during World War II, forming a close friendship with another skipper, Jack Kennedy. After the war, and a clerkship with Chief Justice Fred Vinson, White practiced law in Colorado, where he managed Kennedy's presidential campaign in 1960. Kennedy named him as deputy attorney general in 1961, and White spent a turbulent year in the Justice Department, stamping out civil rights fires in the Deep South. During 33 years on the Court, White consistently supported civil rights, but he took a hard-line position in criminal cases, as we saw in the *Miranda* case. He also opposed abortion rights, from the *Roe* decision in 1973 until his retirement in 1993.

President Kennedy pleased both the Jewish community and the labor movement when he named Arthur Goldberg to replace Justice Felix Frankfurter in 1962. Goldberg was general counsel of the steelworkers' union, and had advised Kennedy on labor issues during the 1960 campaign. Frankfurter had served for 23 years, but Goldberg remained on the Court for just three. After President Kennedy's assassination in November of 1963, Lyndon Johnson moved from the vice-presidency into the White House. Kennedy had sent several hundred American troops to Vietnam, and Johnson inherited what started as a small conflict, but soon escalated into a major war. Looking for ways to end the war, Johnson persuaded Goldberg to leave the Court and become the United Nations ambassador. Under his deal with Johnson, Goldberg would help to mediate an American exit from Vietnam, and then return to the Court. But the war ended Johnson's presidency in 1968, and Goldberg returned to law practice. During his brief judicial service, Goldberg had a consistently liberal voting record.

Goldberg's departure opened a seat for one of Johnson's closest legal and political advisors, Abe Fortas. A native of Memphis, Tennessee, he became editor in chief of the Yale Law Journal and joined Yale's law faculty after his graduation in 1933. Fortas worked in several New Deal agencies, and was solicitor of the Interior Department when he met Johnson, who was then a young Texas congressman. Johnson owed his Senate election in 1948 to Fortas, who persuaded the Supreme Court to keep federal judges from looking into Johnson's 87-vote primary victory, which earned him the nickname of "Landslide Lyndon." As we saw in our previous lecture, Chief Justice Warren appointed Fortas to argue for Clarence Gideon, in the case that established the right to counsel for criminal defendants. We'll discuss the sordid end to Fortas's brilliant legal and judicial career in our next lecture. But his three years on the Court were marked by several landmark opinions, one of which we'll discuss very shortly.

Johnson made history with his second nominee to the Court. Justice Tom Clark retired in 1967, and the president named Thurgood Marshall to replace him. We've looked at Marshall's brilliant record as the NAACP's chief counsel from 1938 to 1961. During those years, he won all but three of the 32 cases he argued before the Supreme Court. President Kennedy named Marshall in 1961 to the federal appellate court in New York, and he resigned from the bench in 1965 when President Johnson offered him the post of solicitor general in the Justice Department. Marshall became the first black person to hold that position.

Several justices had served as solicitor general before moving to the Supreme Court, and many people assumed that Johnson was grooming Marshall for the Court. The president told Marshall that wasn't the case. "You know, this has nothing to do with any Supreme Court appointment," he said when Marshall visited the Oval Office to discuss the job. But in fact, that was the case. "I did not tell Marshall my intentions at this time," Johnson later said. "But I fully intended to eventually appoint him to the Court. I believed that a black man had to be appointed to that body." When President Johnson named Marshall to the Court, many southern senators did not relish the prospect of a black man on the high bench.

Led by Strom Thurmond of South Carolina, southern senators grilled Marshall during his confirmation hearings, and stalled a vote for more than two months. But Johnson was a former senate majority leader, and he twisted enough arms to secure Marshall's confirmation by a vote of 89 to 11, with all the "nays" coming from the Deep South. We'll look at several of Marshall's landmark opinions in later lectures. But his 24 years on the Court were marked by more than his written opinions. He brought the perspective of a black American to the Court, for the first time in its history. "What do they know about Negroes?" he once asked of his white colleagues. "You can't name one member of this Court who knew anything about Negroes before he came to the Court." His fellow justices knew a great deal more about the impact of race in America after Marshall joined them.

We've looked at the justices who joined Earl Warren between 1962 and 1967, because they made up the core of the Warren Court, during the years it reshaped American law and society. The Court's most liberal members during this period included Justices Hugo Black, William O. Douglas, Earl Warren, Arthur Goldberg, Abe Fortas, and Thurgood Marshall. Justice Brennan was fond of saying, "With five votes, you can do anything around here." And there were at least five votes to support an expansive reading of the Bill of Rights between 1962 and 1969, when Chief Justice Warren and Justice Fortas both left the Court. The list of landmark decisions during these years is long, and the central holdings of most of these rulings are still intact. We've looked at some of these decisions in earlier lectures, cases that dealt with school prayer, the right to counsel for criminal defendants, search and seizure, and protections against self-incrimination.

We're going to look now at three of the Warren Court's other landmark decisions. We'll begin with a case that reshaped the American political landscape. The background of this case lies in decades of rural domination of state legislatures. Many state constitutions had provided that each county would have the same number of seats in their legislatures. But as population shifted from farms and small towns to cities and suburbs, the number of voters each lawmaker represented became grossly unequal. For example, the largest state legislative district in Tennessee had 19 voters for each one in the smallest. And in Alabama, the largest senatorial district had 40 times more residents than the smallest. Many state constitutions required periodic reapportionment of legislative districts, but rural lawmakers simply ignored these provisions.

The first challenge to unequal representation reached the Court in 1946, in a case from Illinois, called *Colegrove v. Green.* But Justice Felix Frankfurter wrote for a majority, holding that state legislative apportionment was a "political question" and did not raise any constitutional issue. Sixteen years later, in 1962, Justice Brennan wrote for a new majority of the Warren Court in the case of *Baker v. Carr.* Six justices voted to reverse the *Colegrove* decision, granting urban voters in Tennessee the right to challenge their state's unequal apportionment in federal court. Justice Frankfurter, who retired from the Court that same year, wrote one of his final dissents in the *Baker* case, joined by Justice John Harlan. Frankfurter repeated his claim in *Colegrove* that legislative apportionment was a matter of "political controversy" and was "unfit for federal judicial action." But the *Baker* ruling prompted a rush to federal courts by urban voters in more than a dozen states.

In 1964, Chief Justice Warren wrote for the Court in deciding six of these cases. His opinion in *Reynolds v. Sims*, which challenged Alabama's unequal districts, included these memorable words: "legislators represent people, not trees or acres. Legislators are elected by voters, not farms or cities or economic interests." The "one-person, one-vote" standard of the *Reynolds* opinion has changed the faces in every state legislature, with urban and suburban lawmakers now controlling those bodies. Black and Hispanic voters in big cities, most of them Democrats, benefited from Warren's ruling, but suburban Republicans have gained even more political clout in recent years. Surprisingly, Chief Justice Warren later said that he considered his *Reynolds* opinion even more important than his landmark ruling in the *Brown* case, striking down school segregation.

Another segregation case showed the determination of the Warren Court to protect the civil rights of black Americans. There's a revealing story behind this case. Shortly before the *Brown* decision in 1954, Chief Justice Warren set off with his black chauffeur to visit Civil War battlefields in Virginia. He heard echoes of those battles the next morning. Warren emerged from his nice hotel to find that his driver had slept in the car. He asked why. "Well, Mr. Chief Justice," his driver said, "I just couldn't find a place to stay." Warren suddenly realized that nice hotels in Virginia did not admit black guests. Ten years later, in 1964, Congress passed a sweeping civil rights act that outlawed racial segregation in "public accommodations" like hotels and restaurants. Congress based the law on its constitutional power to regulate "commerce among the several states."

As we saw in an earlier lecture, back in 1883, the Supreme Court had struck down a federal civil rights law based on the equal protection clause of the Fourteenth Amendment, and Congress feared the justices might feel bound by that precedent. The owners of the Heart of Atlanta Motel, which filled most of its rooms with out-of-state guests, promptly challenged the new law. The motel's lawyer asked the justices to listen, as he said, to the "43 million white people in the South" who believed that a business owner's right to discriminate "is more important and more paramount than the commerce of the United States." But Earl Warren listened to the echoing voice of his black chauffeur. He assigned the Court's unanimous opinion to Justice Tom Clark, who wrote in *Heart of Atlanta Motel v. United States* that Congress may employ its commerce powers to legislate against what Clark said was the "moral and social wrong" of racial discrimination.

We'll look at one final decision of the Warren Court in this lecture. This case stemmed from national discord over American

©2003 The Teaching Company Limited Partnership

involvement in the Vietnam War, which sparked massive demonstrations in big cities like Washington and New York. But opposition to the war soon reached the nation's conservative heartland, where protesters often faced hostility from the war's defenders. During the Christmas holiday period in 1965, Senator Robert Kennedy proposed an American bombing halt in Vietnam. A small group of high school students in Des Moines, Iowa, decided to show their support for Kennedy's proposal by wearing black armbands to their classes. One of them was Mary Beth Tinker, a seventh-grader at Warren Harding Junior High.

School officials got wind of the plan and promptly banned the wearing of armbands. Mary Beth was suspended after she wore her armband in her algebra class. She talked with me later about what happened, after newspapers and radio stations covered the armband controversy in Des Moines. "After all the publicity about what we did, we got a lot of repercussions. People threw red paint at our house, and we got lots of calls. We got all kinds of threats to our family, even death threats. They even threatened my little brothers and sisters, which was really sick. I was leaving for school one morning, and the phone rang and I picked it up. This woman said, Is this Mary Tinker? And I said yes. And she said, 'I'm going to kill you!' It's made me a lot more hardened in certain ways, when you learn in a personal way what the repercussions are for doing unpopular things."

Mary Beth and other students who had been suspended asked a federal judge to overturn the armband regulation as a violation of their First Amendment rights. The judge ruled against them, and they appealed to the Supreme Court. We're going to listen now to brief excerpts of the oral arguments in *Tinker v. Des Moines*. Dan Johnston, a young lawyer for the American Civil Liberties Union, argues for the students. He tells the justices that the armband protest was entirely peaceful.

> Johnston: "The difficulty we have with this particular policy as it was enacted is that there was no indication, no testimony by teachers, by administrators or anyone else, of any reason to believe that it would be disruptive. And when the students in fact did wear the armbands, the record quite clearly shows that it was not in fact disruptive."

Chief Justice Warren is troubled by the prospect of disruption in the schools, and he pushes Johnston on this issue.

> Warren: "I suppose you would concede that if it started fistfights, or something of that kind, and disrupted the school, that the principal could prevent the use of them?"

> Johnston: "The suggestion I believe we're making, Your Honor, is that there should not be any special rule for freedom of expression cases for schools."

Johnston concedes that school officials have the right to deal with disruptive activities. But he repeats his argument that schools are not exempt from the First Amendment.

> Johnston: "I should not think that there would have to be a special rule for schools or any other part of our society for the First Amendment. Now the evidence of disruption might be different. But as far as the principles applied, we'd like to have the same principles applied in the schools, or perhaps especially in the schools, that are applied elsewhere."

Allen Herrick argues for the Des Moines school board. He's some 40 years older than Dan Johnston, and he voices the sentiments of his generation.

> Herrick: Now, in substance, if we understand the petitioners' position in this case, it is that the school officials are powerless to act until the disruption occurs. Respondents believe that should not be the rule. Sometimes an ounce of prevention is a lot better than a pound of cure, and I think the subsequent history of such activities bear out the judgment of the school officials in their discretion."

When the Court decided the *Tinker* case, seven justices sided with the students, and only two backed the school board. Justice Abe Fortas wrote for the majority, and put his views in these words: "First Amendment rights, applied in light of the special characteristics of the school environment, are available to teachers and students. It can hardly be argued that either students or teachers shed their constitutional rights to freedom of speech or expression at the schoolhouse gate." Fortas used strong words in his opinion: "In our system, state-operated schools may not be enclaves of totalitarianism. School officials do not possess absolute authority over their students. They are possessed of fundamental rights which the State must respect, just as they themselves must respect their obligations to the State."

The Court's oldest member, Hugo Black, was known for his absolute defense of the First Amendment, but he dissented in the *Tinker* case, along with the next oldest justice, John Harlan. Black endorsed what he called "the old-fashioned slogan that children are to be seen, not heard." He warned that the Court's approval of armbands marked "the beginning of a new revolutionary era of permissiveness in this country." Black ended his dissent with these words: "This case, wholly without constitutional reasons in my judgment, subjects all the public schools in the country to the whims and caprices of their loudest-mouthed, but maybe not their brightest, students." Mary Beth Tinker is still proud of her stand in junior high. She now works as a nurse in a Veterans Administration hospital, and her patients include many Vietnam veterans. And she's still a peace activist. "I'm really proud we had a part in ending the crazy Vietnam War," she told me.

The Supreme Court handed down its *Tinker* decision in March of 1969. This was one of the last rulings of the Warren Court. But the era of the Warren Court had already ended. The year before, in June of 1968, Earl Warren had announced his intention to retire, after the Senate confirmed his successor. Two months after the *Tinker* decision, President Richard Nixon nominated Warren Earl Burger as the next chief justice. In our next lecture, we'll look at the complicated and confusing story of Warren's retirement and Burger's nomination to replace him. This episode in the Court's history illustrates the impact of political factors on the shape of constitutional law.

Lecture Twenty-Eight
Earl Warren Leaves, Warren Burger Arrives

Scope:

The context of this lecture stems from the retirement of Earl Warren as chief justice in 1969 and his replacement by Warren Burger. We first recount the story of Warren's effort to allow President Lyndon Johnson to name Justice Abe Fortas as his successor and the political miscalculations that gave that choice to President Richard Nixon, who picked Burger for his "law and order" opinions as a federal appellate judge. We also look at Burger's career and his role as an ineffective leader of justices who still revered Warren. This lecture focuses on two cases that involved controversial issues. In *Swann v. Charlotte-Mecklenburg School District*, the Court upheld a busing plan to achieve racial balance in the schools of Charlotte, North Carolina. The second case began with the publication in 1971 by the *New York Times* and *Washington Post* of excerpts from a top-secret history of the Vietnam War, known as the *Pentagon Papers*. The Nixon administration sought injunctions to prevent further publication, and the Court ruled that government officials could not impose a "prior restraint" on the press in this case.

Outline

I. This lecture discusses Chief Justice Warren's resignation in 1969 and his replacement by Warren Burger. We also examine two landmark rulings of the Burger Court, on school busing and the *Pentagon Papers* case.

II. President Lyndon Johnson announced in March 1968 that he would not seek another term.

    A. Chief Justice Warren wanted to retire and name Justice Abe Fortas as his successor.

        1. Johnson told Warren in June 1968 that he would accept his resignation "at such time as a successor is qualified."

        2. Johnson nominated Fortas as chief justice, but Senate Republicans mounted a filibuster to delay his confirmation, with the November election in mind.

        3. The press uncovered embarrassing details of Fortas's financial dealings, and Johnson withdrew his nomination in October 1968.

4. Warren remained as chief justice until June 1969, after Richard Nixon was elected president.

B. Nixon named Warren Burger of Minnesota to replace Warren.

  1. Burger was born in 1907 and worked his way through law school at night.

  2. He was active in Republican politics and was placed on the federal appellate bench by President Eisenhower in 1956.

  3. Burger took a conservative position as an appellate judge, particularly in criminal cases.

  4. Nixon chose Burger as a "law and order" judge, hoping to move the Court to the right.

C. However, Burger was, in my opinion, not an effective leader, and the Court did not reverse the landmark Warren Court rulings.

  1. Burger upset other justices by switching his vote in several cases to be able to assign the majority opinion.

  2. Justice William Douglas wrote a memo to his colleagues, saying that Burger's moves would create "a frayed and bitter Court, full of needless strains and quarrels."

III. Justice Abe Fortas resigned in May 1969, after further press reports of his financial improprieties.

A. President Nixon was determined to place southern conservatives on the Court, part of his electoral strategy to appeal to white voters.

B. Nixon's first nominee to replace Fortas was Clement Haynsworth of South Carolina, a federal appellate judge.

  1. Haynsworth had voted in one case for a company in which he owned stock, which led several Senate Republicans to oppose his confirmation.

  2. Civil rights and labor groups also opposed Haynsworth, and his nomination was defeated by a 55–45 vote.

C. Nixon then nominated another federal appellate judge, Harrold Carswell of Florida.

  1. Reporters discovered a 1948 speech in which Carswell defended white supremacy.

2. The Senate rejected his confirmation by a 51–45 vote.

D. Nixon then abandoned his "southern strategy" and nominated Harry Blackmun of Minnesota.

    1. Blackmun was a boyhood friend of Chief Justice Burger and had represented the Mayo Clinic as a lawyer; he later served as a federal appellate judge.

    2. The Senate confirmed Blackmun by unanimous vote; he took a conservative position on the Court but moved to the liberal side after several years.

IV. The Burger Court decided a landmark case in 1971, upholding school busing to achieve racial balance.

    A. The case of *Swann v. Charlotte-Mecklenburg School District* involved the schools in North Carolina's largest district.

        1. A federal judge ordered busing to provide a racial balance of 79 percent white students and 21 percent black.

        2. President Nixon opposed school busing, and it became a heated political issue.

        3. A federal appellate court reversed the busing order.

    B. During the Court's deliberations in the *Swann* case, Chief Justice Burger first voted to uphold the appellate court ruling against busing.

        1. Under the Court's tradition, Justice William Douglas had the power to assign the majority opinion, but Burger said he would write it; Douglas objected strongly, but Burger went ahead.

        2. He produced a unanimous opinion that took a narrow approach, which allowed school districts to maintain all-white or all-black schools if student assignments were not based on racial discrimination.

V. The Burger Court also handed down a landmark ruling on government press censorship in 1971.

    A. The *New York Times* and *Washington Post* printed excerpts of a top-secret Pentagon history of the Vietnam War.

        1. The so-called Pentagon Papers had been given to the newspapers by Daniel Ellsberg, a former Pentagon official who had turned against the war.

2. Government lawyers obtained judicial injunctions to bar further publication of the Pentagon Papers.
B. The legal issue in *New York Times v. United States* was the *prior restraint* doctrine, which prohibits censorship before publication without strong evidence of harm to national security.
   1. Government lawyers argued that further publication would "materially affect the security of the United States" and would complicate efforts to end the Vietnam War.
   2. The newspapers' lawyers replied that only evidence of "immediate and irreparable" harm to national security could justify the government's "heavy burden" against prior restraint.
C. The Court ruled for the newspapers by a six-to-three margin.
   1. The Court issued a one-paragraph, unsigned opinion, but several justices added their own opinions.
   2. Justice Hugo Black called the government's actions a "flagrant" violation of the First Amendment.
   3. In dissent, Justice Burger criticized the "unseemly haste" in bringing the case to the Court.

Suggested Readings:

Bernard Schwartz, *Swann's Way: The School Busing Case and the Supreme Court* (1986).

Sanford J. Ungar, *The Papers and the Papers: An Account of the Legal and Political Battle over the Pentagon Papers* (1989).

Questions to Consider:

1. Do you think Chief Justice Warren was justified in conditioning his retirement on the confirmation of his chosen successor?

2. Should the government be allowed to prohibit the publication of material that might inform hostile nations or terrorist groups about American military or diplomatic plans?

Lecture Twenty-Eight—Transcript
Earl Warren Leaves, Warren Burger Arrives

We have devoted the previous five lectures in this course to the Supreme Court's landmark decisions over the 16 years that Earl Warren served as chief justice of the United States. We began with the Court's historic ruling in *Brown v. Board of Education*, holding in 1954 that school segregation violated the equal protection clause of the Fourteenth Amendment. We then looked at school cases that followed the *Brown* decision, including the conflict over school integration in Little Rock, Arkansas. We followed with lectures that discussed the Court's rulings in cases that involved religion, criminal law, and such areas as legislative reapportionment, civil rights, and free speech. And we looked at the backgrounds and philosophies of the justices who made up the Warren Court.

During the years between 1962 and 1969, the justices who were named by Presidents John Kennedy and Lyndon Johnson gave the Court a liberal majority. Their decisions expanded constitutional rights for minorities and dissenters. But these rulings upset many conservatives, who accused the liberal justices of "making law," and of writing their personal views into the Constitution. During the presidential campaign of 1968, Richard Nixon claimed the Warren Court had "gone too far," as he put it, in siding with criminals and Communists. Nixon promised to name justices who believed in the "strict construction" of the Constitution if he became president.

These political factors form the backdrop for this lecture. We're going to begin with the events that surrounded Chief Justice Warren's resignation, and that culminated in Nixon's appointment of Warren Burger to replace him as the Court's leader. We'll also look at Nixon's effort to place *strict constructionists* on the Burger Court, and the Senate's rejection of his first two nominees, who were both conservative southern judges. Finally, we'll discuss two of the Court's most important rulings, during the first years of the Burger Court. One case dealt with the controversial issue of school busing to achieve racial integration, and the other is the famous *Pentagon Papers* case. As we'll see, both of these cases drew the Supreme Court into heated political conflicts.

In my view, the most important factor that affected the Supreme Court in 1968 was the war in Vietnam. Let me explain how this

©2003 The Teaching Company Limited Partnership

faraway military struggle inflicted casualties in the Court's marble building. Growing opposition to American participation in the Vietnam War had eroded President Johnson's popular support. He felt wounded by criticism of his policies, and feared that his "Great Society" programs would not survive the wartime drain on the federal budget. Johnson announced in March of 1968 that he would not seek another term in the White House. But he would remain in office for another 10 months. Earl Warren also felt drained after 16 years as chief justice. He was 77, and wanted to retire while he still enjoyed good health. Warren also wanted to give Johnson the choice of naming his successor, and he knew that Johnson wanted to elevate his long-time friend and advisor, Justice Abe Fortas, to the chief's position.

Warren worked out a deal with Johnson, one that had no precedent in the Court's history. The chief justice met with Johnson in the Oval Office on June 13 of 1968, and told the president of his plan to retire. Warren handed Johnson a letter: "I hereby advise you of my intention to resign as chief justice of the United States effective at your pleasure." Two weeks later, Johnson released his own letter, stating that he would accept Warren's resignation "effective at such time as a successor is qualified." At the same time, Johnson sent his nomination of Abe Fortas to the Senate. But the deal between the two experienced politicians ran into political trouble.

With a presidential campaign underway, many senators balked at giving a "lame-duck" president the choice of a new chief justice. Republican senators mounted a filibuster against Fortas's confirmation, hoping to block any vote before the November election. During this political struggle, the press uncovered several embarrassing facts about Justice Fortas. One involved his acceptance of $15,000 for speaking at nine sessions of a law school seminar in Washington. This was a large payment for a small investment of time, almost half of Fortas's annual salary as a justice. The Senate voted against cutting off the filibuster on October 1 of 1968, just a month before the election. The next day, Fortas asked Johnson to withdraw his nomination. The president then asked Chief Justice Warren to remain on the Court "until emotion subsides," as Johnson put it.

Warren became a "lame-duck" chief justice during his last term on the Court. This was a painful experience for Warren, who detested

Richard Nixon. Nixon held an equally negative view of Warren, going back to political feuds within the California Republican Party in the 1940s. It's ironic that Nixon stood at the lawyer's podium in the Supreme Court chamber on Warren's last day as chief justice, June 23 of 1969. The president had come for the swearing-in of Warren Earl Burger as Earl Warren's successor. On this ceremonial occasion, Nixon had only words of praise for a man he considered dangerous to the Constitution. The president lauded Warren for the qualities of dignity, integrity, and fairness he exhibited as chief justice. The 16 years of the Warren Court, Nixon said, "will be described by historians as years of greater change in America than any in our history." Over the course of that history, Nixon added, the Supreme Court had provided both "change" and "continuity" to American government and society.

Nixon's nomination of Warren Burger certainly made a change in the Court. Whether the new chief justice would provide continuity in the Court's functioning as an institution remained to be seen. In many ways, there was continuity in the transition from Warren to Burger. The new chief justice resembled his predecessor in several respects. Both men came from humble origins, and both had fathers who worked for railroads. Burger was born in St. Paul, Minnesota, in 1907, and began working at the age of nine, delivering newspapers to help the family's finances. He kept working all through high school and college, taking extension courses at the University of Minnesota for two years. Burger attended the St. Paul College of Law as a night student, and practiced in small firms after his graduation in 1931.

Like Earl Warren, Burger became active in Republican politics as a young man. He was a Minnesota delegate to the Republican national convention in 1948, at which Warren was chosen as the party's vice-presidential candidate. Four years later, Warren and Burger both supported Dwight Eisenhower over Senator Robert Taft for the party's presidential nomination. After his election, Eisenhower rewarded Burger with the job of heading the Justice Department's civil division. In 1956, the president named Burger to the federal appeals court in Washington, D.C. This court was then controlled by liberal judges, and Burger often dissented from its rulings, particularly in criminal cases. Earl Warren was then serving as chief justice, and Burger showed little deference to the Warren Court's rulings.

In one dissenting opinion, Burger attacked Warren's opinion in the *Miranda* case, which required police to warn criminal suspects of their right to remain silent. Burger criticized what he called "the seeming anxiety of judges to protect every accused person from every consequence of his voluntary utterances." His strong "law and order" views impressed Richard Nixon, who quoted one of Burger's speeches during the 1968 presidential campaign. Once he reached the White House, Nixon quickly decided on Burger to replace Chief Justice Warren. When the president announced Burger's nomination in May of 1969, he used these words of praise: "He is a *strict constructionist* as far as the Constitution is concerned." Nixon also noted that Burger's stand on criminal law was the minority view on the Supreme Court. "I would hope it would become the majority view," Nixon added.

It quickly became apparent that Burger's views would not become the Court's majority view, at least until its membership changed. Justice Brennan assumed the leadership of the Court's liberals, who included Justices Black, Douglas, and Marshall. On many issues, Justices White and Stewart joined this group, which left Justice Harlan as the only real conservative. Even Harlan sided with the liberal and moderate justices on some issues, most often in free speech cases, so Chief Justice Burger was far more conservative than his seven colleagues. One seat was vacant on the bench when Burger arrived. Three weeks earlier, Justice Abe Fortas had resigned from the Court, the victim of his own ethical failings. We'll discuss those events very shortly. But it's important to note that the four liberal justices could block the other four in any divided case. That's because the Court's rules provide that cases cannot be decided by tie votes. In such cases, the lower-court decision remains in effect, and the Court issues no opinion.

It's also fair to say that Burger was not greeted with open arms by the justices who served under Earl Warren. In truth, Warren was a hard act to follow. Burger lacked his natural warmth and hearty manner, and several of Burger's initial steps on the Court turned into stumbles. He upset the other justices by changing sides in closely divided cases, switching from the minority to the majority. This allowed him to exercise the chief's prerogative to assign majority opinions, often to himself. Some justices thought this practice indicated a lack of principle on Burger's part. In several cases, he assigned majority opinions after voting with the minority. This outraged Justice Douglas, who sent his colleagues a caustic memo, saying that Burger's efforts to control the assignments would create, in his words, "a frayed and bitter Court, full of needless strains and quarrels." It's only fair to admit my own view, that Burger tried to manipulate the Court, and that he lacked the essential qualities of leadership. But this view may be colored by my disagreement with many of Burger's votes and opinions.

We saw that Justice Abe Fortas resigned from the Court in May of 1969. Fortas had remained on the bench after he withdrew his nomination as chief justice. But the press had continued digging into his financial records. *Life* magazine reported that Fortas had accepted a lifetime payment of $20,000 a year from a millionaire friend who was later convicted on fraud charges, and who boasted that Fortas would help him. Chief Justice Warren had been appalled by these revelations, and he pressured Fortas to spare the Court further embarrassment by resigning. Fortas's departure gave Nixon the chance to shift the Court to the right. The four liberal justices might even find themselves outvoted in cases with political overtones. But Nixon made a blunder that matched Earl Warren's effort to name his own successor.

During the 1968 campaign, Nixon pursued what the press called his "southern strategy." The Republicans courted the votes of white southerners by claiming that federal judges were pushing too hard for school integration. Nixon also promised to fill the next Supreme Court vacancy from the South. The "southern strategy" worked for voters, but it quickly backfired with the court. Nixon's first choice to replace Fortas was Clement Haynsworth, a federal appellate judge from South Carolina. Labor and civil rights groups mounted a campaign against Haynsworth that echoed their successful effort, back in 1930, to keep another southern judge, John Parker, off the Supreme Court. Moderate Republicans joined the campaign when they discovered that Haynsworth had voted in one case for a company in which he owned stock. The amount wasn't large, but the political fallout was deadly. The Senate rejected Haynsworth by a vote of 55 to 45, but President Nixon refused to surrender his "southern strategy."

He asked the Senate to confirm another federal appellate judge, G. Harrold Carswell of Florida. But this nomination died even more

©2003 The Teaching Company Limited Partnership

quickly than Haynsworth's. Reporters dug into old newspapers, and pulled out a 1948 speech by Carswell, who backed the segregationist presidential campaign of Strom Thurmond. "Segregation of the races is proper, and the only practical and correct way of life in our states," Carswell said. The Senate rejected him by a vote of 51 to 45. The day after this defeat, Nixon vented his anger to the press: "I will not nominate another southerner and let him be subjected to the kind of malicious character assassination accorded both Judges Haynsworth and Carswell." But Nixon had no one but himself to blame for the defeat of his "southern strategy." Failing to check the records of his judicial nominees was a fatal mistake, so he turned to a northern judge with a flawless record, Harry Blackmun of Minnesota.

Blackmun had been Phi Beta Kappa at Harvard College, and then graduated from Harvard Law School. He practiced in St. Paul for 16 years, including nine years as general counsel of the Mayo Clinic, one of the nation's leading medical centers. President Eisenhower had placed Blackmun on the federal appellate bench in 1959, where he almost always voted to uphold state laws and sided with governments in conflicts over individual rights. President Nixon met with Blackmun and was impressed with his conservative judicial record. Blackmun had another advantage; he and Warren Burger had attended grade school together, and Blackmun was the best man at Burger's wedding. During his Senate confirmation hearings, Strom Thurmond of South Carolina praised Blackmun as a *strict constructionist*. With that endorsement, Blackmun sailed through the hearings without a ripple. The Senate confirmed him in June of 1970 with a sigh of relief, and without a single dissent.

We're going to look now at two cases that were decided in 1971, during Chief Justice Burger's second year at the Court's helm. As we'll see, each case provoked heated debate and division within the Court, and behind-the-scenes maneuvers to affect their outcome. The first case involved school integration in Charlotte, North Carolina— the state's largest city. Charlotte and the surrounding area of Mecklenburg County had been joined in a school district that covered some 500 square miles. Almost all of the district's black children lived in Charlotte, while the county schools were almost all white. The school board for the consolidated district had adopted an integration plan that included a so-called "minority to majority" provision. This plan allowed white students who lived near all-black schools to transfer into largely white schools. In 1965, a black parent, named Darius Swann, filed a lawsuit that challenged this plan.

Swann was a Presbyterian minister, and his six-year-old son, James, had been turned away from the mostly white school that was closest to their home. School officials had assigned James to an all-black elementary school. Swann's lawsuit noted that 88 of the district's 109 schools remained all black or all white. The federal judge who presided over the case, James McMillan, issued an order in April of 1969. At that time, about one-third of the district's 84,000 students rode buses to school, mostly in the rural areas of Mecklenburg County. McMillan directed school officials to implement a plan that would involve busing an additional 13,000 children. White children from the county schools would be bused into the city, and black children would ride buses to outlying schools. McMillan's plan was designed to achieve a racial balance in each school that reflected the district's make-up of 79 percent white students and 21 percent black.

White parents reacted with outrage at the busing plan. They delivered an anti-busing petition with 67,000 signatures to the White House. President Nixon was sympathetic with their protest, but he avoided any public comment at the time. After a federal appellate court reversed Judge McMillan's busing order, the Supreme Court accepted the *Swann* case for review. The justices heard oral argument on October 12 of 1970. One week later, Nixon visited North Carolina to stump for Republican candidates, telling voters that he opposed "the use of busing solely for the purpose of achieving racial balance" in the schools. What happened inside the Supreme Court during its deliberations in the *Swann* case is a fascinating story.

During the Court's first conference on the case, all but two justices supported the power of federal judges to order busing as a remedy for school segregation. Chief Justice Burger and Justice Hugo Black were the sole opponents of this approach. As the senior justice in the majority, William O. Douglas was entitled under the Court's rules to assign the opinion. But Douglas was astounded when Burger said he would draft an opinion that spoke for all the justices. Burger wanted to write the narrowest possible opinion, sending the case back to Judge McMillan for what Burger called "reconsideration" of his order. Douglas objected strongly, but Burger persisted. The chief

 ©2003 The Teaching Company Limited Partnership

justice finally produced an opinion that supported busing as a remedy for school segregation, but allowed districts to retain all-black and all-white schools if they showed that student assignments were not based on racial discrimination. In other words, busing was a judicial remedy of last resort. The Court's liberal justices swallowed their objections to Burger's opinion, but President Nixon considered it a vindication of his position. He told the press: "I do not believe that busing to achieve racial balance is in the interests of better education."

The Court handed down its decision in *Swann v. Charlotte-Mecklenburg Board of Education* on April 20 of 1971. That morning's newspapers reported that American forces in Vietnam now numbered close to 300,000. American planes had begun bombing villages in Laos that harbored North Vietnamese troops. The Vietnam War had become the most divisive issue in American politics. And the Supreme Court got dragged into this conflict when the *New York Times* published a front-page story on June 13 of 1971, under the headline "Vietnam Archive: Pentagon Study Traces Three Decades of Growing U.S. Involvement." The *Times* had obtained copies of a 47-volume, top-secret history of American involvement in Vietnam from a former Pentagon official named Daniel Ellsberg. He was a former Marine Corps officer who had turned against the war. Ellsberg had worked on the Pentagon study, and he felt the American people should learn about what he considered lies and deception by military officials and presidents.

Ellsberg had secretly copied what became known as the *Pentagon Papers*, and delivered them to the *Times* and the *Washington Post*. The Nixon administration reacted to the *Times* article by running to a federal judge in New York, who promptly issued an injunction against further publication. But the *Washington Post* printed more excerpts from the Pentagon Papers, and federal lawyers sought an injunction against that paper. But Judge Gerhard Gesell turned them down, and the legal situation quickly turned into a major battle over the First Amendment. Confronted by conflicting rulings, the Supreme Court agreed to decide whether the government could block the publication of documents it considered dangerous to national security. Chief Justice Burger called a special session of the Court on June 26 of 1971, just two weeks after the first story in the *New York Times*.

The legal issue in *New York Times v. United States* was over the doctrine of *prior restraint* of the press. Back in 1931, the Court had ruled that government officials could not stop the presses before they rolled. But in this case, *Near v. Minnesota*, Chief Justice Charles Evans Hughes wrote that the government could restrain the publication of what he called "the sailing dates of transports or the number and location of troops" during wartime. This became known as the "troop-ship" exception to the ban on prior restraint. Government lawyers relied on this ruling in their arguments to the Court in the *Pentagon Papers* case. We're going to listen now to brief excerpts of the oral arguments on both sides of this landmark case. Solicitor General Erwin Griswold takes the podium for the federal government. He's a former dean of Harvard Law School and a respected lawyer. Griswold points the justices to the "closed brief" in which the Justice Department included documents in the Pentagon Papers it considered especially damaging to national security. Only the justices could look inside this brief.

> Griswold: "But I also think the heart of our case is that the publication of the material specified in my closed brief will, as I have tried to argue there, materially affect the security of the United States. It will affect lives. It will affect the process of the termination of the war. It will affect the process of recovering prisoners of war. I cannot say that the termination of the war, or recovering prisoners of war, is something which has an 'immediate' effect on the security of the United States. I say that it has such an effect on the security of the United States that it ought to be the basis of an injunction in this case."

Griswold warns that further publication of the Pentagon Papers might endanger American troops in Vietnam.

> Griswold: "I haven't the slightest doubt, myself, that the material which has already been published, and the publication of the other materials, affects American lives, and is a thoroughly serious matter. And I think that to say that it can only be enjoined if there will be a war tomorrow morning, when there's a war going on now, is much too narrow."

Alexander Bickel speaks for the *New York Times*. He's a Yale Law School professor and a noted legal scholar. Justice Potter Stewart asks Bickel a tough question.

> Stewart: "Let me give you a hypothetical case. Let us assume that when the members of the Court go back and open up this sealed record, we find something there that absolutely convinces us that its disclosure would result in the sentencing to death of a hundred young men whose only offense had been that they were 19 years old and had low draft numbers. What should we do?"

Stewart's question puts Bickel on the spot. He tries to duck the question, but Stewart demands an answer.

> Stewart: "You would say the Constitution requires that it be published and that these men die. Is that it?"

> Bickel: "No. No, I'm afraid I'd have, I'm afraid that my, the inclinations of humanity overcome the somewhat more abstract devotion to the First Amendment, in a case of that sort."

After these arguments, the justices continued arguing about the *Pentagon Papers* case. Justice Hugo Black was amazed at Theodore Bickel's answer to Stewart's question. "Too bad the *Times* couldn't find someone who believes in the First Amendment," he said. Black and Douglas took an uncompromising stand against prior restraint under any circumstances, but four other justices felt that the Court shouldn't issue such a broad ruling. They agreed, however, that the government had not met its "heavy burden" of showing that further publication of the Pentagon Papers would damage national security. Six justices voted to lift the injunction and let the *Times* resume its publication. Chief Justice Burger, along with Justices Harlan and Blackmun, voted to send the case back for additional hearings in the lower court and to continue the injunction until those proceedings ended.

But the *Pentagon Papers* case ended with an unusual twist. The Court handed down its ruling in a crowded chamber on June 30 of 1971, four days after the oral arguments. The six justices in the majority were astounded when Burger insisted on reading the one-paragraph, unsigned opinion that lifted the injunctions against the

Times and the *Post*. Burger had also written his own dissenting opinion, criticizing the "unseemly haste" with which the case had been handled. Justice Black, who felt he should have read the Court's opinion, issued his own. He blasted the government for what he called "a flagrant, indefensible, and continuing violation of the First Amendment."

There's a footnote to the *Pentagon Papers* case. Several years after the decision, Solicitor General Griswold said that he hadn't read his own closed brief before the oral argument. When he later read the documents it contained, he decided that none of them could have damaged the nation's security. They all dealt with past events, not with current or future military or diplomatic plans. The *Pentagon Papers* case left several questions open for debate. What if the press obtained secret war plans for a pre-emptive attack on another country, or was going to publish detailed instructions for making deadly biological weapons? Has the age of the Internet made any prior restraint impossible? Has public safety become more important than the public's right to know? Questions like these might come before the Court, and its answers cannot be forecast with any certainty.

Our first look at the Burger Court revealed both the change and the continuity that President Nixon discussed in its chamber. During this crucial period, the Court's leadership changed, but most justices remained. The integration issue changed from opening doors to busing students, but one-race schools remained. The press changed its views on the Vietnam War, but the Court's defense of the First Amendment remained. In our next lecture, we'll focus on an issue that created major changes in American law and society: the conflict over abortion. We'll examine the conflicts within the Burger Court over this difficult and divisive issue.

©2003 The Teaching Company Limited Partnership

Lecture Twenty-Nine
"A Right to Privacy"

Scope:

This lecture begins with a look at two justices placed on the Supreme Court by President Richard Nixon: Lewis Powell and William Rehnquist. We will examine in some detail the background and judicial philosophy of Justice Rehnquist, who was named to lead the Court in 1986. We will then discuss the controversies, going back to the 19th century, over such "personal autonomy" issues as forced sterilization, access to contraceptives, and criminal abortion laws. The major judicial figures in this area include Justices Oliver Wendell Holmes, whose 1927 opinion in *Buck v. Bell* upheld Virginia's forced sterilization law; William O. Douglas, who wrote for the Court in 1965, striking down a state ban on contraceptive use in *Griswold v. Connecticut*; and Harry Blackmun, whose 1973 opinion in *Roe v. Wade* ruled that states could not make abortion a criminal offense. We will look at the differing personal views and judicial approaches these justices brought to each case. We will also hear the stories of Carrie Buck, who was sterilized for bearing an illegitimate child; Estelle Griswold, who headed a Planned Parenthood clinic; and Norma McCorvey, the "Jane Roe" in the abortion case. This lecture follows the *Roe* case from its beginning through the Supreme Court arguments over the Texas law that banned all abortions unless the life of the pregnant woman was endangered.

Outline

I. This lecture begins our discussion of the Court's rulings on abortion and examines the backgrounds and careers of two justices who joined the Court in 1972.

II. Justices Hugo Black and John Harlan both retired in September 1971, and both died before the year ended.

    A. President Richard Nixon nominated Lewis Powell of Virginia to replace Black.

        1. Powell was a prominent lawyer in Richmond, who had chaired both the city and state school boards.

      2. He had served as president of the American Bar Association and had opposed the "massive resistance" program of Virginia's segregationist politicians.

      3. Powell had earlier turned down a Supreme Court nomination, but he agreed to join the Court at Nixon's request.

      4. On the Court, Powell was a moderate conservative and often cast the swing vote in crucial cases.

B. Nixon nominated William Rehnquist of Arizona to replace Harlan.

      1. Rehnquist graduated at the top of his Stanford law school class and had served as law clerk to Justice Robert Jackson.

      2. He practiced law in Phoenix and was active in Republican politics.

      3. Rehnquist served in the Justice Department as legal counsel to the attorney general in the Nixon administration.

C. He was an advocate of *legal positivism*, the doctrine that laws have no moral content and should be obeyed because they reflect majority sentiment.

      1. He took very conservative positions on civil rights, arguing against "public accommodation" laws and school integration plans in Phoenix.

      2. During his Senate confirmation hearings, he was confronted with a memo he wrote to Justice Jackson in 1953, arguing, "*Plessy v. Ferguson* was right and should be reaffirmed."

      3. Rehnquist was only 47 when he joined the Court; Nixon said he chose him because he could serve another 25 years or more.

III. We will examine the origins of the "right to privacy" in American law.

A. In 1890, Louis Brandeis wrote a *Harvard Law Review* article on the right to privacy.

      1. He was concerned about the invasion of privacy by tabloid newspapers.

2. Brandeis argued that a basic principle of law was "the right to be let alone" in personal matters, although he did not mention abortion.

B. However, Brandeis joined the opinion of Justice Oliver Wendell Holmes in the 1927 case of *Buck v. Bell*.
   1. In this case, Holmes upheld a Virginia law that allowed the forced sterilization of "feeble-minded" and "morally delinquent" inmates of state institutions.
   2. Holmes said the state had a right to prevent those who were "manifestly unfit from continuing their kind."

C. In 1942, the Court ruled against the forced sterilization of three-time felons in state prisons, in *Skinner v. Oklahoma*.
   1. Justice William Douglas said that sterilization could be abused by officials with "evil or reckless hands," a reference to the policies of Nazi Germany.
   2. He also said that marriage and procreation were among "the basic civil rights of man."

IV. In 1965, Douglas again wrote for the Court in striking down a state law that banned the use or distribution of contraceptives, in *Griswold v. Connecticut*.

A. This case involved a challenge by the director of the Planned Parenthood clinic in New Haven.

B. Douglas found a "right of privacy" in the Constitution that stemmed from the protections of the Bill of Rights.

C. Justice Hugo Black dissented in *Griswold*, saying that the Constitution does not mention privacy.

D. In my view, the split between Black and Douglas, two of the Court's most liberal justices, says a great deal about the power of ideas.
   1. Douglas believed the Constitution should be read broadly to protect "fundamental rights" against governmental interference. He believed that conceptions of these fundamental rights should reflect changes in society.
   2. Black felt strongly that new rights could be created only by amending the Constitution.

V. The case of *Roe v. Wade* confronted the Court with the abortion issue in 1971 and 1972.

    A. This case began in Dallas, Texas, when a pregnant woman named Norma McCorvey approached two young lawyers, Linda Coffee and Sarah Weddington.

    B. They filed a suit on behalf of McCorvey, protecting her identity as "Jane Roe." Henry Wade, the Dallas district attorney, was the lead defendant.

    C. Texas law banned all abortions, except those necessary to save a pregnant woman's life.

    D. A panel of federal judges struck down the law as a violation of the Ninth Amendment, which protects rights that are "retained by the people" from government abridgment.

VI. The oral arguments before the Supreme Court in *Roe v. Wade* focused on two issues.

    A. Does the Constitution protect a "right to privacy" that includes abortion?

    B. Is a fetus a "person" with rights to life under the due process clause of the Fourteenth Amendment?

    C. Our next lecture discusses the Court's deliberations and decision in the *Roe* case.

Suggested Readings:

Peter Irons, *A People's History of the Supreme Court*, chapters 32–33 (1999).

David J. Garrow, *Liberty and Sexuality: The Right to Privacy and the Making of Roe v. Wade* (1994).

Questions to Consider:

1. Do you think there should be any circumstances in which people could be sterilized without their consent, such as profound mental retardation?

2. If the Constitution does not mention a "right to privacy," should judges have the power to find one in other constitutional provisions?

 ©2003 The Teaching Company Limited Partnership

Lecture Twenty-Nine—Transcript
"A Right to Privacy"

In our previous lecture, we looked at the transition in the Supreme Court, from the leadership of Earl Warren to that of Warren Burger as chief justice. We discussed the political factors that surrounded Warren's effort to name Justice Abe Fortas as his successor, and President Nixon's choice of Burger, hoping to move the Court in a more conservative direction. We also examined two of the Burger Court's most important rulings, both handed down in 1971. One case dealt with the controversial issue of busing as a judicial remedy for school segregation. The other involved the government's effort to block the press from publishing excerpts of the so-called Pentagon Papers, a top-secret history of American involvement in the Vietnam War. Both of these cases reflected deep-rooted conflicts between liberals and conservatives, among the public and within the Court, and they illustrate the theme of continuity and change, a theme we have examined throughout this course.

In this lecture, and the one that follows, we'll pursue this theme in discussing an issue that has created greater conflict in American society than any other over the past three decades. This is the issue of abortion. Public opinion has shifted on the abortion question, over the years since the Court decided the case of *Roe v. Wade* in 1973. Polls show that most people support a woman's basic right to obtain an abortion in the early stages of pregnancy. But most people also feel there should be limits on abortion, and large majorities believe some abortion procedures should be banned. We'll look at cases involving these questions in a later lecture.

But on both sides of this difficult issue, there are people who find no room for compromise. For them, abortion involves what professor Laurence Tribe of Harvard Law School calls "the clash of absolutes." How can the Supreme Court resolve this clash of absolutes? Or should the Court stay out of this controversy altogether, and leave the abortion issue to elected lawmakers, for resolution by the political process? These are questions we'll discuss in this lecture and the next, by looking at the opposing views of the justices who decided the *Roe* case.

Before we reach the *Roe* case, we'll look first at the two men who joined the Burger Court in January of 1972. As we'll see, they took opposite sides on the abortion issue. And then we'll examine the development of what became known as the "right to privacy." This constitutional doctrine first emerged in the 1890s, and then took shape in several cases that dealt with sterilization and contraception. These are fascinating cases, raising basic issues of people's rights to have, or not to have, children.

We'll begin with changes on the Supreme Court bench. Justices Hugo Black and John Harlan both retired from the Court in September of 1971, just a few weeks before the Court's term began, on the first Monday in October. And both men died before the year ended. Their departures gave President Nixon the rare opportunity to place two justices on the Court at the same time. As we saw, the Senate had frustrated Nixon's "southern strategy" by rejecting two highly conservative nominees to replace Justice Abe Fortas in 1969, so the president adopted a variant of that strategy. He picked a moderate—but highly respected—southerner, Lewis Powell of Virginia. Nixon also named a highly conservative—but little known—Justice Department lawyer, William Rehnquist of Arizona. We'll look at these two men in turn.

Powell was a classic lawyer's lawyer, much like John W. Davis, who opposed Thurgood Marshall in the school segregation cases. Powell's ancestors had landed in Virginia in 1607, three centuries before his birth in 1907. He graduated from Washington and Lee University's law school, and spent a year in graduate study at Harvard before returning to his native Richmond. During 40 years in corporate practice, Powell devoted many hours to public service. He chaired both the Richmond and state boards of education in the 1950s and early 60s.

Powell took a "go-slow" approach to school integration. He opposed both the "massive resistance" program of his state's die-hard segregationists, and he also opposed busing students to achieve racial balance in the schools. The only senator who voted against Powell was Fred Harris of Oklahoma, who called him "an elitist who has never shown any deep feeling for little people." There was some truth to this. Powell's clients and friends came from the corporate elite and the first families of Virginia. But he also supported legal services for the poor when he headed the American Bar Association. I think it's fair to call Powell a southern aristocrat with a sense of noblesse oblige.

President Nixon's choice for the Court's other vacant seat had a very different background. We'll take a closer look at William Rehnquist, because he later became chief justice, and because his judicial views have a distinctive character. Rehnquist was born in 1924, in Milwaukee, Wisconsin. During the previous century, only Justices William O. Douglas and Byron White were younger when they joined the Court. Nixon later said: "Rehnquist's most attractive quality was his age. He was only 47 and could probably serve on the Court for 25 years." He passed that mark in 1997.

Rehnquist grew up in the Milwaukee suburb of Shorewood. As its name suggests, the town is on Lake Michigan and its streets are shaded with oaks and maples. Only nine blacks lived in Shorewood, and they all worked as live-in maids in the lakefront mansions of the bankers and brewers who made Milwaukee a prosperous city. Rehnquist's father was the son of Swedish immigrants, and made a comfortable living as a wholesale paper salesman, although the family lived in a modest brick home. Rehnquist absorbed his parents' strong Republican loyalties, and dinnertime included lively political discussion. He started college in 1942, but left after one quarter to join the Army Air Corps, which posted him to North Africa as a weather observer. When he mustered out, the GI bill paid his tuition to Stanford University in California. "I wanted to find someplace like North Africa to go to school," Rehnquist later said.

He majored in political science, and won a Phi Beta Kappa key. He then earned two master's degrees, one at Stanford and the other from Harvard. Rehnquist returned from chilly Massachusetts and entered Stanford's law school. He graduated in 1952 at the top of his class, and then he served for a year as law clerk to Justice Robert Jackson at the Supreme Court. Rehnquist left Washington for Arizona in 1953, and practiced law in Phoenix until 1969. He worked on the presidential campaign of Arizona Senator Barry Goldwater in 1964, and his political contacts later helped Rehnquist land a job with the Justice Department, as director of the Office of Legal Counsel, which functions as the attorney general's in-house law firm. Rehnquist provided legal advice on such issues as antiwar protests, the Equal Rights Amendment, wiretapping, and detention of criminal suspects without bail. His strong conservative views on these issues impressed White House officials, and helped Rehnquist win his Supreme Court nomination.

But they also provoked opposition from liberal senators, who grilled Rehnquist on his public criticism of the Warren Court's rulings. During his confirmation hearings, the senators compiled a big folder of Rehnquist's speeches, articles, and letters to newspapers, going back to his college days. In one magazine article, Rehnquist had blasted the Court for what he called its "extreme solicitude for the claims of Communists and other criminal defendants." These rulings were not based, he told the senators, on "a fair reading of the Constitution." In his view, they reflected "the personal philosophy" of the justices. But Rehnquist impressed other senators with his forthright answers, and the Senate confirmed him by a vote of 68 to 26. It's worth taking a close look at the personal philosophy of Justice Rehnquist for two reasons. First, he's been an articulate and consistent advocate of this philosophy for his entire career. Secondly, Rehnquist has expressed his views in scores of judicial opinions, at first in dissent and more recently for the majority, as the Court has swung to the right.

We'll begin with an editorial Rehnquist wrote for the Stanford Daily in 1948, which was entitled "Emotion v. Reason." What bothered Rehnquist, as he said, was "the implication that humanitarianism is desirable" as a moral value. He argued, "moral standards are incapable of being rationally demonstrated. One personal conviction is no better than another." This may have been youthful rhetoric, but I think the moral neutrality it expresses is consistent with the *legal positivism* that Rehnquist espouses. The term "legal positivism" means that laws have no moral content. Laws should be obeyed without question, simply because they are laws. As he said in 1969, "the minority, no matter how disaffected or disenchanted, owes an unqualified obligation to obey a duly enacted law." People like Rosa Parks, who refused to obey laws they considered unjust, get no sympathy from Rehnquist.

Legal positivism is a concept that Rehnquist has repeatedly expressed, even as a justice. For example, he argued to a law school audience in 1976 that laws, as he said, "take on a form of moral goodness because they have been enacted into positive law." Constitutional protections have been accepted, Rehnquist said, "not because of any intrinsic worth, but simply because they have been incorporated in a constitution by the people." The consequence of this philosophy is that Rehnquist almost always votes to uphold laws that are challenged as violating the Bill of Rights. He has taken the

 ©2003 The Teaching Company Limited Partnership

approach of judicial deference to elected lawmakers far beyond any other justice in the past century. One study of his voting record showed that Rehnquist sided with the government close to 90 percent of the time, in cases ranging from criminal law to civil rights. But Rehnquist has often voted to strike down laws that were designed to protect racial minorities. His attitudes on racial issues, in my view, raise serious doubts about his commitment to equal justice under law.

Back in 1964, Rehnquist opposed a school integration plan in Phoenix, with these words: "We are no more dedicated to an 'integrated' society than we are to a 'segregated' society." This statement expressed Rehnquist's moral neutrality on social issues, but it also reflected his views on race. He put those views into a memorandum he wrote to Justice Robert Jackson, during his stint as a law clerk in 1952 and 1953. The Court was then considering the school segregation cases, and Jackson asked Rehnquist for his views on the separate but equal doctrine of the *Plessy* case. His answer was forthright. "I think *Plessy v. Ferguson* was right and should be reaffirmed," he told Jackson.

He added a revealing sentence: "In the long run, it is the majority who will determine what the constitutional rights of the minority are." Not the majority of the Supreme Court, but the majority of voters. So, in Rehnquist's view, the Court's role is basically to uphold the judgments of elected lawmakers and government officials. But if those judgments conflict with his conservative views, he'll vote to strike them down. Rehnquist makes no bones about this. "I want to see that version of the law applied when the case comes up," he said in 1985. "If that makes me a partisan, certainly I'm a partisan."

On a personal note, Justice Rehnquist and I are both partisans for the views we hold very strongly. I've disagreed with most of the opinions he's written over the past 30 years. But he and I agree on one thing: ideas matter. As Justice Oliver Wendell Holmes put it, "every idea is an incitement." Ideas about constitutional rights have often incited debate, and those debates have often changed the course of American society. One idea that has sparked the most heated debate is the notion that the Constitution includes a "right to privacy." We're going to look now at the origins of the "right to privacy" in American law. The term "privacy" stems from a Latin word that means "belonging to oneself, not to the state." The English common law used the word for the notion that every person enjoys a right to protect their body from physical assault, not only from other people, but also from the King's agents.

Over the years, the idea of privacy took on a broader meaning. Back in the 1880s, a noted legal scholar defined "liberty" under the Constitution as "the right to be let alone." This phrase appealed to a young Boston lawyer, Louis Brandeis, who wrote an article for the *Harvard Law Review* in 1890 with the title, "The Right to Privacy." What prompted Brandeis to write this article was his concern about the "yellow" press, the ancestors of today's tabloid newspapers. Brandeis felt there should be legal protection against what he called "the unwarranted invasion of individual privacy" by scandal-seeking reporters and photographers. He called for shielding "the private life, habits, acts, and relations of an individual" from unwanted disclosure. Brandeis wrote nothing about contraception or abortion. But the notion of a "right to privacy" in matters of procreation had its roots in this path-breaking article.

Brandeis himself did not adopt the idea that the right of privacy extended to personal decisions about procreation. He joined the opinion of Justice Oliver Wendell Holmes, who ruled for the Court in 1927 that Virginia officials could sterilize inmates of state institutions who were considered "feeble-minded" or "morally delinquent." The case of *Buck v. Bell* reflected the influence of the so-called "eugenics" movement, whose leaders pressed for laws to promote "race betterment" through forced sterilization. Carrie Buck was a young woman who was committed to a state institution for the "feeble-minded." She was not, in fact, mentally retarded at all.

Carrie's offense was that she had had an illegitimate child, the product of a rape by a relative. But state officials requested a court order to sterilize Carrie, and prevent her from having any more children. Justice Holmes had no sympathy for Carrie Buck. "It is better for all the world," he wrote, "if, instead of waiting to execute degenerate offspring for crime, or to let them starve for their imbecility, society can prevent those who are manifestly unfit from continuing their kind." Holmes saw no difference between smallpox and sterilization. "The principle that sustains compulsory vaccination," he wrote, "is broad enough to cover cutting the Fallopian tubes." Thirty other states followed Virginia and passed laws that allowed forced sterilization. But the eugenics movement lost support during the 1930s, after the Nazi regime in Germany adopted a "race hygiene" law, under which some two million supposedly "defective" Germans were sterilized.

The Supreme Court took another look at this issue in 1942, during the war against German Nazis. The case of *Skinner v. Oklahoma* shows the influence of changing ideas about privacy and procreation. Jack Skinner was an Oklahoma prison inmate, with three felonies on his record. His first conviction, as a juvenile, was for stealing chickens, but he later committed two armed robberies. State law allowed the sterilization of "three-time losers" like Skinner, who filed a lawsuit to block a court-ordered vasectomy. Justice William O. Douglas wrote for a unanimous Court in reversing this order. He made a veiled, but pointed, reference to the Nazis in his opinion. "In evil or reckless hands," Douglas said, the power to sterilize "can cause races or types which are inimical to the dominant group to wither and disappear." The *Skinner* ruling opened the door to future cases that raised broader issues than sterilization. "We are dealing here with legislation which involves one of the basic civil rights of man," Douglas added. "Marriage and procreation are fundamental to the very existence and survival of the race."

The *Skinner* case established a "fundamental right" to procreate, allowing people to have children if they want them. Does the Constitution also protect the right *not* to have children? The justices answered this question in 1965, 23 years after the *Skinner* ruling. And once again, Justice Douglas wrote for the Court. The case of *Griswold v. Connecticut* involved a state law that banned the distribution or use of contraceptives like condoms and birth-control pills. The Connecticut law was challenged by Estelle Griswold, who directed the Planned Parenthood clinic in New Haven. She was joined by Dr. Thomas Buxton, the clinic's medical director. They were both arrested for giving contraceptives to married couples, and fined $100 for breaking the law.

There are two important facts about the *Griswold* case. First, the feminist movement had grown rapidly in recent years, attracting members with slogans like, "Keep Your Laws Off My Body." Secondly, the case reached the Court at the height of the Warren Court's "activist" period, and the liberal majority relished the chance to strike down a law they viewed as a relic of Victorian morality.

Justice Douglas wanted to find a "right to privacy" in the Constitution, but that phrase does not appear in its text. So he searched the Court's earlier decisions for precedent, turning up four cases that established a "right of association" under the First Amendment.

Two of these cases upheld the rights of parents to make decisions about their children's education, and the other two protected civil rights groups from harassment by southern officials. "The association of people is not mentioned in the Constitution," Douglas noted, but the Court had recognized the "right of association," based on the protections of the Bill of Rights. Douglas found a similar "right to privacy" in those same amendments. He concluded that Dr. Buxton and his patients enjoyed "a relationship lying within a zone of privacy created by several fundamental constitutional guarantees." In other words, the Bill of Rights erected a shield against government interference in what Douglas called "the sacred precincts of the marital bedroom."

Justice Hugo Black agreed with Douglas in virtually every Bill of Rights case. But he read the Constitution with literal precision, and he was unwilling to create new rights that weren't in the old words. "I like my privacy as well as the next one," Black wrote in his dissenting opinion. "But I am nevertheless compelled to admit that government has a right to invade it, unless prohibited by some specific constitutional protection."

In my view, this split between two of the Court's most liberal justices says a great deal about the power of ideas. Black and Douglas both agreed that privacy was a good idea, a value worth protecting. But they had different ideas on the best way to protect that value. Douglas believed the Constitution should be read broadly to protect "fundamental rights" against governmental interference. He also believed that conceptions of these fundamental rights should reflect changes in society. Contraception was not an issue that concerned the men who framed the Constitution in the 18th century, but it *did* concern people in the 20th century, and Douglas considered their views more important than those of the Framers. Justice Black felt strongly that new rights could be created only by amending the Constitution. He objected to judicial efforts, as he wrote in his *Griswold* dissent, "to keep the Constitution in tune with the times."

With this debate in mind, we're going to look now at the landmark case of *Roe v. Wade*, and the issue of abortion. This issue clearly raises many difficult questions. For example, if states cannot ban abortions altogether, can they place restrictions on abortion procedures, or require that doctors inform pregnant women about the risks of abortion, or alternatives to abortion such as adoption? We'll discuss these questions in a later lecture, on cases that followed the *Roe* decision in 1973. But we'll focus now on the conflicting ideas about the proper role of justices in reading the Constitution.

The *Roe* case began in January of 1970, when a young woman named Norma McCorvey met with two young lawyers at a pizza parlor in Dallas, Texas. McCorvey was unmarried, and was in her third month of pregnancy. She had two little girls and didn't feel able to raise a third child. She told the lawyers, Sarah Weddington and Linda Coffee, that she had been raped when she worked with a traveling circus in Florida. McCorvey wanted to end her pregnancy, but she couldn't find a doctor who would perform an abortion. Texas law allowed abortions only to save the life of a pregnant woman, and imposed a five-year prison term on doctors who broke that law. Weddington and Coffee agreed to help McCorvey, but they cautioned her that a lawsuit might take months or even years to reach a decision. McCorvey agreed to go ahead with the lawsuit, but she never got the abortion. When her third daughter was born in July of 1970, she placed her for adoption and never saw her again.

Weddington and Coffee used the pseudonym of "Jane Roe" to protect their client's identity, and they named district attorney Henry Wade as the defendant. They asked a federal judicial panel to enjoin Wade from enforcing the state's criminal abortion law. The judges issued a two-part ruling in June of 1970. They struck down the Texas law as a violation of the Ninth Amendment, which reads: "The enumeration in the Constitution, of certain rights, shall not be construed to deny or disparage others retained by the people." One of those "unenumerated rights," as lawyers call them, was the right to obtain an abortion. But the judges also declined to issue an injunction in the case. Both sides asked the Supreme Court to review this holding, and the stage was set for arguments over abortion in the Court's chamber.

Actually, the *Roe* case was argued twice, the first time in December of 1971. Justices Hugo Black and John Harlan had retired in

September, and there were two vacant seats on the bench. After the first round of arguments, the Court set the case for a second round, in October of 1972. The justices didn't explain their decision. Most likely, they felt the sensitive issue of abortion should be decided by a full bench. By this time, Justices Lewis Powell and William Rehnquist had replaced Black and Harlan. We're going to listen to brief excerpts of the arguments in 1972. But it's important to outline the legal issues before the Court.

One is whether the Constitution should be read to include a right of privacy, as the Court had ruled in the *Griswold* case. If a majority of justices agree on this issue, a second question arises. Does that right extend from contraception to abortion? If the Court agrees, the justices face another question. The Fourteenth Amendment protects "all persons" from being deprived of their lives without due process of law. Is a fetus a "person" under the Constitution? And, if so, does that "person" have a right to life that outweighs a pregnant woman's right to end that life with an abortion? These are all difficult questions, and the lawyers on both sides have just 30 minutes each to address them, and to answer questions from the bench. Robert Flowers is a deputy attorney general from Texas. He defends the notion of fetal "personhood," and provokes a probing question from Justice Potter Stewart.

> Flowers: "It is impossible for me to trace, in my allocated time, the development of the fetus from the date of conception to the date of its birth. But it is the position of the state of Texas that upon conception we have a human being, a person within the concept of the Constitution of the United States and that of Texas also."

> Stewart: "Now, how should that question be decided? Is it a legal question, a constitutional question, a medical question, a philosophical question, a religious question, or what is it?"

> Flowers: "Your Honor, we feel that it could be best decided by a legislature, in view of the fact that they can bring before it the medical testimony, the actual people who do the research. But we do have...."

> Stewart: "You think then it's basically a medical question?"

Flowers: "From a constitutional standpoint, no sir. I think it's fairly and squarely before this Court. We don't envy the Court for having to make this decision."

Sarah Weddington takes the podium to speak for Jane Roe. None of the justices know her client's actual name. She agrees with Flowers on the Court's responsibility, but disagrees that Texas lawmakers should decide the abortion question.

Weddington: "No one is more keenly aware of the gravity of the issues or the moral implications of this case. But it is a case that must be decided on the Constitution. We do not disagree that there is a progression of fetal development. It is the conclusion to be drawn from that upon which we disagree. We are not here to advocate abortion. We do not ask this Court to rule that abortion is good or desirable in any particular situation. We are here to advocate that the decision as to whether or not a particular woman will continue to carry or will terminate a pregnancy is a decision that should be made by that individual. That in fact she has a constitutional right to make that decision for herself, and that the state has shown no interest in interfering with that decision."

The final round of arguments in the Roe *case* concluded on October 11 of 1972. In our next lecture, we'll follow this story and see the outcome of the *Roe* case. We'll also look at a case with a dramatic caption: *The United States of America v. Richard Nixon, President of the United States*. We know this as the "Watergate Tapes" case, and it set the stage for the greatest conflict between the three branches of the federal government since *Marbury v. Madison* in 1803.

Lecture Thirty
From Abortion to Watergate

Scope:

This lecture begins with the Court's deliberations in the *Roe* case, with a focus on the majority opinion of Justice Harry Blackmun. We will look at the way in which Blackmun based his ruling on several earlier cases that dealt with such issues as search and seizure, wiretapping, possession of pornography, and the right of parents to control their children's education. We will see how Blackmun drew out of these earlier cases a "right to privacy broad enough to encompass a women's decision whether or not to terminate her pregnancy." This lecture also discusses the dissenting opinions of Justices William Rehnquist and Byron White in the *Roe* case, who argued that states should retain the right to decide whether abortion should be legal or banned. Finally, we will look at the so-called "Watergate Tapes" case, in which the Court sustained the power of federal courts to order President Richard Nixon to turn over the Oval Office tape recordings of his conversations about the cover-up of White House involvement in the Watergate burglary of the Democratic National Committee in 1972.

Outline

I. This lecture discusses the Supreme Court's deliberations and decision in the abortion case of *Roe v. Wade*. It also examines the Court's landmark ruling in 1974, in the Watergate Tapes case of *Nixon v. United States*.

II. The Court began its deliberations in *Roe v. Wade* shortly after the oral arguments in December 1971.

  A. Only seven justices heard the arguments; Justices Lewis Powell and William Rehnquist had been confirmed by the Senate but did not take their seats until January 1972.

  B. Chief Justice Warren Burger presided at the conference on the *Roe* case.

  1. Justices William O. Douglas, William Brennan, and Thurgood Marshall were strongly in favor of striking down the Texas abortion law.

  2. Justice Byron White made clear that he would vote to uphold the law.

 ©2003 The Teaching Company Limited Partnership

3. Justices Harry Blackmun and Potter Stewart took a middle-of-the-road position; they supported a doctor's right to use his medical judgment on abortion but were not convinced that the Constitution protected a broad right to privacy.

4. Chief Justice Burger argued for upholding the Texas law but reserved his vote on the *Roe* case.

C. Justice Douglas counted Stewart on his side and said there was a majority to strike down the law.

1. Under the Court's practice, Douglas had the power to assign the majority opinion.

2. However, Burger announced he had assigned the opinion to Blackmun.

3. Douglas protested, but he finally agreed to let Blackmun draft an opinion. He suspected that Burger wanted to hold up the decision to avoid making abortion an issue in the 1972 presidential election.

III. The *Roe* case was argued a second time in October 1972, after Justices Powell and Rehnquist took their seats.

A. The arguments largely rehashed those in the first round.

B. The final vote on the *Roe* case was seven to two.

IV. Justice Blackmun spent several months drafting an opinion in the *Roe* case.

A. He explored the medical history of abortion.

1. Most countries did not ban it until the late 19th century, over concerns about infection.

2. However, modern antiseptic procedures had made abortion safer than childbirth.

B. Blackmun devoted just one paragraph to the constitutional issues.

1. He cited 14 earlier decisions to support his conclusion that the Constitution included a right to privacy that prohibited states from banning abortions.

2. These cases spanned the years from 1886 to 1972.

3. None of them dealt with abortion; they covered such issues as search and seizure, wiretapping, the rights of parents and teachers to educate children, and police "stop-and-frisk" practices.

4. Only the *Griswold* decision of 1965 dealt with issues of personal autonomy in procreation.

5. Blackmun based his opinion on the "liberty" interest in the due process clause of the Fourteenth Amendment.

C. Blackmun's opinion applied the strict scrutiny test, which the Court applied in cases involving fundamental rights under the Constitution.

D. Justice Rehnquist based his dissent on the rational basis test, saying that abortion was "far more appropriate to a legislative judgment than to a judicial one."

E. Justice White also dissented, saying the decision was "an exercise of raw judicial power."

F. Chief Justice Burger finally joined the majority but said in a concurring opinion that the Constitution does not allow "abortion on demand."

V. The public reaction to the *Roe* decision was sharply divided.

A. Catholic leaders denounced the ruling, and abortion supporters praised it.

B. A Gallup poll showed that 46 percent of the public felt that decisions about abortion during the first three months of pregnancy should be left to women and their doctors; 45 percent were opposed.

VI. The Court decided the Watergate Tapes case in 1974.

A. This case began in June 1972 with a break-in at Democratic headquarters in the Watergate complex in Washington, D.C.

B. It was soon discovered that the men arrested for the break-in were tied to President Nixon's reelection campaign.

C. Watergate became a national issue, and President Nixon was forced to appoint a special prosecutor, Archibald Cox.

D. When Cox requested tape recordings of Nixon's Oval Office conversations about Watergate, the president fired him. Cox was replaced by a Houston lawyer, Leon Jaworski.

E. Jaworski pressed for the tapes, and Nixon refused to turn them over to a federal judge for the prosecution of White House officials.

VII. The case reached the Supreme Court, and Nixon's lawyers argued that the tapes were protected under the *executive privilege* doctrine.

   A. Jaworski said the president was no different from any other citizen in providing evidence in criminal cases.

   B. The Court ordered Nixon to turn over the tapes in a unanimous ruling in July 1974.

   C. The next month, Nixon resigned as president.

   D. How the Court would rule in another confrontation between a president and federal judges is a difficult question.

Suggested Readings:

David J. Garrow, *Liberty and Sexuality: The Right to Privacy and the Making of Roe v. Wade* (1994).

Stanley I. Kutler, *The Wars of Watergate: The Last Crisis of Richard Nixon* (1990).

Questions to Consider:

1. Should abortion be a matter for each state's legislature to decide, or should this issue be decided by unelected judges?

2. Under what circumstances do you think the president should have the power to protect his or her private conversations from disclosure to judges?

Lecture Thirty—Transcript
From Abortion to Watergate

In our previous lecture, we first looked at the two men who joined the Supreme Court in January of 1972. Lewis Powell and William Rehnquist took the seats of Hugo Black and John Harlan, who both resigned in September of 1971, and who both died before the year ended. We saw that Powell was a respected and experienced corporate lawyer from Virginia, and was a moderate conservative in his political views. In contrast, Rehnquist brought with him to the Court a highly conservative political outlook, which he followed as a justice. We also looked at the idea of a "right to privacy" under the Constitution, beginning with a path-breaking law review article by Louis Brandeis in 1890. And we followed that idea through the cases that culminated in the abortion case of *Roe v. Wade*. We ended our previous lecture with excerpts of the oral arguments in the *Roe* case in 1972. In this lecture, we're going to look at the Court's deliberations in the *Roe* case, from the first drafting of opinions through the final decision in January of 1973.

We'll focus on the process by which Justice Harry Blackmun, who wrote the majority opinion, turned the idea of privacy into a constitutional guarantee of a woman's right to choose abortion over childbirth. We'll also examine the ideas about the Constitution that led Justices William Rehnquist and Byron White to dissent in the *Roe* case. We'll also look at the dramatic case of the *United States v. Richard Nixon*, which is better known as the "Watergate Tapes" case. This case confronted the justices with the greatest conflict between the three branches of the federal government since the landmark case of *Marbury v. Madison* in 1803. The Court's ruling in the Watergate Tapes case illustrates the delicate balance of powers on which our government has rested for more than two centuries.

We'll begin this story in the justices' conference room, on the morning of December 15 in 1971. This was shortly after the first round of arguments in the *Roe* case, and only seven justices were present at this conference. The Senate had confirmed the nominations of Lewis Powell and William Rehnquist, but they would not take their seats until January of 1972. Chief Justice Warren Burger presided at the conference, and he began with a summary of the facts and the legal issues in the *Roe* case. As the discussion proceeded, it became clear that three of the seven justices were

 ©2003 The Teaching Company Limited Partnership

strongly in favor of striking down the Texas abortion law. Justices William O. Douglas, William Brennan, and Thurgood Marshall argued that the Constitution protected a right to privacy that prevented states from banning abortions. Justice Byron White took the opposing view, and made clear that he would uphold the law.

Justices Harry Blackmun and Potter Stewart took a middle-of-the-road position. They felt the Texas law interfered with a doctor's right to practice medicine, according to his professional judgment. But they weren't ready to support a constitutional right to abortion. Under the Court's long practice, voting proceeded from the "junior" justice, who was then Harry Blackmun, to the "senior" associate justice, William O. Douglas. The chief justice always voted last, to avoid any pressure on the other justices to follow his lead. During the discussion of the *Roe* case, Chief Justice Burger had argued strongly for upholding the Texas abortion law. But, when his turn came to vote, Burger said he would reserve his vote, until he read the draft opinions of the other justices. Several justices, most notably Douglas, objected to Burger's habit of withholding his vote until he saw which side had a majority. But Douglas felt that at least four justices would vote to strike down the Texas law in the *Roe* case. He counted Brennan, Marshall, and Stewart in that group, along with himself. Douglas wasn't sure how Blackmun would vote, but that didn't affect the outcome.

Another long-standing practice allowed the senior associate justice in the majority to assign the Court's opinion. Douglas hadn't decided on the *Roe* assignment, but he was outraged when Burger informed the justices, the day after the conference, that Blackmun would draft the opinion. Douglas sent a scathing memo to his colleagues, telling them *he* would assign the opinion when he saw fit. Burger responded with an apologetic memo, saying that he hadn't marked down any final votes at the conference. He simply thought Blackmun had the most experience with medical issues, as the former counsel to the prestigious Mayo Clinic in Minnesota. Douglas finally dropped his objections to Blackmun's assignment, but he suspected that Burger had ulterior motives.

Blackmun was a notoriously slow writer, and it was unlikely he could produce a final draft of his opinion for several months. This would allow Burger to convince the other justices that the Court should hold off deciding the *Roe* case before the presidential election in November of 1972. This would remove a divisive issue that might hurt the reelection campaign of President Nixon, who favored restrictive abortion laws. Burger's real intentions might have been entirely practical. After all, the Court had only seven members, and there were good arguments for holding up the *Roe* decision until Justices Powell and Rehnquist could hear another round of arguments. And that's what happened.

I've recounted these behind-the-scenes maneuverings to show the personal and political divisions inside the Burger Court. As it turned out, Justice Douglas was right, that a majority would strike down the Texas abortion law. And Justice Blackmun did write the majority opinion in the *Roe* case. But, in my view, it's hard to avoid the conclusion that political factors affected these events. Justice Douglas was a partisan Democrat, and Chief Justice Burger was an equally partisan Republican. Both men knew full well that abortion was an issue that could have swayed voters in the presidential election of 1972. In hindsight, President Nixon's sweeping victory over his Democratic opponent, Senator George McGovern of South Dakota, was not affected by either candidate's views on the abortion question. But the Court's internal battles over the *Roe* case were certainly affected by the political battles that were waged outside its chambers.

We're going to shift our focus now from politics to the privacy issue. During the entire presidential campaign, Justice Blackmun was secluded in the Court's library, sitting at a table that was stacked with law books and medical texts. The opinion he was drafting read more like a history paper than a legal opinion. Blackmun plowed through books on the medical aspects of abortion, from the Greek and Roman era to the present. He discovered that abortion had not been a criminal offense in most countries before the late 19th century. The first American laws on this subject were based on concerns that abortions created a serious risk of infection and even death. But the development of antiseptic procedures had reduced this risk, and abortion had become safer than childbirth.

His library research convinced Blackmun that Texas had no medical grounds for banning abortions. His draft opinion in the *Roe* case devoted more than 20 pages to this issue. That left him with the task of finding a constitutional basis for holding that pregnant women had a right to choose abortion over childbirth. Blackmun dealt with this

    ©2003 The Teaching Company Limited Partnership

difficult question in just one paragraph. We're going to look closely at this paragraph, to see how Blackmun reached the conclusion that the Constitution protects a woman's right to obtain an abortion.

In our previous lecture, we looked at the *Griswold* case, in which the Court struck down a state law against the use of contraceptives. Justice Douglas based his *Griswold* opinion on four cases that established, in his view, a right to privacy under the Bill of Rights. As we saw, none of these cases had anything to do with contraception, or even with the broader issue of procreation. They were simply building blocks from which Douglas constructed the right to privacy. Justice Blackmun added 10 blocks to this pile, citing 14 decisions that spanned the years from 1886 to 1972. We're going to look briefly at the cases Blackmun cited for precedent in his *Roe* opinion. The oldest case, called *Boyd v. the United States*, involved the search of a business that imported window glass. Federal agents were looking for records that import taxes had not been paid. The Court held in this case that records could not be seized without a warrant.

Another 19th century case, *Union Pacific Railroad v. Botsford*, stemmed from an accident in a Pullman sleeping car. Clara Botsford suffered a concussion when a sleeping berth fell on her head, but she refused to allow the company's doctor to examine her. The Court ruled in 1891 that Ms. Botsford had a privacy right to shield her body from medical inspection. Justice Blackmun also cited three cases from the 1920s. The Court struck down a state law that barred schools from teaching the German language in *Meyer v. Nebraska*. The Court also struck down an Oregon law that required parents to send their children to public schools, in *Pierce v. Society of Sisters*. Blackmun also cited the dissenting opinion of Justice Brandeis in *Olmstead v. United States*, in which the Court's majority had upheld a federal law that allowed wiretapping by federal agents. Brandeis had used the phrase, "the right to be let alone," to support his stand in this case.

The case of *Palko v. Connecticut*, which the Court decided in 1937, involved the double-jeopardy clause of the Fifth Amendment. In *Price v. Massachusetts*, the Court upheld in 1944 a law that prohibited children from selling newspapers on the street. Blackmun also cited four rulings of the Warren Court in the 1960s. The Court struck down a Virginia law against racially mixed marriages in

Loving v. Virginia. It extended the Fourth Amendment's protection against unlawful search and seizure to telephone booths in *Katz v. the United States*. The Warren Court upheld the police practice of "stop-and-frisk" searches in *Terry v. Ohio*, and it held in *Stanley v. Georgia* that people had a right to possess pornography in their homes. Blackmun also cited the *Griswold* opinion of Justice Douglas, and a 1972 ruling that struck down the conviction of a birth-control advocate for handing out contraceptives at a public meeting.

We've run through this list of cases to make a point. Only a handful of these rulings used the term "privacy." Several were based on the "search and seizure" clause of the Fourth Amendment. With the exception of the more recent contraception cases, none were even remotely connected to issues of procreation. But they provided the building blocks for Justice Blackmun's conclusion that the right to privacy, as he wrote, "is broad enough to encompass a woman's decision whether or not to terminate her pregnancy." We should keep in mind that justices often rely on cases for precedent that have no factual similarity to the case they're deciding. What's more important is their doctrinal similarity. Blackmun had no abortion cases available as precedent, since the *Roe* case was the first to come before the Court. *Griswold* offered the closest parallel, but the right to prevent a pregnancy through contraception is not the same as that of ending one through abortion. In a sense, Blackmun was sailing through uncharted constitutional waters, using whatever landmarks he could find to reach his destination.

In looking at Blackmun's opinion, it's important to note that he based his ruling on the due process clause of the Fourteenth Amendment, which protects "liberty" against deprivation by the states. We saw in earlier lectures that the Court employed the doctrine of "substantive due process" to strike down state laws that interfered with "liberty of contract." But the Court had buried that doctrine in the 1930s, upholding state power to regulate the economy. The Warren Court had carefully avoided reviving the substantive due process doctrine. In his *Griswold* decision, Justice Douglas had based his ruling on the Bill of Rights, and not the Fourteenth Amendment. He was afraid that future, more conservative justices would rely on this doctrine to strike down laws that protected workers and consumers. But in his *Roe* opinion, Justice Blackmun brought it back to life. As we'll see in later lectures, the justices quickly resumed their old debate over the meaning of "liberty" in the due process clause.

Another aspect of Blackmun's opinion deserves our attention. Because he found that women had a "fundamental right" to obtain abortions, he applied the strict scrutiny test in the *Roe* case. Laws that deprive anyone of fundamental rights can survive this test only if they serve a "compelling state interest." Under Blackmun's version of strict scrutiny, states have no compelling interest in banning abortions before fetal viability, when the fetus can live outside the womb. But states can prohibit abortions after that point, unless the life or health of the pregnant woman is endangered. In other words, Blackmun used a sliding-scale version of the strict scrutiny test, finding a compelling interest in protecting a viable fetus.

Not even the most fervent supporters of abortion rights dispute this holding, but those who oppose abortion at any stage of pregnancy think Blackmun used the wrong test. Justice William Rehnquist took this position in his *Roe* dissent, in these words: "The test traditionally applied in the area of social and economic legislation is whether or not a law has a rational relation to a valid state objective." As we've seen, the rational basis test is hard to fail. Only if judges can find no plausible reason for a law will they strike it down. Using this test, Rehnquist argued that decisions about abortion were, in his words, "far more appropriate to a legislative judgment than to a judicial one." In other words, Texas lawmakers had the power to make abortion a crime.

Rehnquist had opened his dissenting opinion with a respectful bow to the majority and to Blackmun's opinion. He knew how long and hard Blackmun had labored over his opinion, and Rehnquist applauded the "extensive historical fact and wealth of legal scholarship" it contained. But he joined another dissenting opinion that used harsh words about the *Roe* majority. Justice Byron White had cast the first vote against *Roe* at the Court's first conference, and he stuck with his position to the very end of his service in 1993. White began his dissent by criticizing the majority for valuing what he called "the convenience, whim, or caprice of the putative mother more than the life or potential life of the fetus." White followed the lead of Justice Black in opposing any expansion of the due process clause to create new rights. We'll see an example in a following lecture, in a case involving gay rights.

But in the *Roe* case, White made this accusation: "As an exercise of raw judicial power, the Court perhaps has authority to do what it does today. But in my view, its judgment is an improvident and extravagant exercise of the power of judicial review which the Constitution extends to this Court." He faulted the majority for erecting what he called "a constitutional barrier to state efforts to protect human life and by investing mothers and doctors with the constitutionally protected right to exterminate it." Between them, the dissenting opinions of Justices Rehnquist and White expressed two different approaches to the majority, those of respectful disagreement and complete disdain. This may reflect the facts that Rehnquist had only served with his colleagues for one year when *Roe* was decided, and that he was the youngest justice. He was also easygoing by nature and got along well with his ideological opponents. White had a reputation for harsh words and a lack of respect for those he considered lacking in intellectual rigor, and Justice Blackmun fell into this category.

The final vote in the *Roe* case was seven to two. Justice Lewis Powell, the Court's other newcomer, had joined Blackmun's opinion with some reluctance, but he had no deep-seated objection to abortion. Chief Justice Burger, at virtually the last minute, decided to join the majority. But his concurring opinion read more like a dissent. Burger faulted the Texas abortion law for not allowing rape or incest victims to obtain abortions, but he hinted broadly that he would uphold laws with such exceptions, and he pointedly rejected, as he put it, "any claim that the Constitution allows abortion on demand."

The Court announced its decision in the *Roe* case on January 22 of 1973. The public reaction to the ruling was sharper and more divided than any ruling since the Warren Court's school prayer decision a decade earlier, in 1963. Catholic leaders were outspoken in their opposition. Cardinal Terence Cooke of New York found the decision "shocking" and "horrifying." Cardinal John Krol of Philadelphia called it "an unspeakable tragedy for this nation." But abortion advocates were predictably happy. Dr. Alan Guttmacher of Planned Parenthood called the ruling "wise and courageous." And New York's liberal Republican governor, Nelson Rockefeller, praised the decision as "a wonderful thing." Perhaps the most accurate barometer of the public pressure that would build up over the abortion issue was the first Gallup Poll after the Court's ruling.

 ©2003 The Teaching Company Limited Partnership

Asked whether abortion decisions should be left to women and their doctors during the first three months of pregnancy, 46 percent of respondents said yes, and 45 percent said no. This virtually even split guaranteed that arguments over abortion would continue in legislative halls and judicial chambers. As we'll see in a later lecture, the abortion issue continues to divide both the public and the Court. More than three decades after the *Roe* decision, the "clash of absolutes" has produced little ground for compromise.

We're going to turn now to a very different case, one that forced the Court to settle a fundamental conflict between executive powers and judicial authority. The Watergate Tapes case began in the early morning of June 17 of 1972, when a security guard discovered five men in the Watergate office and apartment complex in Washington, D.C. The men were caught placing telephone taps in the offices of the Democratic National Committee. Police and FBI agents soon linked the five men to President Nixon's campaign office. The Watergate burglars were tried and convicted for the break-in before federal judge John Sirica. Before their sentencing, one defendant told the judge that other defendants had been pressured to lie before the grand jury, to cover up White House involvement in the break-in.

Watergate soon exploded into a national scandal. Congress forced the Nixon administration to appoint a special prosecutor, Archibald Cox of Harvard Law School, who had served in the Kennedy administration as solicitor general. During the Senate hearings on the Watergate affair, one of Nixon's aides, Alexander Butterfield, revealed that the president had secretly taped his Oval Office meetings and phone conversations. As the cover-up unraveled, a federal grand jury indicted seven of Nixon's top aides and campaign officials for conspiracy to obstruct justice. Nixon himself was named as an "unindicted co-conspirator." Revelations about the Oval Office tapes prompted Cox to obtain a judicial subpoena for some of the tapes. Nixon fired him for this act, igniting a political firestorm that led Congress to begin impeachment proceedings against the president.

Nixon reluctantly appointed another special prosecutor, a respected Texas lawyer named Leon Jaworski. He obtained another subpoena for the tapes. Nixon's refusal to honor that subpoena brought the Watergate case before the Supreme Court in July of 1974, two years after the break-in. These were years of political turmoil, with the president fighting for his survival in office, and the Court was thrust into this crisis by Nixon's adamant claim that the Watergate tapes were protected by the doctrine of *executive privilege*. Nixon's lawyers claimed the Constitution shields the president from the disclosure of his confidential papers and conversations. Otherwise, he can't freely exchange views with his aides and visitors. Leon Jaworski argued in response that the president was obligated, like every other citizen, to provide evidence in criminal cases. Only the most sensitive foreign policy and military matters were protected by the executive privilege doctrine.

We're going to listen now to excerpts of the oral arguments in the case of *United States of America v. Richard Nixon*. Leon Jaworski speaks first, and stresses the gravity of the issues before the Court.

> Jaworski: "Now the president may be right in how he reads the Constitution. But he may also be wrong. And if he is wrong, who is there to tell him so? And if there is no one, then the president of course is free to pursue his course of erroneous interpretations. What then becomes of our constitutional form of government? So when counsel for the president in his brief states that this case goes to the heart of our basic constitutional system, we agree. Because in our view, this nation's constitutional form of government is in serious jeopardy if the president, any president, is to say that the Constitution means what he says it does, and that there is no one, not even the Supreme Court, to tell him otherwise."

James St. Clair speaks for President Nixon. He's an experienced lawyer from a prestigious Boston firm. St. Clair argues that Nixon's claim of executive privilege shields him from any judicial process. The Court should not even consider the case, and should dismiss the subpoena. This claim provokes a question from Justice Thurgood Marshall.

> Marshall: "Well, do you agree that's what's before this Court, and you're submitting it to this Court for decision?"

> St. Clair: "This is being submitted to this Court for its guidance and judgment with respect to the law. The president, on the other hand, has his obligations under the Constitution."

 ©2003 The Teaching Company Limited Partnership

Marshall: "Are you submitting it to this Court for this Court's decision?"

St. Clair: "As to what the law is, yes."

St. Clair argues that Congress is the only body that can act against the president. He sums up his case in these words:

St. Clair: "As I said earlier, the president is not above the law, nor does he contend that he is. But he does contend that the law can be applied to him in only one way, and that's by impeachment, not by naming as a co-conspirator in a grand jury indictment, not by indictment, or in any other way. Therefore, in this case, I urge this Court to take such action as is appropriate, and overrule Judge Sirica's decision, and order that this case be dismissed."

The day after these arguments, on July 9 of 1974, the justices met in their conference room to decide the Watergate Tapes case. Justice William Rehnquist had worked closely with attorney general John Mitchell, who was one of the defendants in the conspiracy trial, and stepped aside and did not participate. The eight remaining justices agreed with James St. Clair that the Constitution gave the president some power of executive privilege. But they also agreed with Leon Jaworski that this power was limited, not absolute, and must defer to judicial power. Their decision was unanimous. President Nixon must turn over the Watergate tapes to Judge Sirica.

Chief Justice Burger wrote the Court's opinion, which he read to a packed audience in the Court's chamber two weeks later. He rejected the argument that the Constitution provides, as Burger put it, "an absolute privilege of confidentiality for all presidential communications." Such a claim, he said, conflicts with the "constitutional duty of the judicial branch to do justice in criminal prosecutions." Even the president must comply with the judicial "demand for every man's evidence." The Court had decided. But would the president obey? Nixon exploded and threatened defiance of the Court's order. But it was too late; three days later, the House Judiciary Committee voted to impeach the president for obstruction of justice. On August 8 of 1974, Richard Nixon dictated an eleven-word letter: "I hereby resign the office of President of the United States." The next day, he left the White House for the last time as president.

We've looked at two cases that both raised fundamental constitutional issues, and that both involved political conflicts. But the emotions that were unleashed by the *Roe* decision have not yet cooled, and the abortion issue has returned to the Court in dozens of cases. The Watergate case, however, seemingly settled the issue of executive privilege in criminal prosecutions by the Court's unanimous decision. But hardly any constitutional question can have a final answer. The Court's personnel changes over time, and presidents since Nixon have made sweeping claims of executive privilege. How would the Court rule in a similar case? In my view, that's a question with no easy answer. Another question with no simple answer is whether the Constitution allows schools and employers to adopt affirmative action programs, to increase the number of racial minorities and women in their classrooms and work places. We'll examine this question in our next lecture. We'll also look at changes on the Court, with the retirement of Chief Justice Burger in 1986 and his replacement by Justice Rehnquist.

©2003 The Teaching Company Limited Partnership

Lecture Thirty-One
The Court Faces Affirmative Action

Scope:

This lecture focuses on long-standing patterns of discrimination against women and racial minorities in education and employment. In 1964, Congress passed the Civil Rights Act, banning discrimination based on gender or race. The *affirmative action* programs adopted by schools and businesses helped many women and blacks, but they generated a white male backlash that brought several important cases before the Supreme Court. We will examine in detail the landmark case of *Regents of the University of California v. Bakke*, first recounting the story of Allan Bakke, an aerospace engineer who applied for admission to the University of California medical school at Davis. Bakke claimed that the school's minority admissions program, which set aside 16 places in a class of 100 for members of "disadvantaged minorities," discriminated against him as a white applicant. We will look at the Court's split decision in this case, in which Justice Lewis Powell cast the deciding vote to strike down the minority quota, but also to allow race to be used as a factor in medical school admissions.

Outline

I. This lecture examines the issue of affirmative action and the Court's 1978 ruling in the landmark *Bakke* case.

   A. The background of this issue stems from discrimination against racial minorities and women during most of our nation's history.

   B. Inferior education in segregated schools before the *Brown* ruling in 1954 made it difficult for blacks to compete with whites for professional training and good jobs.

   C. In 1960, blacks made up fewer than two percent of doctors, lawyers, engineers, and executives.

   D. Women also sought access to higher education and employment, but the failure of the Equal Rights Amendment in 1974 set them back.

II. Congress passed a Civil Rights Act in 1964 that banned racial discrimination in any program receiving federal funds, including most colleges and universities.

- **A.** The law also banned discrimination against women.
    - **1.** Congressional opponents of civil rights had added the sex-discrimination provision to the bill, hoping to reduce its support.
    - **2.** But this move backfired, and the bill passed with that provision.
- **B.** President Lyndon Johnson began the first major affirmative action program in 1965 with an executive order that banned discrimination by federal contractors.

III. The University of California medical school at Davis began its affirmative action program in 1969.

- **A.** This program set aside 16 places in each entering class of 100 for members of "disadvantaged minorities."
- **B.** Applicants in this group were considered by a separate admissions committee.
- **C.** Between 1970 and 1974, 33 Mexican Americans, 26 African Americans, 12 Asian Americans, and 1 Native American were admitted through the special admission program.

IV. Allan Bakke first applied to the Davis medical school for admission in 1973, along with a dozen other schools.

- **A.** Bakke was an aerospace engineer who had served in Vietnam as a Marine officer.
    - **1.** He was 33 years old, and most schools rejected him because of his age.
    - **2.** Bakke had a B-plus undergraduate record and high scores on the medical college admissions test.
- **B.** He was rejected by Davis, falling two points short of admission under the regular admissions program.
- **C.** Bakke learned of the school's minority admissions program and filed a complaint that he had been rejected on racial grounds.
- **D.** He applied again to the Davis medical school for admission in 1974 and was again rejected.

©2003 The Teaching Company Limited Partnership

V. Bakke found a San Francisco lawyer, Reynold Colvin, who filed a lawsuit against the university's board of regents in 1974.

   A. The suit alleged that Bakke had been discriminated against on racial grounds.

   B. It also said that "less qualified" minority students had been admitted.

   C. The university's lawyers replied that the special admission program was aimed at "promoting diversity" in the medical profession.

   D. Bakke won favorable rulings from California state courts, which ordered his admission to the Davis school.

VI. The Supreme Court heard arguments in *Regents v. Bakke* in October 1977.

   A. For its representation, the university hired Archibald Cox, a former solicitor general and Watergate special prosecutor.

      1. Cox argued that the special admissions program did not result in the admission of "less qualified" medical students.

      2. He said minority students "may have qualities that are superior" to those of white students.

   B. Reynold Colvin replied that "race is an improper classification" in university admissions.

VII. The Supreme Court decided the *Bakke* case in 1978.

   A. The justices were split into two factions of four each in this case.

      1. Four liberal and moderate justices voted to uphold the special admissions program and the quota of 16 places for minority students.

      2. Four conservative justices rejected any consideration of race in admissions.

   B. Justice Lewis Powell cast the swing vote and wrote an opinion with two parts.

      1. He joined the liberal and moderate justices in upholding programs that made race a "plus" factor in admissions.

      2. Powell also joined the conservatives in striking down the quota system and ordered Bakke's admission to the medical school.

C. Since the *Bakke* decision, the University of California has adopted a "race-blind" admissions policy, which has lowered the number of minority students.

D. Affirmative action remains a highly controversial issue, and the Court has continued to struggle with this question in subsequent cases.

Suggested Readings:

Peter Irons, *A People's History of the Supreme Court*, chapter 34 (1999).

Joel Dreyfuss and Charles Lawrence III, *The Bakke Case: The Politics of Inequality* (1979).

Questions to Consider:

1. Do you think colleges and graduate schools should be allowed to take racial and ethnic diversity into account in their admissions policies?

2. Should college and graduate school admissions be based solely on grades and test scores, or should other factors be considered? If so, which ones?

Lecture Thirty-One—Transcript
The Court Faces Affirmative Action

In our previous lecture, we looked at the Supreme Court's rulings in two landmark cases, decided in 1973 and 1974. These cases involved very different issues, and raised very different legal questions. By a vote of seven to two, the Court decided in *Roe v. Wade* that the Constitution protected a pregnant woman's right to obtain an abortion during the period before fetal viability. The justices also decided unanimously that the Constitution did not protect President Richard Nixon from a judicial order to turn over tape recordings of his efforts to cover up White House involvement in the Watergate scandal. As we saw, both the *Roe* and *Nixon* cases forced the justices to apply broadly worded constitutional provisions to the facts of specific cases. Does the Fourteenth Amendment's protection of "liberty" against state deprivation allow "Jane Roe" to obtain an abortion in Texas? Does the Constitution's grant of "executive power" to the President allow Richard Nixon to protect the Watergate tapes from judicial scrutiny?

We also saw that both cases involved concepts—or ideas—that go beyond the Constitution's direct words. The Court based its *Roe* decision on a "right to privacy" that stems from the due process clause of the Fourteenth Amendment. The *Nixon* case involved the doctrine of *executive privilege* that is rooted in Article II of the Constitution. Finally, we saw that both abortion and the Watergate scandal became highly political issues, and divided the American public along lines of religion and party, although opinions on these issues often crossed these lines. In this lecture, we're going to look at another issue in the context of these aspects of the *Roe* and *Nixon* cases.

Affirmative action has become one of the most divisive issues in American society, and the Supreme Court has faced several difficult cases in this area. There's no doubt that schools and employers discriminated against members of racial minorities, and against women, during most of our nation's history. In fact, members of these groups were completely barred from many schools and workplaces before the 1950s and 60s. In one sense, we can see the Court's decision in *Brown v. Board of Education* as a major step toward affirmative action. Black children who were forced by law to attend segregated schools were handicapped in competing equally with whites for higher education and good jobs. But as we saw, the slow pace of school integration during the two decades after the *Brown* decision did very little to remedy the historic patterns of discrimination.

Statistics tell part of this story. In 1960, African Americans made up fewer than two percent of doctors, lawyers, engineers, and business executives. Women held a slightly higher number of professional jobs, but they were still excluded from many graduate programs, and some employers simply refused to hire women, except for low-paid clerical jobs. The broader context of *affirmative action* programs lies in the Civil Rights movement of the 1950s and 60s. In fact, the historic March on Washington in 1963, at which Dr. Martin Luther King delivered his famous "I Have a Dream" speech, was formally called the March for Jobs and Justice. Dr. King and other civil rights leaders recognized that without access to good schools and good jobs, African Americans and other minorities would never achieve the American dream.

The early 60s also saw the rapid growth of a women's movement that adopted "equal pay for equal work" as one of its slogans. The women's movement also pressed for ratification of the Equal Rights Amendment to the Constitution, which read: "Equality of rights under the law shall not be denied or abridged by the United States or by any state on account of sex." The Equal Rights Amendment fell two states short of ratification by the deadline in 1974. But the lobbying effort for this amendment brought millions of women into the political system, and created pressure for including them in affirmative action programs.

The most important step toward affirmative action took place with congressional passage of the Civil Rights Act of 1964. Title VI of that law included this provision: "No person in the United States shall, on the ground of race, color, or national origin, be excluded from participation in, be denied the benefits of, or be subjected to discrimination under any program or activity receiving federal financial assistance." Title VI was directed at colleges and universities, almost all of which received federal funding, including private institutions. It's important to note that Title VI did not ban discrimination against women in higher education. We'll see how the Supreme Court ruled on this issue in a following lecture. But the

 ©2003 The Teaching Company Limited Partnership

Civil Rights Act did include a provision that banned discrimination against women and racial minorities in employment.

Title VII made it unlawful for an employer "to refuse to hire any individual because of such individual's race, color, religion, sex, or national origin." There's a story about how sex got added to Title SVII. One of the southern congressmen who opposed the Civil Rights Act, because it outlawed racial discrimination in employment, was Representative Howard Smith of Virginia, who chaired the powerful House Rules Committee. Smith proposed adding the word "sex" to Title VII, hoping that would swing the opponents of women's rights to his side. But his move backfired and the bill passed with the ban on sex discrimination, making Congressman Smith an unwitting hero of the women's movement.

The Civil Rights Act made it unlawful for schools and employers to keep racial minorities out of classrooms and workplaces. They could be sued for acts of racial discrimination. But the law didn't require schools and employers to actively recruit students and workers from minority groups. That's the basic idea behind affirmative action, to take actions that would increase their numbers in schools and jobs. President Lyndon Johnson initiated the first major affirmative action program in 1965, when he issued an executive order that required firms with federal contracts to ensure their hiring practices did not discriminate. Many businesses set up programs to search out and recruit minority workers, and many colleges and universities followed their lead.

One school in California began its affirmative action program in 1969. The year before, the University of California had opened a medical school at its campus in Davis, just a few miles from the state capitol in Sacramento. The first entering class was only 50 students, but the number soon doubled to 100. During its first two years, the Davis medical school admitted only three minority students, all of them Asian Americans. When the Davis administration set up a faculty and student Task Force to frame an affirmative action program, the school set aside 16 places in the entering class of 100 for members of what were called "disadvantaged" groups. Applicants, who checked a box on the admissions form, putting themselves in this category, were processed through a special committee for the Task Force slots. Between 1970 and 1974, the

Task Force admitted 33 Mexican Americans, 26 blacks, 12 Asian students, and one Native American.

It's worth noting that 41 other Asian students were admitted through the regular admissions program, along with a handful of blacks and Latinos. It's also worth noting that the Task Force program did not define the word "disadvantaged" in racial or ethnic terms. But no white applicants were admitted under the program. With this background, we're going to look at one applicant to the Davis medical school in 1973. Allan Bakke was one of almost 2,500 applicants for the 100 seats in the first-year class. In many ways, Bakke was an unusual candidate for medical school. He was an honors graduate in engineering from the University of Minnesota, and had served four years as a Marine Corps officer, with seven months in Vietnam.

Bakke was working as an engineer with the National Aeronautics and Space Administration in California when he decided to switch fields and become a doctor. In 1973, he applied to a dozen medical schools. Bakke had an impressive academic record. His undergraduate grade average was a solid B plus, and he scored very high on the Medical College Admissions Test. Bakke was in the 96th percentile on the verbal test, the 94th in math, and the 97th in science. But he had a serious problem. Bakke was 33 years old when he applied to medical schools, and most turned him down because of his age. But the Davis medical school invited Bakke for an interview, which put him in the running for admission. However, after his grades and scores were tallied, Bakke fell two points short of the total required for admission under the regular program. Thirty-four other applicants also came within two points, and they all received rejection letters. One of those disappointed applicants would not give up.

Allan Bakke sent another application to the Davis medical school for the entering class in 1974. He also sent a letter to the dean of student affairs. Bakke had learned from one of the school's admissions officers that 16 of the 100 seats had been set aside for "disadvantaged" students, and that no white applicants had been admitted under the Task Force program. Bakke put his complaint in these words: "I realize that the rationale for these quotas is that they attempt to atone for past racial discrimination. But instituting a new racial bias, in favor of minorities, is not a just solution." Bakke accused the medical school of practicing "reverse discrimination" in setting aside places for racial and ethnic minorities. He ended his letter with a strong hint that he might sue the medical school if he was rejected once again. And he was rejected in 1974, along with 42 other applicants with higher scores among the regular admissions group.

Allan Bakke turned his hint of legal action against the Davis medical school into a lawsuit in June of 1974. He was represented by a San Francisco lawyer named Reynold Colvin, who had recently won a case that challenged the exemption of racial minorities from the downsizing of San Francisco's school administration. Colvin took on the *Bakke* case with a missionary's zeal and aggressive legal tactics. He named the university's board of regents as defendants, and he filed a complaint alleging that Bakke "is in all respects duly qualified for admission to the medical school, and the sole reason his application was rejected was on account of his race, to wit, Caucasian and white, and not for reasons applicable to persons of every race."

The heart of Bakke's suit was the claim that he had been forced to compete for one of only 84 places open to white applicants. The other 16 had been reserved as a quota for minority groups, with academic standards well below those for the regular admissions program. Reynold Colvin produced statistics from medical school files to make his case. As we saw, Bakke had a B-plus undergraduate grade average. The 16 "disadvantaged" students who were admitted in 1974 had a C-plus average. Bakke scored above the 90th percentile on the medical school admissions test in the verbal, math, and science sections. The minority students had averages below 50 percent on each section of the test. Bakke's complaint alleged that the Task Force program, as Colvin put it, "resulted in the admission of minority applicants less qualified than plaintiff" to the Davis medical school.

Colvin based the suit on the equal protection clause of the Fourteenth Amendment, the equivalent provision of the California state constitution, and Title VI of the federal Civil Rights Act. The university's lawyers responded that medical school officials were justified, as they put it, in considering the "minority group status of qualified applicants as a factor in filling a limited number of spaces in each first-year class for the purpose of promoting diversity in the student body and the medical profession." Bakke's complaint and the university's response put the affirmative action issue in sharp contrast. Bakke charged the medical school with admitting "less qualified" minority students, while the university said that all those admitted were qualified under the school's basic standards. These conflicting positions raise the difficult question of defining a "qualified" applicant.

Bakke argued that grades and test scores were the best standard. But as we saw, some 42 applicants in 1974 had equal or higher point totals than Bakke and were still rejected. The medical school simply didn't have enough seats for all these equally or more qualified applicants, using Bakke's own standard. On the other hand, all the minority students met the school's basic standard of academic competence. The medical school did not admit any students below this standard, regardless of their race. But this standard was set lower for minority applicants. Otherwise, the school would most likely have no black or Latino students, and very little racial and ethnic diversity.

This factor raises other difficult questions. Is diversity a legitimate goal for medical study and practice? How important should it be, for California or any other state, to educate doctors who will serve a diverse population? Will black and Latino patients feel more comfortable with doctors who share their culture and language? These are questions that are hard to fit within the confines of broad constitutional provisions, such as the equal protection clause. They also come up against the narrow wording of the Civil Rights Act, which seemingly bans any consideration of race or ethnicity by institutions that receive federal funds, including the Davis medical school.

Before we move to the judicial rulings in *Regents v. Bakke*, let me explain why we've taken such a close look at the background and facts in this case. First, they put a human face on the issue of affirmative action. Allan Bakke was just one of the 2,500 applicants for 100 seats in the Davis medical school. He came very close to being admitted, but so did many other applicants. But, as Bakke wrote to the dean, "I won't quit trying." He was determined to become a doctor, which he said was a "goal worth fighting for in every legal and ethical way." Should the school have taken this strong determination into account in deciding whether to admit Bakke?

Secondly, the *Bakke* case raised the question of how to measure the elusive quality of "merit" in choosing medical students. Bakke's grades and test scores were clearly higher than those of the minority students who were admitted. Did this make him more qualified, or were there other, more subjective, factors that should have been entered in the complex equation of the admission decision, factors such as a willingness to practice in low-income areas, or in fields like family medicine or emergency care? Thirdly, the *Bakke* case puts in sharp focus the conflict between individual rights and group rights. Allan Bakke argued that his race was irrelevant to his qualifications for medical school, while the university replied that race was a legitimate factor in deciding which applicants to admit.

Bakke won the first two rounds in the California state courts. The state judges struck down the minority admissions program, and they also ordered Bakke's admission to the Davis medical school. But they stayed this order until the Supreme Court ruled on the case. The justices heard argument in *Regents v. Bakke* on October 12 of 1977. We're going to listen now to excerpts of those arguments in the Supreme Court's chamber. The University of California has retained an experienced constitutional lawyer in this case. Archibald Cox is a Harvard law professor, a former solicitor general, and is most noted as the Watergate special prosecutor who was fired by President Richard Nixon. Cox lays out the issue before the Court.

> Cox: "This case, here on certiorari to the Supreme Court of California, presents a single vital question: whether a state university, which is forced by limited resources to select a relatively small number of students from a much larger number of well-qualified applicants, is free, voluntarily, to take into account the fact that a qualified applicant is black, Chicano, Asian, or Native American, in order to increase the number of qualified members of these minority groups trained for the educated professions and participating in them, professions from which minorities were long excluded because of generations of pervasive racial discrimination."

Cox focuses on the broad issue of discrimination in medical education. He mentions Allan Bakke only once in his argument.

Cox: "While it is true that Mr. Bakke and some others, on the conventional standards for admission, would be ranked above the minority applicant, I want to emphasize that in my judgment, and I think in fact, that does not justify saying that the generally better-qualified people were excluded to make room for generally less-qualified people."

Cox turns his argument to the virtues of racial and ethnic diversity in the medical profession.

Cox: "It's quite clear that for some of the things that a medical school wishes to accomplish, and this medical school wished to accomplish, that the minority applicant may have qualities that are superior to those of his classmate who is not minority. He certainly will be more effective in bringing it home to the young Chicano that he too may become a doctor."

Reynold Colvin takes the podium for Allan Bakke. He points the justices to the scores on the admissions test for both years in which Bakke applied to the Davis medical school.

Colvin: "Look at the record in the case. In 1973, the average—not the range, but the average—of the people in the special admission group was in the 35th percentile in science and in the 46th percentile in verbal. In 1974, the percentile in science—and this is an average and not a range—was 37, and in verbal 34. Allan Bakke, Allan Bakke took the test only once and his record is there. You'll find it on page 13 of our brief. He scored in the 97th percentile in science and in the 96th percentile in verbal. The ultimate fact in this case, no matter how you turn it, is that Mr. Bakke was deprived of an opportunity to attend the school by reason of his race."

Colvin responds to a question from Justice Lewis Powell about the issue of racial quotas in the case.

Colvin: "We have the deepest difficulty in dealing with this problem of quota, and many, many questions arise. For example, there is a question of numbers. What is the appropriate quota? What is the appropriate quota for a medical school? Sixteen, eight, 32, 64, 100? On what basis, on what basis is that quota determined?"

 ©2003 The Teaching Company Limited Partnership

Justice William Rehnquist follows up the discussion of quotas with a question about the constitutional issue in the case.

> Rehnquist: "Well, what's your response to the assertion of the university that it was entitled to have a special program and take race into account, and that under the Fourteenth Amendment there was no barrier to its doing that, because of the interests that were involved? Now, what's your response to that?"

> Colvin: "Our response to that is fundamentally, is fundamentally that race is an improper classification in this situation."

After these arguments ended, it took the justices more than eight months to hand down their final decision in the *Bakke* case. There were several reasons for this lengthy process of drafting and polishing opinions. Most likely, the time would have been shorter if Justice William O. Douglas had remained on the bench and voted in the case. Douglas would almost certainly have supported the Davis medical school's minority admissions program, including the quota of 16 places for "disadvantaged" students. But Douglas had stepped down in November of 1975, after 36 years on the Court, the longest service of any justice in its history. President Gerald Ford replaced Douglas with John Paul Stevens, who had served as law clerk to Justice Wiley Rutledge in the 1940s, and who had practiced antitrust law in Chicago, before President Nixon placed him on the federal appellate bench in 1970. Stevens was a judicial "moderate" when he joined the Court, and he generally voted with the other moderate justices, Lewis Powell and Potter Stewart. Over the years, much like Justice Harry Blackmun, Stevens moved to the liberal side, and he became the senior associate justice when Blackmun retired in 1994.

Another reason for the eight-month span from argument to decision in the *Bakke* case was that the justices split into two factions, with four on each side. Chief Justice Warren Burger, along with Justices William Rehnquist, Potter Stewart, and John Paul Stevens, voted to strike down the Davis program in its entirety, and to rule that race or ethnicity could never be a legitimate factor in college and university admissions. This faction took its motto from the dissenting opinion of Justice John Marshall Harlan in the *Plessy* case, back in 1896: "Our Constitution is color-blind, and neither knows nor tolerates classes among citizens." Another faction of four justices—including William Brennan, Thurgood Marshall, Byron White, and Harry Blackmun—voted to uphold the Davis program, including the quota of 16 places for minority students.

Blackmun answered Harlan with these words, in his separate opinion: "In order to get beyond racism, we must first take account of race. There is no other way. And in order to treat some persons equally, we must treat them differently. We cannot—we dare not—let the Fourteenth Amendment perpetuate racial supremacy." There seemed to be no common ground between these two factions. But Justice Lewis Powell constructed a narrow and shaky bridge across this judicial chasm. Powell fashioned a compromise that produced two separate five-to-four majorities in the *Bakke* case.

He agreed with the four who opposed the Davis program, that quotas violated the Constitution. But he also agreed with the four who supported the program that race was a legitimate factor in medical school admissions. Powell wrote an opinion with two separate parts, each joined by four different justices. Powell based his opinion on the admissions program of Harvard College, his own alma mater, which he described in these words: "In such an admissions program, race or ethnic background may be deemed a 'plus' in a particular applicant's file, yet it does not insulate the individual from comparison with all other candidates for the available seats." Race or ethnicity could be considered along with other qualities, among which Powell included these: "demonstrated compassion, a history of overcoming disadvantage, and ability to communicate with the poor."

Justice Powell's opinion settled the *Bakke* case in two ways. It struck down the quota system, and it put Allan Bakke in the Davis medical school. As a footnote, he graduated in 1982, and returned to his native state of Minnesota, where he now practices in the specialty of anesthesiology. But Powell's opinion raised more questions than answers. In my view, it reads like a scale without numbers. How much does a racial or ethnic "plus" weigh in the admissions scale? If grades and test scores can be quantified, how much weight should be given to subjective evaluations of "compassion" or "overcoming disadvantage?" Confronted with these and similar unsettled questions, some colleges and universities dropped race and ethnicity altogether from their admissions policies. The University of

California regents voted in 1995 to remove any "plus" factors based on race or ethnicity, and adopted a "color-blind" admissions policy for all its programs. By 1998, the first-year class at Davis medical school included just five black and three Hispanic students, and not a single black student entered the university's prestigious law school at Berkeley that year. Those figures have increased slightly in recent years, but they are still far below those of the 1970s, before the Supreme Court decided the *Bakke* case.

Since its decision in the *Bakke* case, the Court has issued several rulings in affirmative action cases that have conflicting outcomes, reflecting the sharp judicial divisions on this issue. In one case, the Court upheld a quota system for adding minorities to a job-training program in a Louisiana factory. But the Court also struck down a program that set aside 30 percent of contracts for minority firms in the city of Richmond, Virginia. These cases illustrate the fact that affirmative action remains an issue that divides both the Court, and the American people.

We've focused in this lecture on just one issue, and just one case. But the *Bakke* case, in my view, deserves the sharp focus that we also gave to the *Brown* and *Roe* cases. The story of Allan Bakke, and his determined struggle to obtain a medical education, shows us how the Court's rulings begin with conflicts between real people, as we've seen in many earlier lectures. But the justices must also apply the broad wording of constitutional provisions, such as equal protection and due process, to the cases of people like Allan Bakke. In our next lecture, we'll look at the Court's application of these provisions in cases that involve people like Myra Bradwell and Michael Hardwick, who belonged to two groups in American society that suffered from historic patterns of discrimination: the majority group of women, and the minority group of gays and lesbians.

Lecture Thirty-Two
Down from the Pedestal, Out of the Closet

Scope:

The historical context of this lecture stems from long-standing discrimination against two groups in American society, women and homosexuals. Women constitute a majority of the population, while gays and lesbians make up a small fraction, but they share a history of both social and legal disabilities. From colonial days until the 20th century, women in many states could not own property, participate in government, or aspire to higher education and well-paying jobs. Gays and lesbians fared even worse, subject to criminal laws against homosexual sodomy and harassment by police in gay bars. We will look at several important Supreme Court cases, including one involving women's rights from the 19th century, when the Court ruled that Myra Bradwell could not practice law in Illinois, until 2000, when the justices struck down exclusion of women from the Virginia Military Institute. We will also examine a landmark gay rights case, *Bowers v. Hardwick*, in which the Court narrowly upheld Georgia's criminal sodomy law against a challenge by a gay man, Michael Hardwick.

Outline

I. This lecture discusses the Supreme Court's rulings in cases that dealt with discrimination against women and against gays and lesbians.

    A. The gender discrimination cases raise issues of how stereotypes about women have shaped laws and judicial decisions.

    B. The gay rights case we will discuss involves the question of society's "moral disapproval" of homosexual behavior.

    C. These cases also raise the question of whether the Court should apply the strict scrutiny test to discrimination against women and gays.

II. We begin with the Court's rulings in gender discrimination cases between 1873 and 1996.

    A. The case of *Bradwell v. Illinois* involved a woman lawyer named Myra Bradwell.

1. She published a legal periodical in Chicago that was highly respected by state judges.
2. Bradwell passed the Illinois licensing exam for lawyers with flying colors.
3. However, the state supreme court rejected her application for bar admission solely because she was a woman.

B. In the Supreme Court, her lawyer argued that the Fourteenth Amendment barred discrimination against any person, regardless of sex.

C. The Court unanimously upheld the state's right to ban women from law practice.

D. In a concurring opinion, Justice Joseph Bradley said that the "timidity and delicacy" of women made them unfit to practice professions such as law. He added, "this is the law of the Creator."

E. The Court followed the *Bradwell* precedent in a 1948 case, ruling in *Goesaert v. Cleary* that states could prohibit women from working as bartenders.

III. The feminist movement of the 1960s and 1970s generated pressure against gender discrimination.

A. The American Civil Liberties Union set up a Women's Law Project, directed by a Columbia law professor, Ruth Bader Ginsburg.

B. This project challenged an Idaho law that preferred men over women as administrators of estates.

C. Sally Reed applied to administer the estate of her deceased son, but the state court chose her former husband for this position.

D. The Supreme Court struck down this decision in a unanimous ruling in 1971.
1. The Court's opinion cited a 1920 case that said, "all persons similarly situated shall be treated alike" under state laws.
2. The Court said the Idaho law made the kind of "arbitrary legislative choice" that violated the Fourteenth Amendment.

IV. In 1973, the Court applied this ruling in the case of *Frontiero v. Richardson*.

    A. Sharron Frontiero was an Air Force lieutenant who applied for dependent's benefits for her husband, who was a full-time college student.

    B. The Air Force regulation gave such benefits to male officers, regardless of their spouse's financial status, but female officers had to show they provided more than half of their husband's support, which Frontiero did not.

    C. Ruth Ginsburg argued for Frontiero, urging the Court to apply the strict scrutiny test in gender discrimination cases.

    D. The Court struck down the Air Force regulation by an eight-to-one margin.

        1. Four justices agreed with the strict scrutiny standard in *Frontiero*, but three others in the majority disagreed.

        2. Justice Lewis Powell said in concurrence that the Court should wait for states to ratify the Equal Rights Amendment, which later failed.

V. In 1996, Ginsburg was sitting as a justice. She wrote the majority opinion in *United States v. Virginia*.

    A. This case involved the Virginia Military Institute, a state-run school that barred women from admission.

    B. After the federal government sued the state, Virginia set up a women-only "leadership training" school.

    C. Ginsburg cited the Court's earlier rulings in school segregation cases in ruling that Virginia had not offered women "substantial equality" in the women-only school.

VI. The Court ruled on gay rights in the 1986 case of *Bowers v. Hardwick*.

    A. This case involved a Georgia law that made sodomy a crime, punishable by 20 years in prison.

    B. Michael Hardwick was arrested in his bedroom for having sex with another man.

    C. He challenged the sodomy law as a violation of "liberty" under the Fourteenth Amendment.

    ©2003 The Teaching Company Limited Partnership

D. A federal appellate court struck down the law, and the Georgia attorney general, Michael Bowers, appealed to the Supreme Court as the defendant in the case.

VII. The Court ruled against Hardwick in June 1986 by a five-to-four margin.

A. The majority said that laws were "constantly based on notions of morality."

B. The Court refused to apply the strict scrutiny test, saying that Georgia met the rational basis test in its citizens' belief that homosexual sodomy was "immoral."

C. The dissenters said that individuals, regardless of sexual orientation, should have the "freedom to choose how to conduct their lives," including sexual behavior.

D. Justice Lewis Powell joined the majority in the *Bowers* case. After he retired in 1987, he said, "I probably made a mistake" in that decision.

E. The Georgia Supreme Court later struck down the state's sodomy law, while other states, including Texas and Alabama, have upheld their state laws against sodomy.

Suggested Readings:

Susan Atkins and Brenda Hoggett, *Women and the Law* (1984).

William Eskridge, Jr., *Gaylaw: Challenging the Apartheid of the Closet* (2002).

Questions to Consider:

1. Women make up a slight majority of the population. Should they be subject to the same strict scrutiny test that courts apply to discrimination against racial and ethnic minorities?

2. Do you think women should be allowed to serve in front-line combat units in the armed forces?

Lecture Thirty-Two—Transcript
Down from the Pedestal, Out of the Closet

In our previous lecture, we looked at the issue of affirmative action, and we focused on the Supreme Court's ruling in the landmark case of *Regents of the University of California v. Bakke*. We saw that Allan Bakke was one of 2,500 applicants for 100 places in the university's medical school at Davis. The medical school set aside 16 places for members of "disadvantaged minorities," and Bakke claimed this policy had prevented his admission. The Supreme Court handed down a split decision in the *Bakke* case, with Justice Lewis Powell casting the swing vote. Four justices joined Powell in striking down the minority quota system, and ordering the medical school to admit Allan Bakke. But another four justices voted with Powell to uphold so-called "race-conscious" admissions programs. The Supreme Court found a middle ground in the *Bakke* case, between conflicting views on issues that divide both the American public and the justices.

We've looked back at the *Bakke* case, to introduce this lecture, because it shows the importance of a swing vote on the Court. We'll see in this lecture how the votes of Justice Powell affected the rulings in two important cases, involving different groups in American society. We'll first discuss cases that deal with discrimination against women, cases that span the years from 1873 to 1996. We'll then discuss a case that challenged discrimination against gays and lesbians, decided by the Court in 1986. We'll focus in these cases on issues of stereotypes and prejudice, and how they affect judicial decisions. The cases we'll examine in this lecture raise important questions. If stereotypes about women's role in society have changed in recent decades, as they move from kitchens and kindergarten classrooms, to law offices and legislative halls, do women still need special protection in the courts? If prejudice toward gays and lesbians has declined in recent years, should the courts strike down laws that reflect "moral disapproval" of their sexual orientation and behavior?

Behind these specific questions are broader questions, which become more relevant as this course nears its conclusion. Should the strict scrutiny test, which the Court adopted in the 1930s to protect groups that suffered from public hostility and prejudice, be scrapped as an outdated and unnecessary judicial relic? Should groups like women and gays be directed from the courts to the political arena, to run candidates and use the tools of lobbying and education that other groups have employed over the years? We'll look at these questions through cases that involve people like Myra Bradwell, Sally Reed, Sharron Frontiero, and Michael Hardwick. They each have a story that puts a human face on the pages of the Supreme Court's rulings in their cases.

We'll begin with Myra Bradwell, who brought a case before the Supreme Court in 1873. She had all the makings of an outstanding lawyer. She was educated in the best schools in Illinois and taught school before she married a state judge. Although she raised two children, she wanted a career outside the home, so she established a weekly periodical called the *Chicago Legal News*. Bradwell's legal reporting was so highly respected that state courts made the contents of her journal admissible as evidence in trials. Her husband encouraged her to study law, and she passed the licensing exam with flying colors. The final step to law practice in Illinois was admission by the state supreme court, which was a formality in most cases.

To her surprise, Myra Bradwell received a letter stating her application had been rejected. The only reason given was her sex: women could not practice law in Illinois. This was a clear case of sex discrimination, and Bradwell appealed to the Supreme Court. Senator Matthew Carpenter of Wisconsin argued her case. The right to practice law, he told the justices, belonged to "every American citizen as a matter of right," and could not be denied to Bradwell "on the ground of her sex alone." Carpenter rested his case on the due process clause of the Fourteenth Amendment. That constitutional provision, he argued, "protects every citizen—black or white, male or female."

But, as we saw in an earlier lecture, the Supreme Court ruled in the Slaughterhouse Cases in 1873 that the Fourteenth Amendment was intended only to protect blacks from official discrimination. The Slaughterhouse majority expressed doubt that any other group "will ever be held to come within the purview of this provision." Justice Joseph Bradley dissented from this ruling, arguing that the Fourteenth Amendment protected "every right and privilege" of every citizen. Ironically, Bradley ignored his own words in *Bradwell v. Illinois*. The Court unanimously upheld the state's right to ban women from law practice.

Bradley wrote a concurring opinion, in which he expressed the prevailing male stereotypes about women. "Man is, or should be, woman's protector and defender," he wrote. "The natural and proper timidity and delicacy which belongs to the female sex evidently unfits it for many of the occupations of civil life," including the legal profession. Bradley argued, "The family institution is repugnant to the idea of a woman adopting a distinct and independent career from that of her husband." He looked beyond the Constitution for precedent, which he put in these words: "The paramount destiny and mission of women are to fulfill the noble and benign offices of wife and mother. This is the law of the Creator."

It's tempting to dismiss Justice Bradley and his colleagues as relics of Victorian chivalry. But their attitude toward women lasted well into the 20th century, even after the suffragist movement persuaded Congress and the states to adopt the Nineteenth Amendment in 1920, giving women the right to vote. But the laws of many states reflected gender stereotypes, and erected legal barriers against women in many areas of life. As late as 1948, the Supreme Court relied on the *Bradwell* case to uphold laws that barred women from various occupations. The Court upheld a Michigan law that kept women from tending bar. Justice Felix Frankfurter wrote in *Goesaert v. Cleary* that the Fourteenth Amendment, as he put it, "does not preclude the states from drawing a sharp line between the sexes, certainly in such matters as the regulation of the liquor traffic."

But the legal victories of the Civil Rights movement in the 1950s and 60s prompted feminist groups to attack discrimination through the courts. The American Civil Liberties Union set up a Women's Law Project under the direction of Ruth Bader Ginsburg. She had recently become the first tenured female professor at Columbia law school, and she later became the second female to join the Supreme Court. Ginsburg found an unlikely case to challenge state laws that discriminated against women, an obscure probate case from Idaho. *Reed v. Reed* had none of the elements of legal drama. Richard Reed, a teenager, had died in 1967 and left no will to devise his estate, which was valued at less than $1,000. His parents had divorced, and Sally Reed and her former husband, Cecil, both applied to administer Richard's modest estate. The county probate judge appointed Cecil Reed, relying on an Idaho law that stated, "males must be preferred to females" in selecting administrators. Sally Reed appealed to the Idaho Supreme Court, arguing the law violated the Fourteenth

Amendment's equal protection clause, but the state judges upheld the statute as a reasonable way to spare probate courts the burden of conducting hearings to choose estate administrators.

Ruth Ginsburg prepared the ACLU brief in the case, and secured supporting briefs from a wide range of women's and civil rights groups. The Supreme Court struck down the Idaho law in a unanimous decision. Chief Justice Warren Burger, who always opened doors for women, opened the probate court door for Sally Reed. Because all the Court's prior decisions in gender discrimination cases—going back to *Bradwell* in 1873—had upheld the challenged laws, Burger reached for precedent to an unlikely source. He cited a 1920 case that involved state taxation of a fertilizer company, quoting from *Royster Guano Company v. Virginia* for the proposition that "all persons similarly situated shall be treated alike" under state laws. Burger did not apply the strict scrutiny test, because the Idaho law failed even the lenient rational basis test. The mandatory preference for males, he wrote, was "the very kind of arbitrary legislative choice" the equal protection clause forbids.

Two years after the *Reed* decision, in 1973, the Court accepted an appeal from another unlikely crusader for women's rights. Sharron Frontiero was an Air Force lieutenant who served at a base in Alabama. Her husband, Joseph, was a Vietnam veteran and a full-time college student. Lieutenant Frontiero applied for housing and medical benefits, and listed her husband as a dependent. The military brass rejected her application because her husband's veteran's benefits covered more than half of his monthly expenses. But if their genders were reversed, the Frontieros would have automatically received benefits. The federal law providing military benefits included a legislative "presumption" that wives of personnel were financially dependent on their husbands, with no requirement of proof.

Lieutenant Frontiero sued the Secretary of Defense, Elliot Richardson, with the aid of the ACLU project. Ruth Bader Ginsburg made the first of her six arguments in women's rights cases before the Supreme Court, winning all but one. Her argument in *Frontiero v. Richardson* urged the justices to apply the strict scrutiny test, and to extend "suspect class" protection to women. As we've seen in past lectures, the Court had long applied that test in cases involving racial and religious minorities, requiring governments to prove a "compelling" reason for discriminating against members of those classes. Ruth Ginsburg won the case, but she lost the argument over adding women to the "suspect class" category, and subjecting women's rights cases to the strict scrutiny test.

There's a story about this aspect of the *Frontiero* case. Justice William Brennan drafted an opinion for the eight justices who voted to strike down the gender-based provision in the military benefits law. He cited the *Reed* case for precedent and flunked the statute under the rational basis test. But Justice Byron White persuaded Brennan to apply the strict scrutiny test in his opinion. However, Justice Lewis Powell sent Brennan a note saying, "I see no reason to consider whether sex is a suspect classification in this case." Powell noted that Congress had recently sent the proposed Equal Rights Amendment to state legislatures, which would ban laws that discriminated against women. Powell wrote a concurring opinion in *Frontiero*, arguing that the Court should avoid deciding, as he put it, "sensitive issues of broad social and political importance at the very time they are under consideration within the prescribed constitutional processes."

Ironically, the Equal Rights Amendment fell short of ratification by two states, and Brennan's effort to give women equal rights through judicial action fell one vote short of a majority. Brennan did, however, take a swipe at Justice Bradley's views of the "proper role" of women in the *Bradwell* case. Brennan noted the nation's "long and unfortunate history of sex discrimination," which is "rationalized by an attitude of 'romantic paternalism,' which put women, not on a pedestal, but in a cage. As a result of notions such as these, our statute books gradually became laden with gross, stereotyped distinctions between the sexes." Ruth Ginsburg had paved the way for women's rights in the 1970s, as an exceedingly persuasive advocate before the Supreme Court. Sitting as a justice in the 1990s, she applied that same standard to the state of Virginia's effort to keep women out of the Virginia Military Institute.

This state-funded college had trained young men since 1839 to become what it called "citizen-soldiers," capable of assuming leadership roles in military and civilian life. VMI subjected its cadets to hard physical training, and housed them in barracks with little privacy. After a female high school student was turned away by VMI in 1990, the federal government sued the state of Virginia on equal protection grounds. This lawsuit produced a classic federal-state conflict, reminiscent of cases we discussed in early lectures about the Court under Chief Justice John Marshall. Marshall imposed the Court's will on his native state in those rulings, and Justice Ginsburg followed his lead in *United States v. Virginia*. Another aspect of this case is reminiscent of our earlier discussion of cases in which Oklahoma and Texas established separate law schools for black students, after they were sued for maintaining all-white schools. Virginia responded to the federal lawsuit by setting up the Virginia Women's Institute for Leadership, on the campus of a private women's college.

Justice Ginsburg wrote for a majority of eight in ruling that Virginia, as she put it, "has not shown substantial equality in the separate educational opportunities" it offered at VMI and the new, women-only school. Ginsburg put Virginia to the test of providing an "exceedingly persuasive justification" for keeping women out of VMI. She cited the Court's 1950 ruling in the Texas law-school case, *Sweatt v. Painter*, for precedent in her 1996 opinion. Almost 50 years later, women gained the right to attend schools with males that blacks had achieved in cases argued by Thurgood Marshall, another "exceedingly persuasive" lawyer who later joined the Supreme Court. In many ways, Ruth Ginsburg was to the women's movement what Marshall had been to the Civil Rights movement.

We're going to look now at the Supreme Court's ruling in a case that involved gays and lesbians. Once again, we'll see Justice Powell's crucial role as a swing vote in landmark cases, as he was in the *Bakke* and *Frontiero* rulings. We saw that ancient stereotypes about women had placed them in a cage, as Justice Brennan described their position in American society. Ancient stereotypes about homosexuals had forced them into closets, from which most were afraid to emerge. Both the cage and the closet, of course, are metaphors, but they illustrate the reality of confinement, both psychological and physical. Until the late 1960s, most gays and lesbians were realistically afraid of the hostility, and even the violence, that might await them outside their closets. But that fear was replaced by anger on a hot July night in 1969.

Police officers in New York City raided the Stonewall Inn in Greenwich Village, a popular gay bar. The cops later claimed the bar was overcrowded and too noisy, but the patrons said they shouted anti-gay epithets and pushed them out with nightsticks. This confrontation turned into bloody battles that lasted for three nights. Out of the "Stonewall riots" came the Gay Liberation Movement, which soon moved its agitation from the streets into courtrooms and legislative chambers. The main targets of gay activists were state laws that made sodomy a crime.

Georgia had a typical statute, which stated, "a person commits the offense of sodomy when he performs or submits to any sexual act involving the sex organs of one person and the mouth or anus of another." In 1960, every state made sodomy a crime, but these laws were enforced almost exclusively against gays. But the lobbying and litigation efforts of the gay movement paid off. By 1975, more than half the states had repealed or invalidated their sodomy laws by legislative or judicial action. However, none of those states were below the Mason-Dixon line, where hostility toward gays drew on Biblical sanctions and traditions of southern masculinity.

We're going to focus now on the gay-rights case that reached the Supreme Court in 1986. We've looked in this lecture at determined women like Myra Bradwell and Sharron Frontiero. Michael Hardwick was an equally determined gay man, and his story began on a hot July night in 1982, outside a gay bar in Atlanta, Georgia. Hardwick worked as a bartender, and he stepped outside after the bar closed, to get some fresh air. He was holding an open beer bottle when Officer R.D. Torick drove by in his police cruiser. Torick was noted for hassling gays, and he hassled Michael Hardwick, who had dropped the beer bottle in a trashcan when he saw the police car. Torick gave Hardwick a ticket for drinking in public, which he took to municipal court and paid a $50 fine. But there was a mix-up in the court records, and Officer Torick obtained a warrant for Hardwick's arrest for failing to appear in court.

Hardwick later talked with me about what happened on the morning of August 3 in 1982. He was in his bedroom, with a male friend. "The door opened up" Hardwick told me, "and I looked up and there was nobody there. I just blew it off as the wind and went back to what I was involved in, which was mutual oral sex. Then I heard another noise and I looked up, and this officer is standing in my bedroom. He said, 'My name is Officer Torick. Michael Hardwick, you are under arrest.' I said, 'For what? What are you doing in my bedroom?' He said, 'I have a warrant for your arrest.' I told him the warrant wasn't any good. I had paid my fine. He said, 'It doesn't matter, because I was acting in good faith.'"

Officer Torick handcuffed Hardwick and his friend and took them to the downtown police station, where they were booked for sodomy and tossed into the drunk tank. Hardwick got bailed out after 12 hours, and three days later he was contacted by a lawyer for the American Civil Liberties Union. The ACLU had been looking for someone to challenge Georgia's sodomy law, which carried a maximum 20-year prison term. Hardwick volunteered as a test-case plaintiff, and the ACLU lawyers appeared in the Atlanta municipal court for his arraignment. But the district attorney dropped the charges when he learned that Officer Torick's arrest warrant had expired. However, Hardwick still faced prosecution before the statute of limitations ran out.

The ACLU lawyers filed a suit in federal court in Atlanta, challenging the sodomy law on due process and equal protection grounds. They named the state's attorney general, Michael Bowers, as the lead defendant. The federal district judge who heard the case ruled against Hardwick, but an appellate court panel reversed his decision. Judge Frank Johnson relied on the Supreme Court's rulings in the *Griswold* and *Roe* cases, which established a "right to privacy" that protected contraceptive use and abortion rights. Johnson held that "private consensual sexual behavior among adults" was protected from criminal punishment. "For some," he added, "the sexual activity in question here serves the same purpose as the intimacy of marriage."

The year before Judge Johnson's ruling, the Supreme Court had declined to hear an appeal from another federal appellate court, upholding Virginia's sodomy law. But the justices agreed to consider Georgia's appeal in *Bowers v. Hardwick*. Leaving Johnson's decision in place would have the result of striking down the sodomy laws in most of the Deep South states, and would most likely have precipitated a political uproar. But the outcome of the *Bowers* case was far from certain when arguments began on March 31 in 1986. There's an important point in the argument of Michael Hobbs, who defended the Georgia sodomy law.

One justice asked Hobbs this question: "Do you think it would be constitutional or unconstitutional to apply it to a married couple?" Hobbs did not equivocate. "I believe that it would be unconstitutional," he conceded, because of "the right of marital privacy as identified by the Court in *Griswold*." Marital privacy included not only contraception, but also sexual practices that were illegal for any couple under Georgia law. But this concession raised two serious questions. First, the Supreme Court had extended the *Griswold* ruling to protect contraceptive use by unmarried couples. Did that mean the Georgia sodomy law could not be used to prosecute any heterosexual couple? Secondly, would its application only to homosexual sodomy allow an equal protection challenge? Hobbs did not face these questions from the justices. He concluded his argument with this appeal: "It is a right of the nation, and of the states, to maintain a decent society, representing the collective moral aspirations of the people."

Professor Laurence Tribe of Harvard Law School presented the argument for Michael Hardwick. He put the case in these words: "This case is about the limits of governmental power. The power that the state of Georgia invoked to arrest Michael Hardwick in the bedroom of his own home is not a power to preserve public decorum. The power invoked here is the power to dictate in the most intimate and, indeed, I must say, the most embarrassing detail how every adult, married or unmarried, in every bedroom in Georgia will behave in the closest and most intimate personal association with another adult." Tribe ended his argument with this appeal: "It is not a characteristic of governments devoted to liberty that they proclaim the unquestioned authority of Big Brother to dictate every detail of intimate life in the home." So, the two lawyers asked the justices to choose between morality and liberty in deciding the case. It's worth noting that Tribe did not raise the equal protection claim in his argument, which rested on the "liberty" interest in the Fourteenth Amendment.

The Court decided Michael Hardwick's case on June 30 of 1986. The justices were narrowly divided, five to four. The two sides were far apart on constitutional issues. Justice Byron White, one of the two dissenters in the *Roe* case, wrote for the majority, in upholding the Georgia sodomy law. His opinion made a clear choice between morality and liberty. "The law is constantly based on notions of morality," he wrote, "and if all laws representing essentially moral choices are to be invalidated under the due process clause, the courts will be very busy indeed." Justice White rejected any notion that engaging in homosexual sodomy was a "fundamental right" and that Georgia's law should be subjected to the strict scrutiny test. He found a rational basis for the law in what he called "the belief of a majority of the electorate in Georgia that homosexual sodomy is immoral and unacceptable."

Chief Justice Warren Burger took White's position a step further in his concurring opinion. Condemnation of homosexual sodomy, he wrote, "is firmly rooted in Judeo-Christian moral and ethical standards. To hold that the act of homosexual sodomy is somehow protected as a fundamental right would be to cast aside millennia of moral teaching." Justice Harry Blackmun, who had based his *Roe* opinion on the "right to privacy," wrote for the four dissenters in the *Bowers* case.

Blackmun directed his barbs at Justice White's reliance on the "ancient roots" of hostility towards homosexuals as justification for modern-day sodomy laws. Blackmun quoted the words of Justice Oliver Wendell Holmes: "It is revolting to have no better reason for a rule of law than that it was laid down in the time of Henry IV. It is still more revolting if the grounds upon which it was laid down have vanished long since, and the rule simply persists from blind imitation of the past." Blackmun stressed the "liberty" claim in Professor Tribe's argument, in these words: "A necessary corollary of giving individuals freedom to choose how to conduct their lives is acceptance of the fact that different individuals will make different choices."

Let's return to Justice Lewis Powell as the Court's swing vote in several landmark cases. Two weeks after the Court handed down the *Bowers* ruling, the *Washington Post* ran this front-page headline: "Powell Changed Vote in Sodomy Case." The *Post* story revealed that Powell had initially voted to strike down the Georgia law, which would have produced a different five-to-four majority. But Powell had switched his vote before the ruling was announced. Four years later, after his retirement in 1987, Powell gave a speech to a law-school audience, and was asked about the report of his vote-switching in the *Bowers* case. "I think I probably made a mistake in that one," he confessed. "When I had the opportunity to reread the opinions a few months later, I thought the dissent had the better of the arguments." But his second thoughts came too late to change the outcome.

Let me add a couple of footnotes to this case. Michael Hardwick died of AIDS a few years after the Court rejected his challenge to the Georgia sodomy law. But the law itself died in 1998, when the Georgia Supreme Court struck it down as a violation of the "right to privacy" in the state constitution. Other state courts, however, including those in Texas and Alabama, have upheld their state's laws against sodomy. The gay rights movement has continued its lobbying campaign to repeal the remaining sodomy laws, and the "ancient roots" that nourished these laws have withered, as public hostility toward gays and lesbians has shifted to greater tolerance. But the moral condemnation of homosexual behavior is still reflected in the continuing debate over gay and lesbian rights and the persistence of hate crimes against members of this group.

We've looked in this lecture at the Court's rulings in cases that involved two very different groups in American society, the majority group of women and the minority of gays and lesbians. It's worth noting that both of these groups have gained public support and political influence in recent years. In our next lecture, we'll shift our focus to a group that is much smaller, and that most Americans condemn in heated terms: those few people who have burned American flags and crosses. We'll see how the Court has responded to acts of political and racial hatred, testing the limits of the First Amendment.

 ©2003 The Teaching Company Limited Partnership

Lecture Thirty-Three
Burning Flags and Burning Crosses

Scope:

This lecture examines two acts of "symbolic speech" that have generated much controversy in American society: burning the American flag as an act of political protest and burning crosses to express racial hatred against blacks. We will focus on two cases in this area. In 1989, a sharply divided Court struck down a Texas law under which Gregory Johnson was sentenced to jail for burning the American flag. The majority opinion of Justice William Brennan ruled that flag burning was protected by the First Amendment. The four dissenters, led by Chief Justice William Rehnquist, argued vehemently that the flag held a "unique place" as our national symbol and could be protected by law against destruction or defacement. The Court later invalidated a municipal hate crime ordinance under which Robert Viktora was convicted for burning a cross on the lawn of a black family. We will analyze the conflicting opinions in these cases and look at the continuing debate over efforts to ban the symbolic expression of controversial views.

Outline

I. This lecture examines the Supreme Court's rulings in cases that involve "desecration" of the American flag and burning of crosses as an expression of racial hostility. It also discusses major changes in the Court's membership in 1986 and 1987.

II. Chief Justice Warren Burger announced his retirement in June 1986. He said that he would direct the preparations for celebrating the Constitution's bicentennial in 1987.

   A. President Ronald Reagan nominated Justice William Rehnquist to replace Burger.

   B. Reagan had already placed Justice Sandra Day O'Connor on the Court, the first woman to serve in that post. She replaced Justice Potter Stewart.

   1. O'Connor had graduated from Stanford law school but could not find employment in any major law firm.

   2. She found a job in a California county attorney's office and later established a law practice in Phoenix, Arizona.

3. O'Connor was elected to the Arizona senate, then became a state judge.

4. During her Senate confirmation hearings, she pledged to follow the judicial restraint position.

C. Justice Rehnquist was opposed by many Senate Democrats as too conservative.

1. His opposition to abortion rights in the *Roe* case prompted pro-choice groups to lobby against him.

2. Rehnquist was also questioned about his 1953 memo to Justice Jackson, saying, "*Plessy v. Ferguson* was right and should be reaffirmed."

3. He was finally confirmed as chief justice, with 33 votes against him.

D. Reagan nominated Antonin Scalia to fill the vacancy created by Rehnquist's elevation to chief justice.

1. Scalia was a former law professor and Justice Department official and had served on the federal appellate court in Washington, D.C.

2. He was an outspoken conservative and opponent of abortion, but he was confirmed without dissent.

E. Justice Lewis Powell retired in June 1987, and Reagan nominated Robert Bork to replace him.

1. Like Scalia, Bork was a former law professor, Justice Department official, and federal appellate judge.

2. He was also an outspoken conservative, who denounced the *Roe* decision.

3. Pro-choice groups mounted a lobbying campaign against Bork, and the Senate rejected his confirmation by a 58–42 margin.

F. Reagan chose another appellate judge, Douglas Ginsburg, but withdrew his nomination after reports that Ginsburg had smoked marijuana as a Harvard law professor.

G. Reagan finally replaced Powell with Anthony Kennedy, a federal appellate judge from California. Kennedy was a judicial moderate with a "squeaky-clean" reputation and was confirmed without dissent.

©2003 The Teaching Company Limited Partnership

III. In 1989, the Court struck down a Texas law against "desecration" of the flag in *Texas v. Johnson*, by a margin of five to four.

    A. This case began with a Communist-led demonstration at the 1984 Republican convention in Dallas, at which protestors burned an American flag. Gregory Johnson was sentenced to a year in jail for this act.

    B. Justice William Brennan wrote for the majority, saying Johnson could not be punished for the "content" of his message.

    C. Brennan said the "bedrock principle" of the First Amendment was that society may not punish "the expression of an idea because society finds the idea offensive."

    D. Chief Justice Rehnquist wrote in dissent that the flag was a "special" symbol that deserved protection.

    E. The Court's ruling ignited a firestorm of public protest, and efforts to reverse it by constitutional amendment, but the Senate rejected this effort.

IV. The Court struck down a municipal hate crimes law in the 1992 case of *R.A.V. v. City of St. Paul, Minnesota*.

    A. Robert Viktora was a juvenile who burned a cross on the lawn of a black family in St. Paul. He was convicted under a law that made the placing of a burning cross on private or public property a crime if the act would arouse "anger or alarm" on the basis of race, religion, or gender.

    B. The Court unanimously struck down the law, ruling that it violated the doctrine of *content neutrality*.

    C. Justice Scalia wrote for the Court: "The government may not regulate speech based on hostility—or favoritism—towards the underlying message expressed."

V. The Court's ruling in the *R.A.V.* case did not end the judicial debate over cross burning. The issue returned to the Court in April of 2003, when the justices decided three separate cases from Virginia.

    A. In 1952, the Virginia state legislature had passed a law making cross burning a crime, if its purpose was to "intimidate" anyone who witnessed the act, but the law permitted judges to instruct jurors that they could "infer" that any cross burning was meant to intimidate.

B. In one case, a Ku Klux Klan leader named Barry Black had presided at a Klan rally that included cross burning and Klan rhetoric about white supremacy, but no African Americans had witnessed the rally or the cross burning.

C. In the other cases, two white men had burned a cross on a black neighbor's lawn after the neighbor had complained about the two men shooting firearms on their own property.

D. In deciding these cases, the justices were deeply split.

    1. Justice Sandra Day O'Connor wrote for the majority of six in *Virginia v. Black*, holding that states could outlaw cross burning "as a particularly virulent form of intimidation." However, she also held that Virginia's law was unconstitutional, because it required jurors to find that any act of cross burning was meant to intimidate those who witnessed it.

    2. O'Connor wrote that burning a cross at a Klan rally could be protected by the First Amendment as a form of "symbolic speech." But burning a cross on a neighbor's lawn, regardless of race, could be seen as a "true threat," with no symbolic meaning and no First Amendment protection.

    3. Justices Souter, Kennedy, and Ginsburg dissented, arguing that the "content discrimination" in the Virginia law could not "rescue" it from the *R.A.V.* precedent.

    4. Justice Clarence Thomas also dissented, arguing that cross burning was not speech at all, but simply "terroristic conduct" whose only purpose was to intimidate blacks.

VI. Public opinion polls show that most people oppose the Court's rulings in the flag-burning and cross-burning cases. But as Justice Kennedy wrote in his concurring opinion in the flag-burning case, "sometimes we must make decisions we do not like."

Suggested Readings:

Robert J. Goldstein, *Flag Burning and Free Speech: The Case of Texas v. Johnson* (2000).

Cass R. Sunstein, *Democracy and the Problem of Free Speech* (1993).

Questions to Consider:

1. Do you think the First Amendment should protect those who burn the American flag as an act of political protest?

2. Burning a cross has long been associated with the Ku Klux Klan and other racist groups. Should that act be treated as a criminal offense?

Lecture Thirty-Three—Transcript
Burning Flags and Burning Crosses

In our previous lecture, we looked at the Supreme Court's rulings in landmark cases that involved two groups in American society: women and homosexuals. Women are the majority of the population, but in many ways they were treated under the law as a minority. We saw how the Court viewed women in the 19th century as too "delicate" and "timid" to engage in professions such as law. Not until the 1970s did the justices apply the equal protection clause of the Fourteenth Amendment to discrimination against women, striking down state and federal laws that barred them from probate administration and military benefits. We also looked at discrimination against gays and lesbians, and the Court's ruling in 1986 that states could single out homosexuals for criminal prosecution under laws that banned the act of sodomy.

In this lecture, we're going to shift our focus to much different acts, those of burning American flags and crosses as expressions of political protest and racial prejudice. On the surface, there seems little or no connection between homosexual sodomy on one hand, and burning flags and crosses on the other. But on a deeper level, laws that criminalize these unrelated acts express the moral condemnation of those who undermine or attack "sacred" institutions and symbols in American society. In my view, it's worth noting that laws against homosexual sodomy have "ancient roots" in the sacred texts of Judaism and Christianity, as the Court stated in the *Hardwick* case. Flag "desecration" laws have similar roots in notions of the American flag as a "sacred" symbol of national unity. In fact, the word "desecration" means "to take away the sacredness" of an object or symbol. And it's obvious that burning a cross, the sacred symbol of Christianity, to express racial hatred is a form of desecration.

We'll look in this lecture at the Court's response to acts of desecration of the sacred symbols of the flag and the cross. But we're going to begin with major changes in the Court itself. We ended our previous lecture with the Court's ruling on the Georgia sodomy case of *Bowers v. Hardwick*. That decision was handed down on June 30 of 1986. Ten days earlier, President Ronald Reagan had nominated Justice William Rehnquist to replace Warren Burger as chief justice. Burger had served for 17 years, and had never placed a distinctive stamp on the Court. He relished the ceremonial role of chief justice,

 ©2003 The Teaching Company Limited Partnership

but he lacked the personal warmth and political savvy that had made his predecessor, Earl Warren, the undisputed leader of a generally united Court. Burger explained that he was stepping down to chair the group that was planning ceremonies to celebrate the Constitution's bicentennial in 1987, just the kind of pomp and circumstance that Burger enjoyed.

President Reagan had already filled the first vacancy on the Court, shortly after he took office in 1981. Reagan had defeated the incumbent Democratic president, Jimmy Carter, who became the only 20th century president who didn't place a single justice on the Court. Reagan promised during his campaign to add a woman to the Court if he was elected. The retirement of Justice Potter Stewart in July of 1981 gave Reagan that chance. Stewart had stayed in the Court's moderate bloc during his 22 years of service, and he joined the majority that upheld abortion rights in the 1973 *Roe* decision. By the time of Stewart's retirement, abortion had become the most heated issue in American politics. The Republican platform in 1980 had denounced the *Roe* decision and called for a constitutional amendment to reverse it. Abortion was sure to become a factor in choosing Stewart's replacement, with both sides on this issue closely scrutinizing the nominee.

President Reagan also had a very small pool of women lawyers and judges to choose from, since few women had more than 10 years of legal experience and even fewer were Republicans. But he reached into this pool and picked Sandra Day O'Connor, who had served for seven years as an Arizona state judge. O'Connor had an impressive legal pedigree. She was born in 1930 and grew up on a ranch in Arizona. O'Connor was both independent and ambitious, and she attended Stanford University in California, moving to its law school after completing undergraduate studies. She graduated third in her law school class, two places behind her classmate, William Rehnquist. He won a prize clerkship on the Supreme Court, but O'Connor had no offers from the law firms she applied to in Los Angeles and San Francisco. None of these firms, in fact, had ever hired a woman lawyer. So she took a job with a county attorney's office in California, and then worked for the Army in Germany, where her husband was stationed.

They returned to Arizona, and O'Connor opened a small law practice with another lawyer in Phoenix. She later spent four years as an assistant state attorney general. O'Connor became active in Republican politics, and was appointed to fill a vacancy in the state senate in 1969. She won election for two full terms, and became the senate's majority leader in 1973. She was elected the following year to the superior court in Phoenix, and was appointed to the state court of appeals in 1979. With this record of experience in law practice, elective office, and judicial service, O'Connor topped the class of women candidates for the Supreme Court. During her Senate confirmation hearings, she deflected questions about her views on abortion and the *Roe* decision, pledging only to exercise judicial restraint as a justice. "I do not believe that it is the function of the judiciary to step in and change the law because the times have changed," she proclaimed. The most fervent anti-abortion groups opposed O'Connor's confirmation, because she had once voted as a state senator to liberalize Arizona's abortion law. But the Senate confirmed her without dissent in September of 1981.

Five years later, President Reagan's nomination of Justice Rehnquist to replace Chief Justice Burger provoked considerable dissent. Twenty-six senators had voted against Rehnquist when he was first named to the Court in 1971, most of them Democrats who considered him too conservative. But no senator had ever opposed the elevation of a sitting justice to the chief's position. Rehnquist did not receive this senatorial courtesy. He had compiled the most conservative voting record on the Court, most notably in First Amendment and civil rights cases. And he had dissented in the *Roe* case, which turned pro-choice groups against him.

Rehnquist's views on racial issues also sparked opposition. Liberal senators grilled him about the memorandum he wrote as a Supreme Court clerk, stating that "I think *Plessy v. Ferguson* was right and should be reaffirmed" in the school segregation cases. Senators also discovered that Rehnquist owned houses in Arizona and Vermont, whose deeds included restrictive covenants against their sale to blacks. The racial covenants couldn't be enforced, but many senators were skeptical about Rehnquist's explanation that he'd never read his property deeds, although he'd practiced real estate law in Arizona. The second time around, 33 senators voted against his confirmation as chief justice. The self-proclaimed conservative "partisan" on the Court had not won over the liberal partisans in the Senate.

    ©2003 The Teaching Company Limited Partnership

But another conservative partisan sailed through the Senate without a ripple. Moving Rehnquist to the center seat had opened up his position on the bench, and President Reagan took advantage of the opening to name the first justice of Italian descent. Antonin Scalia was born in 1936, the son of an Italian immigrant who taught romance languages at New Jersey colleges. Scalia was a brilliant student at Georgetown University, earning a summa cum laude degree, which he followed with a magna cum laude from Harvard Law School in 1960. After seven years in private practice, he joined the University of Virginia law school faculty, and later served in both the Nixon and Ford administrations.

In fact, Scalia filled the same position in the Justice Department that William Rehnquist had occupied, heading the Office of Legal Counsel for the attorney general. President Reagan placed him on the District of Columbia federal appellate court in 1982, where he wrote bristling dissents from opinions by that court's liberal majority. Scalia argued for an "original intent" approach to the Constitution, and he made no bones about his opposition to abortion. But the pro-choice lobby did not mount a campaign against his confirmation, which was approved by the Senate in a voice vote, with no objections. However, Reagan's next choice sparked a ferocious battle over the abortion issue. Justice Lewis Powell retired in June of 1987, and Reagan turned to another conservative partisan, who matched Scalia in his background and his views.

Robert Bork was a former law school professor, who served as solicitor general in the Reagan administration. He had also served with Scalia on the District of Columbia federal appellate court. Bork was equally outspoken in his opposition to abortion, and pro-choice groups feared he would add the decisive fifth vote to reverse the *Roe* decision, assuming that Justice O'Connor would join the conservatives on this issue. Under the glare of television lights, Bork faced the Senate Judiciary Committee in hearings that quickly became contentious. Liberal senators grilled him with hostile questions, which Bork answered with none of Scalia's charm and wit. Outside the Senate chamber, abortion supporters and opponents mounted lobbying campaigns unequaled in Supreme Court history. After weeks of intense and often bitter debate, the Senate rejected Bork by a vote of 58 to 42. The fact that 47 senators who had voted to confirm Scalia, turned around and voted against Bork the following year, offers a striking illustration of the increasingly political nature of Supreme Court nominations.

Bork's defeat only stiffened President Reagan's resolve to place another anti-abortion vote on the Court. His advisors combed the federal appellate bench for potential justices and came up with two names: Anthony Kennedy of the Ninth Circuit in the western states, and Douglas Ginsburg, who served for one year with Bork on the District of Columbia court after teaching antitrust law at Harvard. Ginsburg got the nod, largely because of his youth—he was just 41—and his rock-solid conservative views. But his nomination in October of 1987 went up in smoke after former colleagues at Harvard told reporters that Ginsburg had smoked marijuana at parties with students. The First Lady, Nancy Reagan, was conducting her "Just Say No" campaign against drug use, and Ginsburg withdrew his name just a week after the president announced his nomination.

Reagan then turned to Kennedy, whose moderate judicial record and "squeaky-clean" personal life made him palatable to senate liberals. Kennedy was born in 1936, like Scalia, and was also a devout Catholic. He graduated from Stanford University and Harvard Law School, and spent 14 years in corporate practice in California before he joined the appellate court. Reagan's conservative supporters harbored doubts about Kennedy's devotion to the anti-abortion cause, but the president was convinced he would vote to overturn the *Roe* decision. As we'll see in our next lecture, Kennedy later became the swing vote to save *Roe* from reversal. He's also emerged as the Court's leading defender of First Amendment rights, despite his conservative votes in criminal law and civil rights cases. But in 1987, with Kennedy's confirmation, the Court appeared to have a narrow, but solid, conservative majority.

We're going to look now at one of the Court's most controversial rulings in the past two decades, the flag-burning case of *Texas v. Johnson*. This case began in 1984, at the Republican convention in Dallas, where the delegates shouted their approval of President Reagan's nomination for a second term. Outside the convention hall, protesters shouted their disapproval, most of them peacefully. But one small group, the Revolutionary Communist Youth Brigade, marched through downtown Dallas, spray-painting slogans on the walls of corporate buildings. One marcher pulled an American flag from its pole outside a bank, and handed it to Gregory Lee Johnson,

 ©2003 The Teaching Company Limited Partnership

who led the noisy band to City Hall. Johnson unfurled the flag, doused it with lighter fluid, and flicked a cigarette lighter.

While the flag burned, the protesters chanted, "America, the red, white, and blue, we spit on you!" No fights broke out, and the police did not break up the demonstration. One spectator, a man named Daniel Walker, gathered the burned remains of the flag and buried them in his backyard. Police later arrested Johnson under a Texas law that punished anyone who "desecrates" a flag with knowledge this act would "seriously offend" an observer. Walker told a jury that he was offended by the flag burning, and Johnson received a one-year jail term from the judge. A panel of state judges reversed the conviction, holding that Johnson's act, as they wrote, "was clearly speech contemplated by the First Amendment." The Supreme Court accepted the state's appeal from this ruling in 1989.

We're going to listen now to excerpts of the oral arguments in *Texas v. Johnson*. Kathi Drew, an assistant district attorney in Dallas, argues for the state. She agrees that flag burning is a form of "symbolic speech." But she claims that Texas has the right to protect the physical integrity of the American flag because, in her words, "its symbolic effect is diluted by certain flagrant public acts of flag desecration." Her argument provokes a question from Justice Antonin Scalia.

> Scalia: "What is the juridical category you're asking us to adopt in order to say we can punish this kind of speech? Just an exception for flags? It's just a, there's just a flag exception of the First Amendment?"

> Drew: "To a certain extent, we have made that argument in our brief. With respect to the 'symbolic speech' standard, we believe that there are compelling state interests that will—in a balancing posture—override this individual's 'symbolic speech' rights, and that preserving the flag as a symbol, because it is such a national property, is one of those."

Scalia agrees that the flag is a national symbol, but he's troubled by the state's decision to punish only those who burn the flag to show their contempt for this symbol. He presses Drew on this issue.

> Scalia: "I understand that. But we—up to now—have never allowed such an item to be declared a national symbol and to

be usable symbolically only in one direction, which is essentially what you're arguing. You can honor it all you like, but you can't dishonor it as a sign of disrespect for the country."

William Kunstler replaces Drew at the podium. Kunstler has represented many unpopular clients, from black militants to Communists like Johnson. He focuses on the sacred nature of the American flag.

> Kunstler: "When you use the word 'desecrate,' you don't mean really in essence praising the flag. Desecrate has a meaning, and I just looked in Webster's Second International about it, and desecrate means 'to divest of a sacred character or office, to divert from a sacred purpose, to violate the sanctity of, to profane, the opposite of consecrate.'"

Chief Justice Rehnquist had dissented from rulings in earlier cases that struck down convictions for wearing the flag on the seat of a pair of jeans, and taping a peace symbol on the flag to protest the Vietnam War. Kunstler responds to Rehnquist's claim the flag is a "unique national symbol" that deserves special protection from desecration.

> Kunstler: "I understand that this flag has serious important meanings. The chief has mentioned many times that it's not just pieces of material, blue and white and red. That it has real meaning to real people out there. But that does not mean that it may have different meanings to other people out there, and that they may not—under the First Amendment—show their feelings by what Texas calls 'desecration of a venerated object.' I think it's a most important case. I sense that it goes to the heart of the First Amendment. To hear things or to see things that we hate tests the First Amendment more than seeing or hearing things that we like. It wasn't designed for things we like. They never needed a First Amendment."

On June 21 of 1989, the Court struck down the Texas law by a vote of five to four. Justice William Brennan wrote for the majority, which included Justices Kennedy and Scalia, who rarely agreed with Brennan and the Court's liberals. Brennan acknowledged, as he put it, "there is a special place reserved for the flag in this nation." But that made its treatment by Gregory Johnson an act that deserved special protection by the First Amendment. Johnson was punished, Brennan said, "because of the content" of his message, however hateful to most Americans. Brennan put the issue in these words: "If there is a bedrock principle underlying the First Amendment, it is that government may not prohibit the expression of an idea because society finds the idea offensive." He suggested an answer to Johnson's act: "We can imagine no more appropriate response to burning a flag than waving one's own."

This was a hard case for justices on both sides. The Court's newest member, Justice Kennedy, joined the majority with a brief concurring opinion. "The hard fact," he said, "is that sometimes we must make decisions we do not like. We make them because they are right, right in the sense that the law and the Constitution, as we see them, compel the result." The four dissenters disagreed. Chief Justice Rehnquist did not see the flag as just another symbol, or Johnson's act as just another message. The flag was more than special to Rehnquist. "Millions of Americans," he said, "regard the flag with an almost mystical reverence." "The government tells Americans," Rehnquist said, "they must fight and perhaps die for the flag." He cited the Marines who raised the flag over Iwo Jima in World War II, after fighting "hand to hand against thousands of Japanese."

The Court's decision in the flag-burning case ignited a firestorm of public outrage. Newspapers printed thousands of heated letters, and political leaders in both parties condemned the ruling. President George Bush, whose 1988 campaign featured the flag, proposed a constitutional amendment to protect it. But the campaign to amend the Constitution ran out of steam after the speeches ended and second thoughts began. Senator Bob Kerrey of Nebraska, who lost a leg in Vietnam and won a Medal of Honor, dampened the rhetorical flames with a dramatic speech against a constitutional amendment.

"At first I was outraged by the Supreme Court's opinion," he said. Later, during the Senate's Fourth of July recess, he read the opinions. "I was surprised to discover that I found the majority argument to be reasonable, understandable, and consistent with those values that I believe make America so wonderful," he said. Kerrey recalled "the smell of my own burning flesh" on the Vietnam battleground. "I don't remember giving the safety of our flag anywhere near the thought that I gave the safety of my men." By a slim margin, the

Senate refused to amend the Constitution, and to make the First Amendment exception for the flag that Justice Scalia had questioned.

If burning the American flag offends most people, burning a cross is especially offensive to black Americans. This act evokes painful images of hooded Klansmen and lynchings. But if flag burning is protected by the First Amendment, does cross burning also deserve constitutional protection? The Supreme Court faced this question in 1992, three years after its ruling in *Texas v. Johnson*. Justice Scalia gave the Court's answer, in a case known as *R.A.V. v. City of St. Paul, Minnesota*. The Court used the initials of the defendant, because he was prosecuted as a juvenile. But his full name was Robert A. Viktora, and he was a 17-year-old high school dropout, who called himself a "skinhead" and filled his bedroom with racist posters and Nazi swastikas.

On the night of June 21 in 1990, Viktora and several friends fashioned a cross out of broken chair legs. They set it on fire inside the yard of a black family, Russell and Laura Jones and their five children. Russell Jones called the police, and they quickly tracked down Viktora, who lived down the block. He was charged, not with trespass or arson, but with violating St. Paul's "hate crime" ordinance. This law made it a crime to "place on public or private property a symbol or object, including a burning cross or Nazi swastika, which one knows—or has reasonable grounds to know— arouses anger or alarm, or resentment, in others—on the basis of race, color, creed, religion, or gender." Viktora was convicted in juvenile court, and the Minnesota Supreme Court upheld the ordinance as a means of "protecting the community against bias-motivated threats to public safety and order."

Viktora's appeal to the United States Supreme Court rested on the ordinance's limitation of its protection to groups that were specified by race, religion, or gender. Justice Scalia wrote for a unanimous Court in striking down the ordinance. He based his ruling on the doctrine of *content neutrality*. Scalia put that doctrine in these words: "The government may not regulate speech based on hostility—or favoritism—towards the underlying message expressed." He ruled that St. Paul could not punish Viktora for the message he conveyed to the Jones family by burning a cross on their lawn. Scalia pointed out that Viktora could have been properly charged and convicted for trespass or for arson. This may seem to be a distinction without a difference. After all, the Jones family was terrified by the burning cross.

But there were state laws to punish acts that cause people to fear their physical safety is threatened. Justice Scalia made this point in these words: "Let there be no mistake about our belief that burning a cross in someone's yard is reprehensible. But St. Paul has sufficient means at its disposal to prevent such behavior without adding the First Amendment to the fire." The Court's ruling in the *R.A.V.* case did not end the judicial debate over cross burning. This issue returned to the Court in April of 2003, when the justices decided three separate cases from the state of Virginia. Back in 1952, the state legislature had passed a law that made cross burning a crime if its purpose was to "intimidate" anyone who witnessed this act. But the law also permitted judges to instruct jurors that they could "infer" that any cross burning was meant to intimidate. In other words, the mere act of burning a cross, regardless of where it was done or who witnessed this act, would allow a conviction.

The facts in the Virginia cases were quite different. In one case, a Ku Klux Klan leader named Barry Black had presided at a Klan rally in an open field that belonged to one of the group's members. Along with the cross burning, Black made a speech that included Klan rhetoric about white supremacy. But there weren't any African Americans who witnessed the rally and the burning cross. In the other cases, two white men, Richard Elliott and Jonathan O'Mara, burned a cross on a black neighbor's lawn, after the neighbor had complained about the two men shooting firearms on their own property. Elliott pleaded guilty under the cross-burning law, and O'Mara was convicted after the jury was instructed to find that he meant to intimidate his black neighbor. The Virginia Supreme Court later reversed all three convictions, relying on the *R.A.V.* decision. The state's lawyers asked the U.S. Supreme Court to reinstate the convictions, arguing that the Virginia law did not involve the kind of "content discrimination" the Court had struck down in the *R.A.V.* case.

In deciding these cases, the justices were deeply split. Justice Sandra O'Connor wrote for a majority of six in *Virginia v. Black*, holding that states could outlaw cross burning as "a particularly virulent form of intimidation," as she put it. But she also held that Virginia's law was unconstitutional, because it required jurors to find that any act of cross burning was meant to intimidate those who witnessed it. Defendants should be allowed, O'Connor said, to argue that they burned a cross simply to express the message of white supremacy, and not to intimidate anyone. In other words, burning a cross at a Klan rally could be protected by the First Amendment as a form of "symbolic speech." But burning a cross on a neighbor's lawn, regardless of their race, could be seen as what O'Connor called a "true threat," with no symbolic message and no First Amendment protection.

Justices David Souter, Anthony Kennedy, and Ruth Ginsburg dissented from this ruling, arguing that the "content discrimination" in the Virginia law could not "rescue" it from the *R.A.V.* precedent, as Justice Souter put it. On the other side, Justice Clarence Thomas also dissented, arguing that cross burning was not speech at all, but was simply "terroristic conduct" whose only purpose was to intimidate blacks. The Court's majority left open the question of whether a cross-burning law that didn't require jurors to find an intent to intimidate would pass constitutional muster. In my view, this remains an issue that is still clouded by the smoke of judicial debate.

We've seen in this lecture that the Supreme Court has taken unpopular stands in the flag-burning and cross-burning cases. Public opinion polls show that most people feel these acts deserve criminal punishment. But these cases, in my view, illustrate the wisdom of Justice Kennedy's comment: "sometimes we must make decisions we do not like." In our next lecture, we'll see how Kennedy played a key role in cases that involved school prayer and abortion. As we've seen, the Court's first rulings on these issues, in the 1960s and 70s, provoked much public disagreement. Those who supported school prayer, and those who opposed abortion, brought political pressure on lawmakers at every level of government, to test the Court's resolve. The laws they passed in response to these campaigns brought new cases, for decisions by new justices. We'll look at those cases from the 1990s and the first years of the 21st century.

Lecture Thirty-Four
Prayer and Abortion Return to the Court

Scope:

This lecture reflects the fact that some of the Supreme Court's decisions in controversial cases do not resolve the issues they raise but, in fact, provoke even more controversy and produce more cases for the justices to decide. In this lecture, we look at cases in which the Court was forced to revisit issues involving school prayer and abortion that had been decided in earlier cases. The Court ruled in 1962 and 1963 that official prayers in public schools violated the establishment of religion clause of the First Amendment, but many schools continued to offer prayers. We will examine two recent cases in which the Court faced challenges to prayers at school commencement ceremonies and football games, *Lee v. Weisman* and *Santa Fe School District v. Doe*. We will also discuss two cases in which the Court ruled on federal and state laws to limit access to abortions, *Harris v. McRae* and *Webster v. Reproductive Health Services*. The Court upheld a federal ban on Medicaid funding for abortions in the *Harris* case and state restrictions on abortion access in the *Webster* case.

Outline

I. This lecture discusses the Supreme Court's rulings in cases that involved school prayer and abortion in the years after its landmark decisions on these issues in the 1960s and 1970s.

   A. Efforts to overturn the earlier decisions through constitutional amendments came close to passage in Congress but were defeated.

   B. However, state and federal lawmakers passed many laws to limit or circumvent these decisions, producing cases that came before the Court.

II. In 1985, the Court struck down an Alabama law that allowed the recitation of a state-composed prayer in public schools.

   A. This case began in Mobile, Alabama, when Ishmael Jaffree, a lawyer and religious agnostic, objected to prayers in his children's grade-school classrooms.

B. After Jaffree filed a lawsuit to stop the prayers, the state legislature adopted an official prayer that was drafted by the governor's son.

    1. The legislature also provided that if the law was struck down by the courts, schools could establish a "moment of silence" for meditation or prayer.

    2. The lawmakers made clear the religious motivation for this law.

    3. A federal judge upheld the law, ruling that states were not bound by the First Amendment and could adopt an official state religion.

    4. A federal appellate court reversed this decision, saying that judges must obey "the controlling decisions of the Supreme Court."

C. The Supreme Court struck down the Alabama law by a six-to-three vote in *Wallace v. Jaffree.*

    1. The majority said both the official prayer and moment of silence were motivated by religious sentiment and violated the First Amendment.

    2. Justice William Rehnquist said in dissent that the First Amendment does not require government "to be strictly neutral between religion and irreligion."

III. In 1992, the Court struck down the practice of having ministers offer prayers at school graduation ceremonies in the case of *Lee v. Weisman.*

A. The parents of a Jewish student objected to prayers by a rabbi at their daughter's graduation from a middle school in Providence, Rhode Island.

B. The Court ruled by a five-to-four margin that prayers offered by ministers who were invited by school officials violated the First Amendment.

    1. Justice Anthony Kennedy based his majority opinion on the school's "endorsement" of religion.

    2. He also said that students were subjected to "coercion" and "peer pressure" by having to choose between attending their graduations and hearing prayers or staying away from these ceremonies if they objected.

    3. Justice Antonin Scalia dissented, saying the Court's decision was a "jurisprudential disaster" and that graduation prayers reflected the "historic practices of our people."

IV. The Court struck down the practice of offering prayers at high school football games in the 2000 decision in *Santa Fe School District v. Doe.*

    A. Parents of Catholic and Mormon students filed a lawsuit against the prayers, saying their children were harassed because of their objections.

    B. The Court ruled by a six-to-three margin that the football game prayers, which were led by students, were nonetheless "authorized by a government policy" and violated the First Amendment.

    C. Chief Justice Rehnquist said in dissent that the majority opinion "bristles with hostility to all things religious in public life."

V. The Court faced several abortion cases after its landmark ruling in *Roe v. Wade* in 1973.

    A. In 1980, the Court upheld, by a five-to-four margin in *Harris v. McRae,* the so-called Hyde Amendment, in which Congress barred the use of Medicaid funds to pay for abortions for poor women.

        1. The majority said the inability of poor women to obtain abortions under the Medicaid program was not based on "governmental restrictions on access to abortions" but resulted from their "indigency."

        2. The dissenters said the Court's ruling would have a "devastating impact on the lives and health of poor women."

    B. In 1989, the Court upheld, by a five-to-four vote, several state restrictions on access to abortions in *Webster v. Reproductive Health Services,* which involved a Missouri law.

        1. Four justices were willing to reverse the *Roe* decision in *Webster,* but Justice Sandra O'Connor said *Webster* was not a "proper case" to reexamine that decision.

        2. Justice Harry Blackmun, writing in dissent, expressed his fear that a new justice might create a majority to overturn *Roe.*

VI. Two new justices did join the Court after the *Webster* decision.

    A. Justice William Brennan retired in 1990 after 34 years of service.

    B. President George Bush replaced him with David Souter of New Hampshire.

        1. Souter was a former state attorney general and supreme court judge and had served on the federal appellate court in Boston for just seven months before his nomination.

        2. During his Senate confirmation hearings, Souter said the Constitution protected a right to privacy, but he did not express his views on the *Roe* decision.

    C. Justice Thurgood Marshall retired in 1991 after serving since 1967.

        1. President Bush named Clarence Thomas to replace him.

        2. Thomas was an outspoken black conservative, who had served in the Reagan administration and, later, on the federal appellate court in Washington, D.C.

        3. During his Senate confirmation hearings, a former Thomas aide, Anita Hill, accused him of sexual harassment, but Thomas denied the charges and was confirmed by a 52–48 vote.

    D. With Souter and Thomas on the bench, the Court faced a crucial abortion case in 1992, with the reversal of *Roe* a distinct possibility.

Suggested Readings:

Peter Irons, *A People's History of the Supreme Court*, chapter 34 (1999).

Barbara H. Craig and David M. O'Brien, *Abortion and American Politics* (1993).

Questions to Consider:

1. Do you agree that offering non-sectarian prayers at school functions, such as graduations, violates the Constitution?

2. Should state and federal lawmakers have the power to ban public funding of abortions?

Lecture Thirty-Four—Transcript
Prayer and Abortion Return to the Court

In our previous lecture, we looked at the Supreme Court's rulings on two issues that have sparked continuing debate, and have even prompted efforts to reverse the most controversial decision by constitutional amendment. We discussed cases that involved burning the American flag as a form of political protest, and burning a cross to express racial hatred. The flag-burning case divided the justices by a five-to-four margin, with those on each side taking sharply opposed views of the First Amendment. Justice William Brennan argued for the majority in the flag-burning case that government cannot punish the expression of any political message, no matter how much it offends the public. Chief Justice William Rehnquist replied that the American flag holds a "special place" as a national symbol, and that most people regard it with "reverence."

The Court ruled unanimously in one cross-burning case that governments cannot punish the expression of views on the basis of their content alone, however hateful and offensive. In a later case, the Court ruled that cross burning could be made unlawful under certain circumstances. We made the point in the previous lecture that both the flag and the cross are symbols with "sacred" meanings for most Americans. In a sense, the Court's rulings in these cases had religious overtones. We're going to return in this lecture, and the one that follows, to issues that have clear religious significance: school prayer and abortion.

We saw in earlier lectures that the Court's first decisions on these issues, in the 1960s and 70s, prompted efforts to reverse them by constitutional amendments. These efforts came close to passage, but they ultimately failed to gain the necessary two-thirds majority in both houses of Congress. However, lawmakers from city councils to Congress passed numerous statutes that were designed to bring back school prayer, and to roll back the Court's approval of abortion rights. We'll look at several cases that challenged these laws, from the 1980s through the last year of the 20th century. These are not the only landmark cases the Court has decided during this period, on issues like capital punishment, civil rights, and the balance of state and federal powers. But the school prayer and abortion cases, in my view, deserve our attention as we near the conclusion of this course. They reflect the deep and almost unbridgeable divisions in American

 ©2003 The Teaching Company Limited Partnership

society over matters at the core of our belief systems. And they also confront the Supreme Court with recurring appeals to reconsider its past decisions.

In this lecture and the one that follows, we'll focus on the role of Justice Anthony Kennedy in two important cases, one involving school prayers, and the other dealing with abortion. As we saw in our previous lecture, Kennedy reluctantly joined the five-to-four majority that struck down the Texas flag desecration law. He put his feelings in these words, which bear repeating: "The hard fact is that sometimes we must make decisions we do not like. We make them because they are right, right in the sense that the law and the Constitution, as we see them, compel the result." Justice Kennedy spoke honestly and openly about the hard choice between personal conviction and judicial duty, in those hard cases when these two values are in conflict. Very few cases pose this dilemma for most justices, whose personal and judicial views are congruent on most issues. But Justice Kennedy offers us a window into a divided mind, on a very divided Court.

We're going to begin with a school prayer case from the city of Mobile, Alabama, on the state's Gulf Coast. Mobile is a very religious city, with churches from more than 60 denominations. Baptists are by far the largest religious group, with 192 churches in the area. The majority of students and teachers in the Mobile schools were Baptists, and they recited classroom prayers and said grace at lunch, well after the Supreme Court ruled that school prayer violated the Constitution. No student or parent objected to these prayers until Chioke Jaffree came home from his kindergarten class in September of 1981. Chioke told his father, Ishmael Jaffree, that his teacher, Charlene Boyd, led the children in reciting this lunchtime grace: "God is great, God is good, Let us thank him for our food. Bow our heads, we all are fed, give us Lord, our daily bread. Amen."

Chioke's father was both a religious agnostic and a lawyer, and he visited his son's classroom to ask Ms. Boyd to stop the prayers. She refused, and both the school's principal and the Mobile superintendent backed her up. Jaffree also learned that his daughter Makeba's third-grade teacher led her students in the Lord's Prayer. But school officials ignored his protests about these religious practices. Jaffree finally filed a lawsuit in federal court, seeking an injunction to end the prayers in Mobile schools. He later talked with me about the reaction to his suit. "I got all kinds of nasty letters, and I got nasty phone calls at all times of night. I used to talk with people and try to let them understand why I did this—that it was a matter of principle and the schools shouldn't be promoting anyone's religion. People in the neighborhood stopped their children from associating with my children. My children got jumped on, laughed at, talked about in school."

Alabama's politicians also jumped on Jaffree after he filed his suit. Governor Forrest James denounced him in a statewide television speech, and the state legislature adopted an official school prayer that was drafted by the governor's son and included these words: "Almighty God, you alone are our God. We acknowledge you as the creator and supreme judge of the world. In the name of our Lord, Amen." The legislature also provided, as a backup to any judicial invalidation of this prayer, for a moment of silence at the beginning of the school day. Jaffree promptly amended his suit to name Governor James as a defendant.

The federal judge in Mobile who first ruled in the case surprised many people with a 20,000-word opinion that rejected decades of Supreme Court doctrine. Judge Brevard Hand wrote that states were not bound by the First Amendment, and were free to establish a state religion, and to adopt official prayers. This was a direct and defiant challenge, and the federal appellate court sharply reminded Hand that judges "are bound to adhere to the controlling decisions of the Supreme Court." By the time the Court ruled on the case in 1985, George Wallace had returned as Alabama's governor, and the case was now called *Wallace v. Jaffree*.

Six justices voted to strike down both the school prayer and the moment of silence, ruling that both were motivated by religious sentiment. Writing for the majority, Justice John Paul Stevens rejected Judge Hand's "remarkable conclusion," as he put it, "that the federal Constitution imposes no obstacle to Alabama's establishment of a state religion." But Hand found an ally on the Court. Justice William Rehnquist argued in his dissenting opinion that the First Amendment was designed solely, in his words, "to prohibit the designation of any church as a 'national' one." Under Rehnquist's reading of the Framers' intent, Alabama was free to make the Baptist church the state church, just like the state bird is the yellowhammer. Nothing in the First Amendment, Rehnquist concluded, "requires government to be strictly neutral between religion and irreligion."

We've looked at the *Jaffree* case for three reasons. First, it shows that school officials and lawmakers in Alabama, and even federal judges, simply ignored the Court's very clear rulings in earlier cases, that school prayer violates the First Amendment. Secondly, the Court stood firm in the face of this defiance and reaffirmed those earlier decisions. And thirdly, Justice Rehnquist's dissenting opinion displays his rejection of the incorporation doctrine, under which the Court has imposed virtually all of the Bill of Rights on the states. If a majority of the justices sided with Rehnquist on this issue, in future cases, the impact on civil rights and liberties would be enormous. That hasn't yet happened, and most likely won't happen in the near future. The only current justices who share this position, Antonin Scalia and Clarence Thomas, have avoided this claim in their own opinions. Perhaps they're biding their time until there is a clear majority of the Court behind them. But, in my view, this is an issue worth watching in the coming years.

We're going to look now at two more school prayer cases that moved the issue out of classrooms and onto graduation stages and football fields. The first case began in 1986, at the Nathan Bishop Middle School in Providence, Rhode Island. Merith Weisman and her family, who are Jewish, attended the graduation ceremony for Merith's eighth-grade class. Her younger sister, Deborah, tells what happened. "I'll never forget how uncomfortable I felt when a Baptist minister led us in a prayer at the ceremony," she said. The minister ended his prayer "in the name of our Savior, Jesus Christ." The school's principal, Robert E. Lee, had followed a long tradition of inviting a Christian minister to offer an invocation and benediction.

The girls' father, Daniel Weisman, sent a letter to school officials, objecting to the prayer, but they never replied. Three years later, when Deborah was graduating from the same school, Weisman called the school to inquire about the prayers. Deborah says, "A teacher told him, We got you a rabbi! They thought we objected to the minister just because we're Jewish. But a rabbi wouldn't have made it any better. Prayer in public school was what we objected to. The school board told us that if we had a problem with the practice, we could sue. And that's just what we did." The Weismans filed a suit in federal court, naming Principal Lee as a defendant, but the judge allowed the ceremony to proceed with prayers by Rabbi Leslie Gutterman. He invoked God's name in blessing the graduates and their families.

The Weismans pursued their case after the graduation ceremony, and they won the first two rounds in the district and appellate courts. The case of *Lee v. Weisman* reached the Supreme Court in 1992. Deborah Weisman talked later about her family's experience. "Throughout the years of waiting for a ruling, we were harassed by hate mail and even death threats, and the media attention bothered me. But I was encouraged by the support we received from friends, and at no time did I regret having taken our case to court." Despite this ordeal, the result was encouraging to the Weismans. By the narrow margin of five to four, the Court ruled against the graduation prayers. Justice Kennedy wrote for the majority, with an opinion that closely resembled Chief Justice Earl Warren's landmark ruling in the school segregation cases, back in 1954.

Warren had based his *Brown* opinion on social science findings that segregation created a feeling of inferiority among black children. Kennedy cited similar studies in his opinion. "Research in psychology," he wrote, "supports the common assumption that adolescents are often susceptible to pressure from their peers toward conformity." Forcing Deborah Weisman to listen to prayers as the price of attending her graduation, Kennedy said, "was too high an exaction to withstand the test of the establishment clause." He fashioned what has become known as the "coercion test" in school prayer cases, which he put in these words: "There are heightened concerns with protecting freedom of conscience from subtle coercive pressure in the elementary and secondary public schools."

Writing for the four dissenters, Justice Scalia turned his rhetorical guns on Kennedy, leveling a withering barrage of sarcasm. He called Kennedy's opinion a "jurisprudential disaster," and an example of "psychology practiced by amateurs." Scalia accused the majority of demolishing what he called the "historic practices of our people" in offering "prayer to God at public celebrations." He took direct aim at Kennedy's coercion test. "As the instrument of its destruction, the bulldozer of its social engineering," Scalia wrote, "the Court invents a boundless, and boundlessly manipulable, test of psychological coercion." He advised Deborah Weisman, when she graduated from high school, to endure what he called the "minimal inconvenience" of standing while her classmates prayed "to the God whom they all worship and seek."

The most recent school prayer case began in 1995, in the town of Santa Fe, Texas, some 20 miles south of Houston. The vast majority of the town's 9,000 residents were Southern Baptists, and the school board was dominated by religious conservatives. One junior high teacher passed out fliers for a Baptist revival in her classes. Other teachers included religious teaching in their lessons, and students were told to bow their heads and pray at lunchtime. The school also invited Christian ministers to give invocations at all school events, including assemblies and Friday-night football games.

Two families in Santa Fe—one Mormon and the other Catholic—objected to these sectarian practices and filed a lawsuit in federal court, after their children were harassed by teachers and other students. One Mormon official reported that when a Mormon student questioned her teacher's promotion of a Baptist revival, the teacher launched into an attack on Mormonism, calling it a "non-Christian cult" and telling the student she was going to hell. The families who filed the suit were so afraid of retaliation that the judge allowed them to use the name "Doe" to protect their identity. The judge also threatened what he called "the harshest possible contempt sanctions" if school officials continued their efforts to learn the names of the plaintiffs.

School officials agreed to end the classroom religious exercises before the case went to trial, but they refused to give up the practice of having students lead prayers at football games, over the stadium loudspeaker. The Supreme Court ruled in June of 2000 on the school district's appeal from lower-court decisions against the football-game prayers. Justice John Paul Stevens wrote for a majority of six in *Santa Fe School District v. Doe*. The only differences between this case and *Lee v. Weisman* were that students led the prayers and they were delivered at football games. Stevens didn't find these differences significant. The prayers in Santa Fe, he wrote, "were authorized by a government policy and take place on government property at government-sponsored school-related events." The prayers sent a message to the Mormon and Catholic students who objected, Stevens wrote, "that they are outsiders, not full members of the political community" in which they live.

Chief Justice Rehnquist wrote a dissenting opinion that denounced the Court's rulings in school prayer cases over the past four decades. He repeated his statements in many earlier prayer cases that offering thanks to God at public ceremonies did not violate the First Amendment. Rehnquist criticized the majority opinion in these words: "Even more disturbing than its holding is the tone of the Court's opinion; it bristles with hostility to all things religious in public life." The chief justice reminded the majority that, as he wrote, "George Washington himself, at the request of the very Congress which passed the Bill of Rights, proclaimed a day of 'public thanksgiving and prayer, to be observed by acknowledging with grateful hearts the many and signal favors of Almighty God.'"

It's clear that the Supreme Court's majority and the American public disagree on this issue. By a margin of two to one, public opinion favors school prayer. But unless the Court itself changes, with the addition of justices who are willing to reverse the prayer cases of the past four decades, there's little chance that judicial opinions on this issue will yield to public opinion. And we see, once again, the impact of Justice Robert Jackson's statement, back in 1943, that constitutional rights are "beyond the reach of majorities; they depend on the outcome of no elections."

We're going to turn now to another issue on which the Court has placed its reading of constitutional rights beyond the reach of legislative majorities. As we've seen, the Court's ruling in *Roe v. Wade* struck down the criminal abortion laws of Texas and other states. But, like school prayer, the abortion issue has returned to the Court in dozens of cases since the *Roe* decision in 1973. Many of those cases involved laws that were based on Justice Harry Blackmun's statement in *Roe* that states had the power, after the first three months of pregnancy, "to regulate the abortion procedure in ways that are reasonably related to maternal health." The Court also decided several challenges to laws that were designed to limit access to abortion, or to discourage women from having them. Most of these laws survived the Court's scrutiny, including parental consent for teenagers who wanted abortions.

The most controversial issue the Court faced in the decade after *Roe* involved federal and state funding of abortions for poor women under the Medicaid program. After several years of lobbying, abortion opponents persuaded Congress to adopt the so-called Hyde

Amendment, named for its House sponsor—Henry Hyde of Illinois—and adopted in 1976. This law banned federal Medicaid funding of abortions, unless childbirth would endanger a pregnant woman's life. The Court faced a challenge to the Hyde Amendment in the case of *Harris v. McRae*. It's ironic that both parties in this case were black women. Patricia Harris was Secretary of Health and Human Services under President Jimmy Carter, and Cora McRae was a welfare mother in New York. After a federal judge in New York struck down the Hyde Amendment, the Supreme Court accepted the government's appeal in 1980.

Pro-choice groups, including Planned Parenthood and the American Civil Liberties Union, submitted briefs with studies that showed many poor women would resort to self-abortions or unlicensed clinics if Medicaid funding was ended. Pro-life groups responded that Congress had the right to promote childbirth over abortion through its funding power. By the narrow vote of five to four, the Court upheld the Hyde Amendment. Justice Potter Stewart wrote for the majority, which accepted the *Roe* decision as its guide. Stewart explained his ruling in these words: "The financial constraints that restrict an indigent woman's ability to enjoy the full range of constitutionally protected freedom of choice are the product not of governmental restrictions on access to abortions, but rather of her indigency." But abortions were the only medical procedure that poor women could not obtain under the Medicaid program.

Stewart explained that Congress had adopted the Hyde Amendment, as he put it, "to encourage alternative activity deemed in the public interest," a rather odd way of saying that Congress preferred childbirth over abortion. The four dissenters in *Harris v. McRae* all wrote separate opinions. Justice Thurgood Marshall spoke the most forcefully about the effect of the Hyde Amendment. "The consequence is a devastating impact on the lives and health of poor women," he wrote. "I do not believe that a Constitution committed to equal protection of the laws can tolerate this result." The Court's ruling on the Hyde Amendment came in the final year of President Jimmy Carter's single term in office. His defeat by Ronald Reagan in the 1980 election gave hope to abortion opponents that the Court would reverse the *Roe* decision.

We saw in the previous lecture that President Reagan named three new justices between 1981 and 1988: Sandra O'Connor, Antonin

Scalia, and Anthony Kennedy. Along with Chief Justice Rehnquist and Justice Byron White, both of whom dissented in the *Roe* case, a five-vote majority to overturn *Roe* seemed likely. During the eight years of the Reagan administration, government lawyers urged the Court in five separate cases to reverse the *Roe* decision. They came the closest to this goal in 1989, in the case of *Webster v. Reproductive Health Services*.

Missouri lawmakers had placed several restrictions on access to abortion, and a majority of five justices upheld most of them. But they declined the invitation of solicitor general Charles Fried, who said during oral argument: "Today the United States asks this Court to reconsider and overrule its decision in *Roe v. Wade*." Four justices were clearly willing to take this step, but Justice Sandra O'Connor held back. She wanted to defer any final judgment on *Roe* until the Court faced a direct challenge to its ruling. "There will be time enough to reexamine *Roe* in a proper case," she wrote, "and to do so carefully." But she also did not rule out a later vote to overturn *Roe*.

Justice Blackmun, who wrote the *Roe* opinion, knew that just one vote would shift the balance. "I fear for the future," he said in his *Webster* dissent. "For today, at least, the law of abortion stands undisturbed. But the signs are very evident and ominous, and a chill wind blows." Blackmun had reason to be fearful. Of the four *Webster* dissenters, three had passed their 80th birthday. Justice Stevens was the youngest at 69. Blackmun knew the next death or retirement might turn the chill wind into a judicial hurricane and blow the *Roe* decision away. And there were two retirements before the next abortion case reached the Court in 1992. The two most liberal justices, William Brennan and Thurgood Marshall, left the Court in 1990 and 1991. As we've seen, Brennan had been the intellectual leader of the Warren Court, ever since he took his seat in 1956. And he kept its legacy alive, as the Court swung to the right during the 70s and 80s.

Many of the Warren Court's landmark decisions had been trimmed by judicial conservatives, but none had been toppled. Brennan's retirement gave the first President Bush his first chance to shape the Court. He surprised many people by naming an obscure federal appellate judge with only seven months of service on the First Circuit bench in Boston. David Souter was born in 1939, and graduated from Harvard Law School. He spent 14 years in the New

Hampshire attorney general's office, the last two in the top post, and had served five years on the state's supreme court before President Bush placed him on the appellate bench in 1990. During his Senate confirmation hearings, Souter resisted efforts to pin him down on abortion, but he asserted his belief that the Constitution protected a right to privacy in matters of personal autonomy. Both sides in the abortion debate waited anxiously to see how Souter would vote, when the time came to "carefully" reexamine the *Roe* decision, as Justice O'Connor had promised in her *Webster* concurrence.

Justice Brennan's departure left Thurgood Marshall feeling lonely on the bench, as the Court turned to the right under Chief Justice Rehnquist. Marshall's health had been declining, and he finally gave up on June 27 of 1991, the last day of the Court's term. "I'm old, and I'm coming apart," he told reporters the next day. He also felt the Court was coming apart. His final opinion was a dissent in a death penalty case, in which the majority had overturned precedents just two years old. "Power, not reason, is the new currency of this Court's decisions," Marshall charged. The Constitution had not changed in two years, he added, "only the personnel of this Court did." With Brennan no longer at his side, Marshall predicted, "scores of established constitutional liberties are now ripe for reconsideration."

One of the cases that were ripe for reconsideration, as everyone knew, was *Roe v. Wade*, and the man President Bush named to replace Marshall was considered a sure vote to overturn the *Roe* decision. Clarence Thomas was an outspoken black conservative, who was then 43, the youngest nominee since William O. Douglas in 1939. Thomas was born into poverty in Pin Point, Georgia, and had been raised by his grandfather after both parents abandoned him. He attended Catholic schools from elementary grades through college, and he won a scholarship to Yale Law School, graduating in 1974. After five years of law practice in Missouri, he moved to Washington as an aide to Republican Senator John Danforth.

Thomas joined the Reagan administration in 1981, moving up to direct the federal Equal Employment Opportunity Commission. President Bush placed him on the District of Columbia federal appellate court in 1990, with speculation that he was being groomed for Justice Marshall's seat. Thomas reportedly told friends that Marshall "wouldn't last forever" on the Court, and that he deserved his seat as the highest-ranking black lawyer in the government. During his confirmation hearings, Thomas dodged all questions on abortion. He even denied having discussed the *Roe* decision with his law school classmates when the Court ruled during his second year at Yale. But his confirmation seemed assured until Anita Hill, a University of Oklahoma law professor and a former aide to Thomas, charged that her former boss had propositioned her and made crude sexual remarks. Thomas vehemently denied her charges, and complained that he was the victim of a "high-tech lynching" by liberals. Thomas won this "he-said, she-said" battle, and the Senate confirmed him by the narrow vote of 52 to 48.

Thomas took his seat as a justice on October 23 of 1991. Two weeks later, the case that gave the Court its chance to carefully reexamine the *Roe* case landed on its docket. In our next lecture, we'll look carefully at this case, *Planned Parenthood of Southeastern Pennsylvania v. Casey*. We'll also examine another abortion case that raised the highly emotional issue of what are called "partial-birth" abortions, in a decision that was handed down in June of 2000. Finally, we'll look at one of the Court's most controversial rulings in the past three decades, the presidential election case of *Bush v. Gore*, which was decided in December of 2000, with a ruling that had a tremendous impact on American government and politics.

Lecture Thirty-Five
One Vote Decides Two Crucial Cases

Scope:

This lecture begins with the Court's continuing struggle to deal with the contentious issue of abortion and ends with its five-to-four decision in the disputed presidential election of 2000. No issue has so sharply divided the Court, and the American public, over the past three decades as abortion. We will follow the cases that were discussed in the previous lecture with two additional landmark rulings on abortion. In the 1992 case of *Planned Parenthood v. Casey*, three moderate justices reaffirmed the central holding of *Roe* but also upheld several restrictions on abortion. They based their decision on concerns about damaging the Court's "legitimacy" if the Court struck down the *Roe* case and upset the "settled expectations" of American women about their right to obtain abortions. In the partial-birth abortion case of *Stenberg v. Carhart*, the Court divided five to four on this controversial abortion method, with the majority holding that states could not prohibit doctors from performing this procedure in late-term abortions. Finally, we will examine the case of *Bush v. Gore*, in which the Court also split five to four in blocking the further recount of votes in Florida, a case that ended with the narrow victory of George W. Bush over Al Gore in the presidential election of 2000.

Outline

I.   This lecture discusses three landmark Supreme Court decisions, in cases that involved abortion and the presidential election of 2000.

II. As background to the abortion cases, the Court in 1989 had upheld restrictions on access to abortion in the *Webster* case.

   A. Four justices were clearly willing to overturn the 1973 *Roe* decision in *Webster*, but Justice Sandra O'Connor said that was not the "proper case" in which to reexamine *Roe*.

   B. Following the *Webster* decision, two justices who supported abortion rights, William Brennan and Thurgood Marshall, retired from the Court.

C. They were replaced by Justices David Souter and Clarence Thomas; many observers felt that one or both would vote to overturn the *Roe* decision.

III. In 1992, the Court decided an important abortion rights case, *Planned Parenthood of Southeastern Pennsylvania v. Casey.*

A. This case involved several restrictions the state legislature had imposed on access to abortion; lower federal courts had upheld the challenged provisions.

1. The Court heard arguments in April 1992, during a presidential election year; most observers felt that abortion would become a major issue in the campaigns.

2. Lawyers on both sides asked the justices to make a clear ruling on whether or not to overturn *Roe*.

B. The lawyer for Planned Parenthood said that access to abortion had been "part of the settled rights and expectations" of women for nearly two decades.

C. The state's lawyer said, "*Roe*, being wrongly decided, should be overruled."

IV. In June 1992, the Court handed down its decision in the *Casey* case.

A. The justices did not agree on a majority opinion in *Casey*.

B. Three moderate justices—Sandra O'Connor, Anthony Kennedy, and David Souter—signed an opinion that said, "the essential holding of *Roe v. Wade* should be retained and once again reaffirmed."

1. They were joined in this holding by two liberal justices, Harry Blackmun and John Stevens.

2. The three moderates noted that public opinion had not shifted against abortion since *Roe* was decided, and reversing it would intensify the debate on this issue.

3. These justices concluded that overturning *Roe* "would subvert the Court's legitimacy beyond any serious question."

C. The four *Casey* dissenters expressed scorn for the "outrageous arguments" of the three moderates. Justice Antonin Scalia wrote: "The imperial judiciary lives."

D. But the three moderates and four conservatives joined in upholding all but one provision of the Pennsylvania law.

 ©2003 The Teaching Company Limited Partnership

V. Justice Blackmun noted in his separate *Casey* opinion that he was 83 and that abortion would likely become the central issue in choosing his successor.

    A. Blackmun retired in 1994, after Bill Clinton defeated President Bush in the 1992 election.

    B. Clinton had already named Ruth Bader Ginsburg, who supported abortion rights, to replace Justice Byron White, who had consistently opposed abortion.

    C. Clinton named Stephen Breyer to replace Blackmun; Breyer was a former Harvard law professor and federal appellate judge who supported abortion rights.

VI. In 2000, the Court struck down a Nebraska law that banned so-called "partial-birth" abortions by a five-to-four margin.

    A. The two new justices, Ginsburg and Breyer, joined the majority in *Stenberg v. Carhart*.

    B. Justice Kennedy, who joined the *Casey* opinion that upheld the central holding of *Roe*, voted with the dissenters in the *Stenberg* case.

    C. Justice Breyer wrote a narrow majority opinion in *Stenberg*, holding that the Nebraska ban on partial-birth abortions was "overbroad" in banning other abortion procedures that were legal under the *Roe* decision.

    D. Justice Scalia wrote in dissent that "a five-to-four vote on a policy matter" by unelected judges should not override the judgment of elected lawmakers.

    E. The partial-birth abortion procedure remains a controversial issue in American politics.

VII. The Court became embroiled in the disputed 2000 presidential election between Texas governor George Bush and Vice President Al Gore.

    A. After Florida election officials awarded the state's electoral votes to Bush, the state supreme court ordered a recount and extended the statutory deadline for reporting the vote to Congress.

    B. Bush asked the Supreme Court to halt the recount, arguing that election officials in different counties applied different standards in deciding the voter's intent.

C. The Court ruled for Bush by a five-to-four margin, ordering the state judges to halt the recount.

D. The majority said that applying different vote-counting standards violated the equal protection clause of the Fourteenth Amendment.

E. All five justices in the majority had been active in Republican politics, which led to criticism that the decision was partisan.

    1. However, two justices named by Republican presidents dissented in *Bush v. Gore*.

    2. This case underscores the observation of Alexis de Tocqueville in the 1830s: "Scarcely any political question arises in the United States that is not resolved, sooner or later, into a judicial question."

Suggested Readings:

Peter Irons, *A People's History of the Supreme Court*, chapter 35 (1999).

E. J. Dionne and William Kristol, eds., *Bush v. Gore: The Court Cases and the Commentary* (2001).

Cass R. Sunstein and Richard A. Epstein, eds., *The Vote: Bush, Gore, and the Supreme Court* (2001).

Questions to Consider:

1. Do you think doctors should be allowed to perform partial-birth abortions? If not, should there be an exception if the fetus has little or no chance of survival?

2. Was the Supreme Court justified in halting the Florida recount in the 2000 presidential election?

©2003 The Teaching Company Limited Partnership

Lecture Thirty-Five—Transcript
One Vote Decides Two Crucial Cases

In our previous lecture, we looked at the Supreme Court's rulings in cases that involved two very controversial issues, school prayer and abortion. The justices had issued landmark rulings in these areas of law in the 1960s and 70s, striking down religious exercises in public schools and state laws that imposed criminal penalties on abortions. Efforts to reverse these decisions by amending the Constitution have come close to passage in Congress on several occasions, but they failed to gain the necessary two-thirds majority in both houses of Congress. However, the school prayer and abortion issues have returned to the Court in dozens of cases over the past three decades.

As we've seen, the justices have stood firmly behind their school prayer rulings, striking down prayers at graduation ceremonies and high-school football games. But the Court has upheld laws that withhold public funding of abortion, and that limit access to abortion in various ways. We also saw in previous lectures that Presidents Ronald Reagan and George Bush named five justices between 1981 and 1991, moving the Court to the right and setting the stage for the possible reversal of the *Roe* decision. In this lecture, we'll look first at the showdown over abortion in 1992, and we'll examine the opinions that exposed the deep split on the Court over this issue. We'll also discuss the Court's ruling in the year 2000, on the emotional question of "partial-birth" abortions. Finally, we'll turn to another controversial ruling in 2000, in which the Court decided the outcome of the presidential election, between Texas Governor George W. Bush, and Vice President Al Gore. This case also created sharp divisions among the justices over the power of state courts to decide election contests.

We're going to look first at the abortion case of *Planned Parenthood of Southeastern Pennsylvania v. Casey* in 1992. As background to this case, we saw in our previous lecture that the Court had been urged in 1989, in the *Webster* case from Missouri, to reverse the *Roe* decision. Four conservative justices were clearly eager to overturn *Roe*, but Justice Sandra O'Connor argued that *Webster* was not the "proper case" to make that decision. Three years later, after the retirements of Justices William Brennan and Thurgood Marshall, there seemed to be a clear majority to reverse the *Roe* decision. The two new justices, David Souter and Clarence Thomas, had declined to give their views on abortion at their confirmation hearings, but most observers felt they would vote to overturn *Roe*.

The *Casey* case involved several restrictions that Pennsylvania lawmakers had placed on access to abortions. The law required doctors to explain the "risks" of abortion to pregnant women, and to provide them with state-approved information about "alternatives to abortion," such as adoption. It also required women seeking abortions to sign a written consent, and to wait 24 hours for an abortion after signing the form. A coalition of abortion providers had sued Pennsylvania's governor, Robert Casey, to block the law, but lower federal courts had upheld the challenged provisions.

The pro-choice groups that backed the challenge to the Pennsylvania law had rushed to file their appeal before the Supreme Court's term ended in June of 1992. They expected the conservative majority to reverse the *Roe* decision, and they wanted to make abortion an issue in the 1992 congressional and presidential campaigns. Public opinion polls showed a pro-choice majority among the electorate, and voters would presumably support candidates who pledged to protect abortion rights. In this political scenario, the Supreme Court would become their target, with future nominations to the Court at stake in campaigns for the Senate and the White House. So, politics were on everyone's mind when the arguments began on April 22 of 1992.

Kathryn Kolbert spoke for Planned Parenthood. She challenged the justices to either flatly reverse the *Roe* decision or to firmly uphold it, and to end the uncertainty about abortion rights. She put her argument in these words: "Never before has this Court bestowed and taken back a fundamental right that has been part of the settled rights and expectations of millions of Americans for nearly two decades." Taking back those rights, she added, "would be incompatible with any notion of principled constitutional decision-making." Pennsylvania's attorney general, Ernest Preate, replied that the Court should apply the *Webster* case as precedent, and uphold his state's law "short of overruling *Roe*," as he put it. But if the two cases could not be reconciled, Preate said, "*Roe*, being wrongly decided, should be overruled."

As the Court's term neared its end, and the public waited for its decision in this case, an interesting article appeared on the front page of the *New York Times*, under the headline, "Changed Path for the Court? New Balance is Held by Three Cautious Justices." Linda

Greenhouse, who covered the Court for the *Times*, wrote, "Effective control of the Court has passed to a subgroup of the majority, a moderately conservative middle group of three justices." Pictured next to her article were Justices Sandra O'Connor, Anthony Kennedy, and David Souter. "The group's hallmarks," Greenhouse wrote, "appear to be a generally cautious approach to deciding cases, a hesitancy to overturn precedents, and a distaste for aggressive arguments. This group does not always vote together, but when it does, its views prevail."

Linda Greenhouse proved to be an accurate prophet. Three days after her article appeared, on June 29 of 1992, the Court handed down its decision in *Casey*. In virtually every case, the Court's ruling is expressed in an opinion that five or more justices have joined. But in this case, what was called "the judgment of the Court" appeared under the names of three justices: O'Connor, Kennedy, and Souter. Their opinion began with these words: "Liberty finds no refuge in a jurisprudence of doubt." The justices in the Court's middle explained their position in these words: "After considering the fundamental constitutional questions resolved by *Roe*, principles of institutional integrity, and the rule of *stare decisis*, we are led to conclude that the essential holding of *Roe v. Wade* should be retained and once again reaffirmed." Justices Harry Blackmun and John Paul Stevens joined this part of the centrist group's opinion, sparing *Roe* from reversal by a one-vote margin.

There were five separate opinions in this case, with overlapping groups of justices who joined parts of each one, but we're going to focus on the joint opinion of Justices O'Connor, Kennedy, and Souter. In my view, the reasoning in their opinion provides much insight about the dilemma that faces justices whose personal values are in conflict with judicial precedent over difficult issues like abortion. We've already seen that Justice Kennedy faced such a conflict in the flag-burning case, and that he voted to protect an act he found personally abhorrent. Kennedy was reportedly the primary force behind the joint opinion in the *Casey* case, despite his personal objections to abortion. The most important and interesting aspect of the joint opinion is the reasons it offered for not reversing the *Roe* decision, despite what its authors called the "personal reluctance any of us may have" to affirm its "central holding."

The three justices frankly acknowledged the political factors that influenced their decision. In a fascinating history lecture, they discussed two landmark cases in which the Court *had* overruled settled precedent, the cases of *Plessy v. Ferguson* and *Adkins v. Children's Hospital*, which we discussed in earlier lectures. *Plessy* had upheld segregation laws in 1896, and *Adkins* had struck down minimum wage laws for women in 1923. The Court overturned *Plessy* in the *Brown* decision of 1954, and the *Adkins* case in the *West Coast Hotel* ruling of 1937. The three justices in *Casey* argued that "changed circumstances" had *required* the Court to reverse those earlier rulings. They stressed, in their words, "the terrible price that would have been paid if the Court had *not* overruled" *Plessy* and *Adkins*. That price would have been the erosion of the Court's "legitimacy" in the public's mind. And that legitimacy is a product, the three justices wrote, "of the people's acceptance of the judiciary as fit to determine what the nation's law means and to declare what it demands."

How did this reasoning lead these justices to reaffirm the *Roe* decision, rather than overrule it? They offered two reasons. First, as they wrote, "An entire generation has come of age free to accept *Roe's* concept of liberty in defining the capacity of women to act in society, and to make reproductive decisions." In other words, the Court should not upset the "settled expectations" of women that they can obtain abortions. Secondly, the *Roe* decision involved what the three justices called an "intensely divisive controversy." Overturning *Roe*, they suggested, would inflame—rather than dampen—the long-standing public debate over abortion. The three justices concluded, as they wrote, that "to overrule under fire in the absence of the most compelling reason to reexamine a watershed decision would subvert the Court's legitimacy beyond any serious question." Their opinion in *Casey*, they said, "calls the contending sides of a national controversy to end their national division by accepting a common mandate rooted in the Constitution."

Whether this argument for reaffirming the "central holding" of the *Roe* decision is persuasive is obviously a matter of opinion. It certainly did not persuade the four dissenters—Chief Justice Rehnquist and Justices Scalia, White, and Thomas. In his dissenting opinion, Scalia deplored what he called the "outrageous arguments" of his three colleagues. He directed particular scorn at the undue burden test that Justice O'Connor had adopted in abortion cases.

 ©2003 The Teaching Company Limited Partnership

O'Connor has applied this test to laws that place what she calls a "substantial obstacle in the path" of women seeking abortions. Scalia denounced the undue burden test as "unprincipled in origin" and "hopelessly unworkable in practice." He said, "The joint opinion's verbal shell game will conceal raw judicial policy choices" about the decisions of elected lawmakers. Justice Scalia concluded his opinion with these scornful words: "The imperial judiciary lives. We should get out of this area, where we have no right to be, and where we do neither ourselves nor the country any good by remaining."

One aspect of the *Casey* ruling was almost ignored in this judicial crossfire. The three centrist justices and the four conservatives agreed on all but one provision of the Pennsylvania law. These seven justices sustained the consent requirement, the 24-hour waiting period, and the requirement of parental consent for unmarried minors. They differed on the provision that required a married woman to notify her husband she was seeking an abortion, unless she faced physical danger from her spouse. The four conservatives supported this provision, but Justices Harry Blackmun and John Paul Stevens joined the three centrists to strike it down.

Nineteen years after Justice Blackmun wrote the *Roe* opinion, he was relieved that it survived the most determined efforts to reverse it. He called the joint opinion of Justices O'Connor, Kennedy, and Souter "an act of personal courage and constitutional principle." But he also recognized that *Roe* had again survived by just one vote. Blackmun ended his opinion with a remarkable personal statement: "I am 83 years old. I cannot remain on the Court forever, and when I do step down, the confirmation process for my successor may well focus on the issue before us today." Blackmun also knew that abortion would become an issue in the presidential contest that was already underway, between President George Bush and his Democratic challenger, Bill Clinton. The two candidates offered voters a clear choice on abortion. Bush favored a constitutional amendment to overturn the *Roe* decision, while Clinton was committed to protecting it from reversal.

Clinton owed his victory in that election over President Bush in part to his stand on abortion rights, although most voters were more concerned with economic issues. Neither candidate said much about the Supreme Court until the week before the election, when Bush told voters that he and Clinton had a "fundamental difference about what should happen on the Supreme Court." The president added that if voters wanted "somebody on there to legislate with a liberal point of view," they should vote for his opponent. Public opinion polls showed that many women who normally voted Republican had supported Clinton because they feared that Bush would lead an assault on the *Roe* decision. As we've seen, Clinton had his first chance to shape the Court when Justice Byron White retired in June of 1993, and he named Ruth Bader Ginsburg as the second female justice.

Clinton's second opportunity came a year later, when Justice Harry Blackmun left the Court in June of 1994. With Ginsburg's confirmation, he felt assured that *Roe* would survive his departure. Although he served for 24 years, and wrote more than 500 opinions, most people associate Blackmun with his *Roe* opinion in 1973. "I suppose I'll carry Roe to my grave," he once said. President Clinton named Stephen Breyer to replace Blackmun. Breyer was born in San Francisco in 1938, and graduated from Harvard Law School. He worked closely with Senator Edward Kennedy on issues like airline deregulation, and he taught administrative law at Harvard before President Jimmy Carter placed him on the federal appellate court in Boston in 1980, where he served briefly with Justice David Souter. Much like Justices Ginsburg and Souter, Breyer has become known as a cautious liberal on most issues, sticking to precedent whenever possible and writing careful, precise opinions that do not stake out any new constitutional ground.

We're going to look now at a case in which Justice Breyer wrote an exceedingly precise opinion, on the highly controversial issue of "partial-birth" abortions. As we saw, three moderate justices had joined the Court's two most liberal justices in 1992, to reaffirm what they called the "central holding" in the *Roe* decision. But the same three moderates had joined the four most conservative justices to uphold most of the restrictive provisions of the Pennsylvania law in *Planned Parenthood v. Casey*. Those three justices—O'Connor, Kennedy, and Souter—held the balance when the Court decided the case of *Stenberg v. Carhart* in the year 2000. This case involved a Nebraska law that banned the procedure known as "partial-birth" abortions. There are two different methods of performing these late-term abortions. As Justice Breyer noted in his opinion, they both strike most people as gruesome, but they require some description, to understand the Court's ruling in this case.

It's important to note that both methods of "partial-birth" abortions are rarely used, in less than one percent of abortions. They're used most often when the fetus has a malformation like hydrocephaly, when the head is swollen with fluid, and when live childbirth is impossible or would endanger the mother's life or health. The most commonly used "partial-birth" method is known by doctors as "dilation and evacuation," or "D & E." Under this procedure, the fetus is dismembered with surgical instruments inside the uterus. Because the head is too large to pass through the cervix, the skull is pierced and the brain matter is sucked out. In some cases, however, doctors use another procedure known as "dilation and extraction," or "D & X." This abortion method involves what's called a "breech delivery," in which the feet are first pulled out from the cervix, and the skull is then pierced and drained to allow its removal from the uterus. The only difference is that "D & X" involves first pulling a body part through the cervix.

The reason we're getting into the details of these two procedures is that the difference between them became a central focus of the Supreme Court's opinion in the case of *Stenberg v. Carhart*. Nebraska was one of 30 states that passed laws to ban "partial-birth" abortions. This law carried a maximum penalty of 20 years in prison, and revocation of a doctor's license to practice in Nebraska. Dr. Leroy Carhart was the only doctor who performed late-term abortions in Nebraska. He sued the state's attorney general, Don Stenberg, to block him from enforcing the law. The case reached the Supreme Court in 2000 after Nebraska lost the first two rounds in the lower federal courts.

Justice Breyer wrote for a majority of five in striking down the Nebraska law. The justices were acutely conscious, he noted, of the "virtually irreconcilable views" that millions of Americans hold on the abortion issue. But he pointed to the *Roe* and *Casey* rulings, in which, he said, "this Court has determined and then re-determined that the Constitution offers basic protection to the woman's right to choose" abortion. "We shall not revisit those legal principles," Breyer stated firmly. "Rather, we apply them to the circumstances of this case." After he explained in graphic detail the abortion procedures known as "D & X" and "D & E," Breyer faulted Nebraska lawmakers for writing their law so broadly that it could be read as banning both procedures, even though the state's lawyers claimed they meant only to ban the "D & X" procedure.

As we saw, the difference between the two is that "D & X" involves pulling a body part through the cervix, rather than dismembering it inside the uterus. Justice Breyer concluded that the law was "overbroad" in subjecting doctors to prosecution for performing a lawful abortion procedure. He also faulted the law for not including an exception, to protect the pregnant woman's health from the complications of pregnancy and childbirth. Breyer noted that both the *Roe* and *Casey* rulings had required states to provide health exceptions in their abortion laws. He put his conclusion in these words: "In sum, using this law, some prosecutors may choose to pursue physicians who use 'D & E' procedures. All those who perform abortion procedures using that method must fear prosecution, conviction, and imprisonment. The result is an undue burden upon a woman's right to make an abortion decision."

It was not surprising that Chief Justice Rehnquist, along with Justices Scalia and Thomas, dissented in the *Stenberg* case. They had all dissented in *Casey* from its reaffirmation of the *Roe* decision. Scalia noted that Justice Breyer's "clinical description" of the "partial-birth" abortion procedure "evokes a shudder of revulsion." He accused the majority of acting as legislators, rather than as judges. "Those who believe that a five-to-four vote on a policy matter by unelected lawyers," Scalia argued, "should not overcome the judgment of 30 state legislatures have a problem, not with the application of *Casey*, but with its existence. *Casey* must be overruled."

It was surprising to some people, however, that Justice Kennedy joined the dissenters, after his vote in *Casey* to reaffirm the *Roe* decision. He accused the majority of misinterpreting the *Casey* decision. But in my view, Kennedy's dissent in the *Stenberg* case reflected the personal and moral revulsion he shared with Scalia about the "partial-birth" abortion procedure. He put his feelings in these words: "The decision nullifies a law expressing the will of the people of Nebraska that medical procedures must be governed by moral principles having their foundation in the intrinsic value of human life, including life of the unborn." It was not the *fact* of the abortions that Kennedy objected to in *Stenberg*, since doctors could use other methods in late-term abortions, some of them more risky than "partial-birth" methods.

It seems clear that it was the admittedly gruesome *method* which offended his moral views. Whether this should be a factor in deciding cases depends, in my view, on the moral perspective each person brings to this question. But it's worth noting that Justice Kennedy did not speak about the "command of the Constitution" in the "partial-birth" abortion case, as he had in the flag-burning case. These are both emotional issues for most people, but it's hard to separate moral and legal views when human life, or the potential for that life, is at stake.

We'll turn now to the final case we'll examine in this course, the case of *Bush v. Gore* in December of 2000. We're not going to review all the details and disputes in this case. As most people recall, the outcome of that presidential election hinged on the 25 electoral votes in Florida. Whichever candidate received those disputed votes would become president. Millions of Americans watched on television at least part of the recount of disputed votes in several Florida counties. As the clock moved toward the final date for states to certify their electoral votes to Congress, the Florida Supreme Court ruled that election officials should continue their counting of disputed votes.

The state judges based their decision on provisions of Florida's election laws. Lawyers for George Bush asked the U.S. Supreme Court to halt the recounts, and to allow the Florida secretary of state to certify the results that gave Bush the state's electoral votes. After the justices heard arguments in early December of 2000, the Court granted Bush's motion and ordered the recounting to end. The legal issues in the case centered on two provisions of Article II in the Constitution. One provides that "each state shall appoint, in such manner as the legislature thereof shall direct, a number of electors, equal to the whole number of senators and representatives to which the state might be entitled in the Congress." The other provides that "Congress may determine the time of choosing the electors, and the day on which they shall give their votes." Congress had passed a law that set a date for states to cast their electoral votes. In this case the date was December 18. The Supreme Court also faced the question of whether state courts had the power to allow recounts to proceed until this final date.

The justices handed down their ruling in *Bush v. Gore* on December 12 of 2000. The Court issued an unsigned opinion that spoke for a majority of five justices: Chief Justice Rehnquist and Justices O'Connor, Scalia, Kennedy, and Thomas. These five justices based their ruling on the equal protection clause of the Fourteenth Amendment. They noted that the Florida Supreme Court had not ordered election officials to adopt a uniform standard for deciding which ballots to count as "legal votes" for each presidential candidate. The five-justice majority put its concern in these words: "When a court orders a statewide remedy, there must be at least some assurance that the rudimentary requirements of equal treatment and fundamental fairness are satisfied." They held that "it is obvious that the recount cannot be conducted in compliance with the requirements of equal protection" before the time for submitting the electoral votes to Congress.

There are two aspects of this ruling that deserve mention. One is that these five justices, most notably Chief Justice Rehnquist and Justice Scalia, were not normally supportive of equal protection claims in most cases. The other is that all five were generally deferential to the decisions of state courts, especially when state judges were interpreting provisions of their own state laws and constitutions. Rehnquist and Scalia, in particular, advocate a notion of federalism that protects states from congressional regulation in many areas. But the five-justice majority in *Bush v. Gore* held that Florida's Supreme Court had erred in its reading of the state's election laws.

The four dissenters in *Bush v. Gore* differed on the equal protection issue. Justices Souter and Breyer felt the Florida Supreme Court should decide on a uniform standard for counting votes and require election officials in each county to follow that standard. But the dissenters agreed that state officials should be given time to complete the recount, before the deadline for casting electoral votes. Justice Stevens used the strongest words in his dissenting opinion. He wrote that Bush's appeal to the Court rested on "an unstated lack of confidence in the impartiality and capacity of the state judges who would make the critical decisions if the vote count were to proceed." He added these words: "The endorsement of that position by the majority of this Court can only lend credence to the most cynical appraisal of the work of judges throughout the land."

  ©2003 The Teaching Company Limited Partnership

As we know, the Court's ruling in *Bush v. Gore* effectively decided the outcome of the presidential election, and put George W. Bush in the White House. The disappointed backers of Vice President Gore noted that all five justices in the majority had been named to the Court by Republican presidents. All five, in fact, had been active in Republican politics before they joined the Court. But this was not a simple partisan division. Justices Stevens and Souter were also nominated by Republican presidents, although neither had been active in party affairs. It's also true that Stevens and Souter were members of the Court's liberal wing, along with Justices Ginsburg and Breyer. So the judicial division in *Bush v. Gore* may reflect political ideologies more than partisan attachments. In any event, this case underscores the perceptive comment of Alexis de Tocqueville, back in the 1830s. "Scarcely any political question arises in the United States," he wrote, "that is not resolved, sooner or later, into a judicial question."

We've seen in this lecture that two very political questions, abortion and presidential elections, became judicial questions in recent years. Virtually all the cases we've discussed in these lectures, in fact, began as political disputes and ended with judicial decisions. But in many cases, those rulings provoked more political debate, and created more cases for the Supreme Court to decide. We'll look back on those cases, and draw some conclusions about the links between law and politics, in our concluding lecture.

Lecture Thirty-Six
Looking Back and Looking Ahead

Scope:

In this lecture, we will first look back at the basic themes we have discussed throughout this course: continuity and change in the Supreme Court's history, consensus and conflict in its rulings, and the impact of the diversity in American society on the cases that reach the Court for decision. We will place some of the Court's landmark rulings in the context of the judicial doctrines the justices have developed as tools for deciding cases. These doctrines reflect political and economic changes in American society, as well as changes in the Court's membership, as presidents add new justices to replace those who die or retire. Our primary focus will be on the doctrines of judicial activism and judicial restraint, which are generally associated with liberal and conservative positions. We will see that these labels are not always accurate, as conservative justices often strike down laws, and liberal justices often uphold them. We will conclude with a look at the Court as a model for other countries that have adopted many provisions of our Bill of Rights in the Universal Declaration of Human Rights.

Outline

I. This lecture looks back at the Supreme Court's history in the context of three basic themes.

A. The first theme is continuity and change.
1. The Constitution and the Court have endured for more than two centuries.
2. But there have been major changes in American society, with rapid growth in population and a shift from an agrarian to an industrial economy.

B. A second theme is consensus and conflict.
1. We have a shared consensus on the values of representative democracy and the rule of law.
2. But there has been much conflict over such issues as race and religion.

 ©2003 The Teaching Company Limited Partnership

C. A third theme is the diversity in American society.

    1. We are not a homogenous nation in such areas as race, religion, politics, and sexual orientation.

    2. But we are not so divided that we have continuing outbreaks of violence over these issues.

II. In this course, we looked at three periods in the Court's history.

    A. The first began with the Constitutional Convention in 1787 and extended through World War I. It was marked by conflicts over slavery and the Civil War.

    B. The second extended from the 1920s through the Court's leadership by Chief Justice Earl Warren. Crucial events included the Great Depression, World War II, and the Court's 1954 ruling against school segregation.

    C. The third period included the Warren Court's landmark rulings on religion, criminal law, and free speech. It extends to the present, with rulings on abortion and affirmative action under Chief Justices Warren Burger and William Rehnquist.

III. The Court has employed various judicial doctrines in reading the Constitution and deciding cases.

    A. These doctrines are affected by changes in the Court's membership.

        1. One example is the Constitutional Revolution of 1937.

        2. After the Court shifted its position on economic regulation, President Franklin Roosevelt named several liberal justices.

    B. Judicial doctrines are also affected by changes in American society.

        1. One example is the 19th-century shift from an agrarian to an industrial economy.

        2. These changes produced conflict between workers and employers and between farmers and railroads.

        3. The Court employed the liberty of contract doctrine to protect business interests.

C. Another example is the Civil Rights movement of the 20th century.

    1. The NAACP was founded in 1909 and campaigned against racial segregation.

    2. The Court developed the strict scrutiny doctrine to protect racial and religious minorities.

IV. The Court's decisions often reflect the complex interaction of personality and politics.

    A. One example is the *Dred Scott* decision in 1857.

        1. Chief Justice Taney held that no black person could be a citizen and that Congress had no power to ban slavery in the territories.

        2. Taney's opinion reflected his uncompromising support for slavery, rooted in his background in southern politics.

    B. Another example is Chief Justice Warren's opinion in the *Brown* case.

        1. Warren based his opinion on the psychological impact of segregation on black children.

        2. He had become sensitive to this issue through its impact on his own chauffeur.

V. This course has looked at the doctrines of judicial activism and judicial restraint.

    A. Activism is generally associated with liberal views and restraint, with conservative ones, but this is not always true.

    B. One example is Chief Justice Marshall's 1803 opinion in *Marbury v. Madison*.

        1. Marshall struck down an act of Congress, which could be viewed as activism.

        2. But Marshall was a political conservative; his real motivation was to assert judicial supremacy over the other branches of government.

    C. During the years from the 1880s to the 1930s, conservative justices employed the liberty of contract doctrine to strike down state and federal economic regulation; this was certainly judicial activism.

D. On the other side, liberal justices showed restraint in upholding state and federal laws during and after the Constitutional Revolution in 1937.

VI. There are two competing approaches to judicial decision making.

   A. One is that the meaning of constitutional provisions, such as due process and equal protection, depends on who determines that meaning. Chief Justice Hughes once said, "The Constitution is what the judges say it is."

   B. The other looks to the "original intent" of the Constitution's Framers.

      1. Justice Antonin Scalia argues that justices should not read their own views into the Constitution.

      2. Justices who hold this view have been called *strict constructionists.*

   C. Efforts to find the Framers' intent in such phrases as "due process" do not provide guidance in particular cases.

      1. Justice William Brennan believed the due process clause was based on "the underlying vision of human dignity."

      2. Justice John Harlan wrote that due process cannot be "reduced to any formula; its content cannot be determined by reference to any code."

VII. The Court has become a model around the world, as an independent body with the power to protect "all persons."

   A. The Universal Declaration of Human Rights was adopted by the United Nations in 1948 and includes the basic protections of our Bill of Rights.

   B. Admiration for our Supreme Court helped in adopting that Declaration.

Suggested Readings:

Peter Irons, *A People's History of the Supreme Court* (1999).

Kenneth Starr, *First among Equals: The Supreme Court in American Life* (2002).

Questions to Consider:

1. Do you think presidents should agree to choose Supreme Court nominees from a short list of the most qualified candidates selected by a nonpartisan committee of eminent lawyers and judges?

2. Would you support a constitutional amendment that provided that Supreme Court justices should be subject to a second confirmation vote after 10 years of service?

 ©2003 The Teaching Company Limited Partnership

Lecture Thirty-Six—Transcript
Looking Back and Looking Ahead

We've come to the final lecture in our course on the history of the United States Supreme Court. It's time to look back on that history, and also to look forward, to use the perspective of the past, in viewing the ongoing role of the Court as an institution in American government. It's impossible, of course, to predict with any degree of certainty what the future holds, for any institution in society. But I think we can apply the basic themes of this course to give us some idea of the role the Court will play in shaping American law, as it decides cases that reflect the changing nature of our society in the 21st century. I'd like to restate the themes that we discussed in our first lecture, and that we've followed throughout the course.

One of those themes is that of continuity and change. On one level, of course, both American society and the Supreme Court have exhibited great continuity over the past two centuries. Ever since the American Revolution freed the original 13 colonies from British rule, and the United States became an independent nation, our system of government has endured with little fundamental change. We have lived under the Constitution that was drafted in 1787, during a hot summer in Philadelphia, for a longer period than any other country in the world. But the continuity of our government and the Constitution is itself based on change in society at large. Many of those changes have profoundly affected the lives of all Americans. Over the past two centuries, the nation has increased dramatically in population, from four million residents in the first census of 1790, to more than 280 million in the census of 2000. There have been profound economic changes as well, as the country moved from a nation of small farmers to an industrial power, fueled by advances in transportation and technology.

These profound changes in American society have been accompanied by the twin factors of consensus and conflict, the second major theme of this course. We've benefited, in my view, from a shared consensus on the principles and values of representative democracy and the rule of law. The old saying that we are a nation of laws, and not of men, is more than a truism. Our commitment to democratic government and the rule of law have spared the American people from rule by demagogues and dictators, while the Bill of Rights has protected those who dissent from the tyranny of the majority. But this basic consensus has endured through periods of great conflict in American society. The political struggles over slavery, the military battles of the Civil War, and more recent conflicts over issues like segregation, all stemmed from the greatest conflict in American history, the conflict over race.

We've also experienced bitter, and sometimes violent, conflicts over issues like religion and abortion. These different sources of conflict reflect a third theme in this course, the theme of diversity. The American people are amazingly diverse in areas such as race and ethnicity, religious belief and disbelief, political ideology, family structure, and sexual orientation. We are not a homogenous nation in any sense, unlike those in which the vast majority of the population shares a common race, religion, or political outlook. But neither are we a nation so divided in these areas that we face continual outbreaks of racial, religious, or political violence. As we know, American history is full of such outbreaks, but they have been generally short-lived and contained by law enforcement. We've revisited these themes from our introductory lecture to place in focus the Supreme Court and its landmark rulings over the past two centuries.

I'd like to briefly review the Court's origins and its later development, in the context of the three periods in its history that we outlined in the first lecture. The first period began with the Constitutional Convention in 1787 and extended through World War I. This period spanned more than a century, marked by conflicts over slavery and the national trauma of the Civil War. The second period extended from the 1920s through the Court's leadership by Chief Justice Earl Warren. The most significant events of that period, and the ones that most dramatically affected the Court, were the Great Depression of the 1930s, World War II, and the Court's ruling in 1954 that public school segregation violated the Constitution. The third period overlapped those years, and was marked by the Court's rulings in such different areas as religion, criminal law, political protest, and abortion. During the last three decades of this period, the Court was led by two conservative chief justices—Warren Burger and William Rehnquist.

Of course, these three periods in the Court's history are not neatly divided and distinct. But they provide us with very different approaches to the ways in which successive generations of Supreme

Court justices have interpreted the Constitution, and have shaped judicial doctrines that affect the outcome of the landmark cases we have discussed in this course. It's important, I think, to look back on the Court's landmark decisions, during these three periods in history, in the context of some of the more philosophical and broad questions that affected its rulings. And it's also important to consider these questions in terms of the judicial doctrines that emerged from the Court's reading of the Constitution.

These doctrines are developed and employed by justices as tools for deciding cases. But they reflect different approaches to judicial decision-making, approaches that are rooted in the political views and judicial philosophies of the justices. And, of course, there are competing doctrines that are often employed in the same case, with justices in the majority expressing one doctrine, and those in the minority another. As we've seen in these lectures, a judicial doctrine that is dominant in one period of the Court's history is later rejected or revised in another. And the factors that influence these changes in doctrine reflect both the Court's membership, and the broader social and political changes outside the Court. We've seen that changes in the Court's membership, through death and retirement, can very quickly and dramatically produce changes in prevailing judicial doctrines.

Perhaps the best example of this was the Constitutional Revolution of 1937, and the addition of several liberal justices by President Franklin Roosevelt. The second factor that has a great impact on the rise and fall of competing judicial doctrines stems from broader changes in American society. One example of this factor was the gradual—but rapidly accelerating—shift in the American economic system during the 19th century. The agrarian economy, based on small farms and small towns, gave way to an industrial economy, of factories and mines and mills. The rapid development of railroads, the production of steel and machine tools, and the mass-production system of turning out huge quantities of consumer goods, required millions of workers, many of them recent immigrants. And these basic economic changes produced conflicts between workers and employers, and conflicts between farmers and the railroads that shipped their goods to markets. We've seen in several lectures how these conflicts brought cases to the Supreme Court, and how the judicial doctrine of liberty of contract became dominant on a conservative Court.

Another example of the great impact of social and political change stemmed from the growing demands of black Americans for racial equality during the 20th century. We've seen how the Civil Rights movement, through groups like the NAACP, launched a campaign against Jim Crow laws and school segregation, a campaign that spanned almost 50 years between the founding of the NAACP in 1909 and the landmark *Brown* decision in 1954. This campaign would not have succeeded in the Court, without pressure outside the Court, as blacks and sympathetic whites began demanding an end to legalized segregation. And the judicial doctrines the Court employed in *Brown* and other civil rights cases, especially the strict scrutiny doctrine and an expansive reading of the equal protection clause of the Fourteenth Amendment, reflected the liberal views of the justices who joined the Court between 1937 and 1953.

What these two examples of doctrinal change illustrate, in my view, is the linkage between the justices and the world outside their chamber. Who sits on the Court, and the views they bring to the bench, is largely determined by who sits in the White House. We have had conservative presidents—like William Howard Taft, Richard Nixon, and Ronald Reagan—who named conservative justices. And we have had liberal presidents—like Franklin D. Roosevelt, John F. Kennedy, and Lyndon Johnson—who placed liberal justices on the Court. And there have been middle-of-the-road presidents—like Harry Truman and Dwight Eisenhower, to name a Democrat and a Republican. Most of their Supreme Court nominees took middle-of-the-road positions on the bench.

We've also seen that not all justices turn out the way that presidents expected them to. Justice Felix Frankfurter came to the Court with a liberal reputation, and became a judicial conservative on many issues. On the other side, Justice Harry Blackmun had a conservative voting record during his early years on the Court, and gradually moved to the liberal side. Supreme Court justices, of course, are people whose views can, and sometimes do, change over time. Exposure to new issues, and the exchange of ideas within a small group like the Court, can change the outlook of a justice. Some adopt a narrower reading of the Constitution, and others a broader reading. My point is, and I think many of our lectures have illustrated this

   ©2003 The Teaching Company Limited Partnership

point, that the outcome of many landmark cases reflects the complex interaction of personality and politics. Let me give two examples, to make this point concrete.

One is the *Dred Scott* decision in 1857, ruling that no black person could be a citizen of the United States. The opinion of Chief Justice Roger Taney said that blacks "have no rights which the white man is bound to respect." Taney also ruled that Congress had no power to ban slavery in the vast territories that stretched from the Mississippi River to the Pacific Ocean. I doubt whether Taney's opinion would have been so dogmatic and uncompromising, if he were not a dogmatic and uncompromising defender of slavery, with a background in southern politics. My second example is the Court's unanimous decision in *Brown v. Board of Education* in 1954, ruling that school segregation violated the Constitution. Chief Justice Earl Warren based his opinion on the "feeling of inferiority" that segregation produced in the "hearts and minds" of black children. I doubt whether Warren's opinion would have been so expansive in its reading of the Constitution, and so understanding of the impact of segregation, if he had not witnessed that impact on people like his own chauffeur, who was barred from sleeping in the same hotel that welcomed Warren during a visit to Civil War battlefields in Virginia.

As I said, the interaction between personality and politics, and its expression in judicial doctrine, is a complex matter. Chief Justice Taney was not just a mirror of the system of slavery in which he grew up and developed his views of blacks. As we saw, other members of his class, both lawyers and politicians, abhorred slavery and fought against it with equally uncompromising determination as Taney defended it. And other members of Chief Justice Warren's class, both lawyers and politicians, defended segregation with as much determination as he opposed it. But each of these chief justices led a Court with a majority of like-minded men, who joined the opinions of forceful and determined leaders. And those like-minded justices had been placed on the Court by presidents whose elections reflected the views of a majority of the American people.

Of course, most voters don't cast their ballots for presidential candidates with any thought of their future Supreme Court nominations. But the outcome of presidential elections reflects the prevailing currents of public opinion—sometimes conservative, sometimes liberal, and sometimes in the middle. And those shifting currents are affected, in my view, by deeper forces of social and economic change. So, the impact of these complex factors on the outcome of particular Supreme Court decisions is often difficult to predict, if not impossible. With this background of the links between judicial doctrine, personality, and politics, I'd like to briefly discuss another issue that has run through this course. This is the conflict between judicial activism and judicial restraint. As we saw in our introductory lecture, this conflict in approaches to deciding cases has often been linked, at least in the public's mind, with liberal and conservative positions on the issues that come before the Court. Many people associate judicial activism with liberal political views.

Judicial activists, in this view, are those who are willing to override the judgments of elected officials who will represent the majority of the voters who elect them to office. On the other side, those who follow the position of judicial restraint are more likely to show deference to elected lawmakers, and are reluctant to strike down laws that reflect majority sentiment. But if we look back at the cases we've discussed throughout this course, the link between liberal activism and conservative restraint is more apparent than real. Just about half of the cases we've discussed resulted in judicial reversal of state or federal laws, or of executive and administrative policies. And the Supreme Court upheld those laws and policies in the other half of the cases. Let me offer a few examples.

The first, and perhaps the most important, came in the landmark decision of Chief Justice John Marshall, in the case of *Marbury v. Madison* in 1803. In this case, Marshall struck down an act of Congress that had conferred jurisdiction on the Court to issue what were called "writs of mandamus." Marshall said that Congress could not add to the Court's "original jurisdiction," which is spelled out in Article III of the Constitution. We can view this as an example of judicial activism. But Marshall was not a political liberal by any means. He was a staunch Federalist, the party that supported the business interests of that time. I think it's more accurate to view Marshall's decision in the *Marbury* case in the context of his firm belief in judicial supremacy over the other branches of government, in carrying out the Court's duty "to say what the law is," as Marshall wrote in his opinion. In a sense, the *Marbury* decision represented conservative activism. The Court exerted its power to decide what the Constitution means. It was clear to Marshall that the Constitution

 ©2003 The Teaching Company Limited Partnership

did not give Congress the power to expand the Court's jurisdiction without a constitutional amendment.

Several other examples come from the Court's rulings during the period from the 1880s, through the early years of the 1930s. During this entire period, the Court was dominated by judicial conservatives, who employed the doctrine of liberty of contract to strike down many state and federal laws. The Court ruled in the *Lochner* case in 1905 that New York did not have the power to set maximum working hours for bakers. The state law in this case had been passed by a majority of New York's lawmakers. The Court also struck down in 1923 a federal law that authorized a commission in the District of Columbia to establish minimum wages for women, in the case of *Children's Hospital v. Adkins*. In both of these cases, the Court displaced the judgment of elected lawmakers, asserting its power to examine the "substance" of laws.

There have been many other examples on the other side of this question. During the later years of the Great Depression of the 1930s, the Court upheld a state law that set minimum wages for women, in the case of *West Coast Hotel v. Parrish*. The Court also upheld a federal law that protected the right of workers to join unions and bargain with their employers over wages and hours. Is it accurate to call these cases examples of judicial restraint? Or is it more accurate to say that a different group of justices, more liberal than their predecessors, read the Constitution differently? As Chief Justice Hughes said in the *West Coast Hotel* case, "the Constitution does not speak of freedom of contract. It speaks of liberty." To Hughes and the four justices who joined his opinion, the due process clause did not prohibit elected lawmakers from carrying out the will of the voters on issues like minimum wages. As Hughes put it, "regulation which is reasonable and is adopted in the interests of the community *is* due process."

In my view, the issue is not judicial activism versus judicial restraint. In most cases, the deciding factor in the Court's decision is the prevailing political balance on the bench. When justices are confronted with laws that conflict with their political and economic views, they will most often vote to strike them down. When the laws agree with their views, they will generally vote to uphold them. This is where judicial doctrines—such as liberty of contract, and strict scrutiny—come into play. In my view, such doctrines, however honestly they reflect the justices' reading of the Constitution, are rooted in the political and economic views of the justices who adopt and employ them. Now, this may seem a simplistic, or even cynical, perspective on the difficult task of determining the meaning of such broad constitutional phrases as "due process" or "equal protection," or the meaning of terms such as "commerce" or "contract." But I think Chief Justice Hughes made a perceptive comment when he said, before he joined the Court, "The Constitution is what the judges say it is." The meaning of constitutional provisions depends on who is on the Court at any given time.

There's another perspective on this issue that deserves some discussion as we conclude this course. Over the past few decades, many influential legal scholars, and several justices, have advocated the position known as "original intent." That is, justices should look for the intent of the Framers in reading the Constitution and deciding cases. The most forceful advocate of this position in recent years has been Justice Antonin Scalia, who is known as a judicial conservative. Scalia has argued that the meaning of the Constitution's provisions was determined by those who framed them, and that justices have no warrant for reading their own views into the Constitution. Conservative politicians—including Presidents Richard Nixon and Ronald Reagan—used the term *strict constructionists* in describing the kinds of justices they wanted to place on the Court, a term that describes those who advocate the "original intent" position.

There is certainly a strong argument for following the intent of the Framers, at least when that intent was clearly stated at the time a constitutional provision was adopted. But, in my view, efforts to find the clear intent of those who framed such provisions as the due process clause of the Fifth Amendment, or the equal protection clause of the Fourteenth Amendment, are not likely to provide much guidance in deciding particular cases. For example, did the framers of the due process clause intend that welfare officials must conduct hearings before they cut off benefits? This was the question in the case of *Goldberg v. Kelly*, which the Court decided in 1970. Justice William Brennan, a firm judicial liberal, wrote in his opinion in this case that welfare recipients were entitled to a hearing, and to be represented by a lawyer, in welfare termination cases. He later said his opinion was based on what he called "the underlying vision of human dignity enshrined in the due process clause." But it's difficult to find the origin of this decision in the intent of those who framed the due process clause.

Another expansive view of the due process clause was expressed by a judicial conservative, the second Justice John Marshall Harlan. Writing in 1961, Harlan said, "due process has not been reduced to any formula; its content cannot be determined by reference to any code." It represents, Harlan added, the "balance which our nation, built upon postulates of respect for the liberty of the individual, has struck between that liberty and the demands of organized society." But that delicate balance has shifted many times over the past two centuries, as both American society and the Supreme Court have adapted to the changes we've discussed in this course.

Before we conclude this course, I'd like to say a few words about my selection of cases and topics for these lectures. We've discussed some 120 of the Supreme Court's landmark decisions over the past two centuries, ranging from 1793 to 2003. But over the course of its entire history, the Court has decided more than 30,000 cases. During the 19th century, the Court often decided several hundred cases each year, many of them in brief opinions, and most with little enduring significance.

It would be impossible, of course, to discuss more than a small fraction of these cases in a course of this length. But I've tried to include cases that illustrate some of the drama and emotion that can make the Supreme Court chamber almost a theater. The tearful arguments of Daniel Webster in the *Dartmouth College* case, and of John W. Davis in the school segregation case from South Carolina, the emotion of Justice Thurgood Marshall's argument in the Little Rock case, and the outrage in Chief Justice Warren's voice in the same case, denouncing the defiance of Arkansas officials to the Court's ruling, are examples of how the Court can become, in fact, a very dramatic chamber. I hope you'll agree that the cases we've discussed in this course will spur us to look more closely at its past decisions—through the books I've suggested for further reading— and to follow the Court's future decisions, with some greater understanding of its crucial role in American society and government.

There's a final point I'd like to make before we conclude this lecture and this course. The Supreme Court is an institution, with a structure and functions that were established in the Constitution more than two centuries ago. But the Court is still a small group of people, who make their decisions around a conference table, through a process of discussion and debate on cases that often have a momentous impact on American society. It is the people—much more than the process—who have been the focus of this course. During our lectures, we've met several dozen of those people, many of whom left a lasting imprint on the Court, and on American society.

Those who stand out, and who have completed their service, include John Marshall, Roger Taney, Oliver Wendell Holmes, Felix Frankfurter, Hugo Black, Earl Warren, William Brennan, and Thurgood Marshall. It bears reminding that the Court decides cases that began with the lawsuits of real people, many of them ordinary people with extraordinary courage, people like Dred Scott, Homer Plessy, Lillian Gobitis, Fred Korematsu, Mary Beth Tinker, and Michael Hardwick. Like the justices, these people differed greatly in background and values. But they all placed their cases in the hands of people who shared a responsibility that is chiseled into the Court's marble facade: "Equal Justice Under Law." To what extent this promise became a reality in the cases we've discussed, certainly depends on our own views and values. But we all share a responsibility, as members of the American community, to think about the meaning of that promise—not only for ourselves but for future generations of Americans.

That brings me to my own thoughts about the Court's future. I have no crystal ball, and no idea of how the Court might change, with the certainty, but also with the uncertainty, of death or retirement at any time. I do feel confident that the Court, and the Constitution, will endure for many years to come. But it will certainly change, as justices depart and their successors arrive. Most likely, the kinds of cases, and the issues they raise, will also change, as American society, and the world outside our borders, also changes. The great diversity of our nation, one of the basic themes of this course, guarantees that conflicts over values and interests will bring many new issues before the Court.

I'm also convinced that other nations will adopt the model set by our Supreme Court, of an independent body with the power to protect the rights of "all persons" to the values that are embodied not only in our Constitution, but in the Universal Declaration of Human Rights. This

 ©2003 The Teaching Company Limited Partnership

document, which was adopted by the United Nations in 1948, recognizes the "inherent dignity" and "inalienable rights of all members of the human family," and incorporates the provisions of our own Bill of Rights, including the right to life, liberty, and security of person, and to the equal protection of the law. These are laudable goals for any nation. But in a world that is torn by wars between nations and within them, by the growing inequality of rich and poor, and by deeply rooted conflicts over race, religion, and ideology, those goals have yet to be achieved for most of the world's people, and even for many in our own country.

I want to end this course with a personal note. I have very much enjoyed preparing and delivering this course for you. Even after three decades of study, teaching, and writing about the Supreme Court, I continue to learn, and I continue to view the Court with respect, despite my frequent disagreement with its decisions. Most of all, I continue to feel both excitement and awe, when I visit the Court and listen to the arguments in its chamber. I hope I have passed on that excitement and awe to you. Thank you for sharing this learning experience with me. I think it's appropriate to end this course with the words that began our first lecture, in the chamber of the United States Supreme Court.

Timeline

1781 ....Articles of Confederation adopted to govern 13 "sovereign" states

1787 ....Constitutional Convention held in Philadelphia to draft a charter for a "federal" government with three branches

1789 ....Constitution ratified and becomes effective

1790 ....Supreme Court holds first meeting in New York City under Chief Justice John Jay

1791 ....Bill of Rights ratified and adds first ten amendments to the Constitution

1793 ....Court decides *Chisholm v. Georgia*, which leads to adoption of the Eleventh Amendment in 1795

1795 ....John Rutledge named to replace Jay as chief justice; he serves five months before the Senate rejects his nomination

1796 ....Oliver Ellsworth confirmed as chief justice to replace Rutledge

1801 ....John Marshall replaces Ellsworth as chief justice

1803 ....Marshall writes opinion in *Marbury v. Madison*, asserting the Court's power of judicial review over laws passed by Congress

1810 ....Court upholds land grants in *Fletcher v. Peck*

1819 ....Court decides landmark cases of *McCulloch v. Maryland* and *Dartmouth College v. Woodward*

          ©2003 The Teaching Company Limited Partnership

1824	Court upholds federal power over interstate commerce in *Gibbons v. Ogden*
1825	Court returns captured slaves to foreign owners in *The Antelope* case
1832	Court upholds Indian land rights in *Worcester v. Georgia*
1835	Chief Justice Marshall dies and is replaced by Roger Brooke Taney in 1836
1836	Court allows state to revise corporate charter in *Charles River Bridge* case
1842	Court upholds fugitive slave law in *Prigg v. Pennsylvania*
1850	Court rules that the status of slaves depends on owner's residence in *Strader v. Graham*
1857	Taney holds in the *Dred Scott* case that no person of African descent can be a citizen of the United States or any state
1864	Taney dies and is replaced as chief justice by Salmon P. Chase
1865	Thirteenth Amendment ratified to abolish slavery
1868	Fourteenth Amendment ratified to overturn *Dred Scott* decision and grant citizenship to former slaves; requires states to provide "due process" and "equal protection of the laws" to all persons
1870	Fifteenth Amendment ratified to protect voting rights of blacks

1873 ....Court upholds state monopoly in Slaughterhouse Case; upholds state ban on women lawyers in *Bradwell* case

1874 ....Morrison Waite replaces Chase as chief justice

1875 ....Court strikes down civil rights enforcement act in *Cruikshank* case

1877 ....Court upholds regulation of grain storage rates in *Munn* case and state ban on liquor trade in *Mugler* case

1883 ....Court holds in Civil Rights Cases that the Fourteenth Amendment does not ban "private" discrimination

1886 ....Court strikes down discrimination against Chinese in *Yick Wo* case

1888 .... Melville Fuller replaces Waite as chief justice

1890 ....Court strikes down railroad rate regulation in *Chicago, Milwaukee* case

1895 ....Court strikes down Sherman Antitrust Act in *E.C. Knight* case; strikes down federal income tax in *Pollock* case; upholds conviction of union leader in *Debs* case

1896 ....Court adopts separate but equal doctrine in *Plessy v. Ferguson*

1905 ....Court applies liberty of contract doctrine in *Lochner v. New York*

1908 ....Court upholds maximum hours law for women in *Muller* case

1910 ....Edward D. White replaces Fuller as chief justice

 ©2003 The Teaching Company Limited Partnership

1919 ....Court decides landmark First Amendment cases in *Schenck*, *Debs*, and *Abrams*; creates clear and present danger doctrine

1921 ....William Howard Taft replaces White as chief justice

1923 ....Court strikes down minimum wages for women in *Adkins v. Children's Hospital*; strikes down ban on teaching foreign languages in *Meyer v. Nebraska*

1925 ....Court upholds conviction of Communist in *Gitlow* case; strikes down ban on private schools in *Pierce v. Society of Sisters*

1927 ....Court upholds conviction of Communist in *Whitney* case; upholds state sterilization law in *Buck v. Bell*

1928 ....Court upholds wiretap law in *Olmstead* case

1929 ....Court upholds ban on citizenship for pacifists in *Schwimmer* case

1930 ....Charles Evans Hughes replaces Taft as chief justice

1932 ....Court strikes down state regulation of ice business in *New York State Ice Co.* case

1934 ....Court upholds state "mortgage moratorium" law in *Blaisdell* case; upholds state regulation of milk prices in *Nebbia* case

1935 ....Court strikes down regulation of oil production in *Panama Refining* case; strikes down National Recovery Act in *Schechter Poultry* case

1936 ....Court strikes down Agricultural Adjustment Act in *Butler* case; strikes down state minimum-wage law for women in *Morehead* case

1937 ....Constitutional Revolution, in which Court's rulings in *West Coast Hotel* and *Jones & Laughlin* cases derail FDR's court-packing plan; Court upholds unemployment benefits in *Stewart Machine* case and Social Security Act in *Helvering v. Davis*; strikes down convictions of Communists in *De Jonge* and *Herndon* cases

1938 ....Justice Stone states strict scrutiny test in *Carolene Products* case; Court upholds separate but equal law schools in *Gaines* case; strikes down licensing of Jehovah's Witnesses in *Lovell* case

1939 ....Court strikes down licensing of Jehovah's Witnesses in *Schneider* case

1940 ....Court strikes down licensing of religious groups in *Cantwell* case; upholds expulsion of Jehovah's Witnesses for refusing school flag salute in *Minersville v. Gobitis*

     ©2003 The Teaching Company Limited Partnership

1941	Justice Harlan Fiske Stone replaces Hughes as chief justice
1942	Court says indigent defendants have no right to lawyer in *Betts v. Brady*
1943	Court strikes down expulsion of Jehovah's Witnesses for refusing flag salute in *Barnette* case; upholds wartime curfew on Japanese Americans in *Hirabayashi* and *Yasui* cases; strikes down sterilization of prisoners in *Skinner* case
1944	Court upholds internment of Japanese Americans in *Korematsu* case
1946	Fred Vinson replaces Stone as chief justice; Court rules that states cannot be sued in reapportionment cases in *Colegrove* case
1947	Court upholds state payment for bus transportation of parochial school students in *Everson* case
1948	Court orders admission of black student to white law school in *Sipuel* case; strikes down school religion classes in *McCollum* case; says states can ban women bartenders in *Goessart* case
1949	Court says that the exclusionary rule against illegally seized evidence does not apply to states in *Wolf v. Colorado*
1950	Court orders admission of black students to law and graduate schools in *Sweatt* and *McLaurin* cases

1951 ....Court upholds convictions of Communist leaders in *Dennis v. United States*

1953 ....Earl Warren replaces Vinson as chief justice

1954 ....Court strikes down school segregation in *Brown v. Board of Education*

1955 ....Court approves "all deliberate speed" in school integration in *Brown* case

1957 ....Court strikes down conviction of Communists in *Yates* and *Watkins* cases; strikes down firing of Marxist professor in *Sweezy* case

1958 ....Court orders Arkansas officials to comply with integration decision in *Cooper v. Aaron*

1961 ....Court upholds Sunday-closing laws in *McGowan* and *Braunfeld* cases; applies exclusionary rule to states in *Mapp v. Ohio*

1962 ....Court rules against school prayer in *Engel* case; says states can be sued on legislative reapportionment in *Baker v. Carr*

1963 ....Court strikes down school Bible reading in *Schempp* case; says states must provide lawyers for indigent defendants in *Gideon* case

©2003 The Teaching Company Limited Partnership

1964	Court strikes down obscenity law in *Jacobellis* case; rules defendants have right to consult lawyers in *Escobedo* case; states "one-person, one-vote" rule in *Reynolds v. Sims*; upholds federal Civil Rights Act in *Heart of Atlanta Motel* case
1965	Court strikes down state ban on contraceptive use in *Griswold* case
1966	Court upholds right against self-incrimination in *Miranda v. Arizona*
1967	Court strikes down state ban on interracial marriages in *Loving* case
1968	Court upholds police stop-and-frisk searches in *Terry v. Ohio*
1969	Warren Burger replaces Earl Warren as chief justice; Court strikes down school ban on armbands as Vietnam War protest in *Tinker* case; strikes down conviction for racist speech by Klan leader in *Brandenburg* case
1971	Court strikes down "prior restraint" on publishing the Pentagon Papers in *New York Times* case; strikes down state ban on women as estate administrators in *Reed v. Reed*
1973	Court upholds abortion rights in *Roe v. Wade*; strikes down Air Force restriction of benefits for women officers in *Frontiero* case
1974	Court rules against President Nixon in Watergate Tapes Case
1978	Court strikes down racial preferences in medical school admissions in *Bakke* case

1980 ....Court upholds federal ban on Medicaid funds for abortions in *Harris v. McRae*

1985 ....Court strikes down school prayer in *Wallace v. Jaffree*

1986 ....Justice William Rehnquist replaces Burger as chief justice; Court upholds Georgia law against homosexual sodomy in *Bowers v. Hardwick*

1989 ....Court strikes down law against flag-burning in *Texas v. Johnson*; upholds state restrictions on abortion access in *Webster* case

1992 ....Court reaffirms *Roe* decision in *Planned Parenthood v. Casey*; rules against prayer at school graduations in *Lee v. Weisman*; strikes down hate-crime conviction for cross burning in *R.A.V. v. St. Paul*

1996 ....Court rules Virginia Military Institute must admit women in *United States v. Virginia*

2000 ....Court decides presidential election in *Bush v. Gore*; rules against prayer at high school football games in *Santa Fe v. Doe*; strikes down state ban on partial-birth abortions in *Stenberg v. Carhart*

2003 ....Court rules that states can punish cross burning in *Virginia v. Black*

 ©2003 The Teaching Company Limited Partnership

Glossary

Note: The best source for the meaning of legal terms is *Black's Law Dictionary*, which is available in most libraries.

Acquittal: A decision by a jury or judge that a person charged with a crime is not guilty.

Affirm(ed): A judicial decision upholding the ruling of a lower court.

Amicus curiae: Latin for "friend of the court"; a person or group that is not a party in the case and submits a brief to the court.

Appeal: A procedure by which the ruling of a lower court is submitted to a higher court for review.

Appellant: In the federal courts of appeals, the party asking for reversal of a district court ruling (see **appellee**).

Appellee: In the federal courts of appeals, the party asking for affirmance of a district court ruling (see **appellant**).

Attainder, Bill of: A legislative act declaring a person guilty of a crime without a trial or hearing; prohibited by the Constitution.

Balancing test: The judicial practice of deciding cases by weighing the rights of one party against the other without applying a strict doctrinal rule.

Brief: The written submission of a party (or *amicus* group) to a court, presenting the legal arguments in a case.

Certiorari, writ of: The Latin name for a request that the Supreme Court review a case; the Court denies most applications for this writ.

Class action: A lawsuit brought on behalf of a class of people with a similar stake in its decision.

Common law: The practice imported from English law of deciding cases on the basis of precedent established by courts in earlier cases, rather than by reliance on legislation or constitutional provisions.

Concurring opinion: An opinion by a judge who agrees with the court's ruling but who writes separately to explain his or her reasoning in the case.

Contempt: A knowing failure or refusal to carry out or abide by a judicial ruling; judges can punish contempt with fines or jail terms.

Courts of appeal: In the federal system, the intermediate layer of courts that hear appeals from the district (trial) courts; rulings of the courts of appeal may be reviewed by the Supreme Court.

De facto: A Latin term for a factual situation that is not imposed by law; applied most often in school segregation cases (see ***de jure***).

De jure: A Latin term for a factual situation that is imposed by law, as in ***de jure*** segregation.

Defendant: The party against whom judicial relief is sought in a lawsuit.

Dicta, obiter dicta: A statement in a judicial opinion that is not related to the ruling and that has no force as law or precedent.

Discretionary jurisdiction: A term for cases that a court is not required by law or the Constitution to decide but may if it chooses to exercise its power of decision (see **mandatory jurisdiction**).

Dissenting opinion: An opinion by a judge (or judges) in the minority in a case, taking issue with the court's ruling.

Distinguish: A judge's explanation of reasons why a prior decision does not apply to a present case as precedent.

District courts: In the federal system, the trial courts in which most cases are heard and decided.

Diversity jurisdiction: The power of federal courts to decide cases brought under state law by parties who are residents of different states.

Due process: The requirement, established in both the Fifth and Fourteenth Amendments, that governments treat all persons fairly in actions that might deprive them of "life, liberty, or property" (see **substantive due process**)

***Ex post facto* law**: A criminal law that punishes a person for acts committed before the law was passed.

Exclusionary rule: The judicial doctrine that courts must not admit illegally obtained evidence in criminal trials.

Habeas corpus, writ of: A Latin term for "you have the body"; a writ ordering an official to bring a person into court to determine if he or she is being unlawfully detained.

Incorporation: The judicial doctrine that provisions of the Bill of Rights were "incorporated" into the due process clause of the Fourteenth Amendment and apply to the states.

Injunction: A judicial order commanding a person to perform or refrain from performing an act required by law.

Judicial activism: A legal philosophy that judges should decide cases to protect the rights of minorities and dissenters, striking down laws if necessary to accomplish this aim.

Judicial restraint: A legal philosophy that judges should defer to the decisions of the legislative and executive branches unless their actions clearly violate a constitutional provision.

Judicial review: The power of courts to determine whether a law or executive act conforms to the Constitution and to strike down those that violate the court's interpretation of the Constitution.

Jurisdiction: The grant of power to courts, by the Constitution or laws, to hear and decide a case.

Litigant: A party to a lawsuit.

Mandamus, writ of: A Latin term from the word for "hand"; a judicial order directing an official to perform an act required by law.

Mandatory jurisdiction: A term for cases that courts are required by law or the Constitution to hear and decide (see **discretionary jurisdiction**).

Motion: A request made to a court for a ruling on a point of law, such as a motion to dismiss a case or to rule on the admissibility of evidence.

Order: A written command of a judge to carry out the court's ruling in a lawsuit.

Per curiam: A Latin term for "by the court"; a judicial opinion that is unsigned or issued by the court as a body.

Petitioner: In Supreme Court procedure, the party asking for reversal of a lower-court decision (see **respondent**).

Plaintiff: The party who brings a lawsuit asking for judicial relief.

Plurality opinion: A judicial opinion that decides the case but is not joined by a majority of the court.

Police powers: The judicial doctrine that governments have the power to pass laws protecting the health, safety, welfare, or morals of the public, originating in English common law.

Precedent: Previously decided cases that establish judicial doctrine that judges follow in ruling on cases before them.

***Pro se* litigant**: A party who appears in court on his or her own behalf, without a lawyer.

Rational basis test: The judicial doctrine that presumes the constitutionality of laws for which any "rational" argument can be found or presumed in its defense (see **strict scrutiny test**).

Respondent: In Supreme Court procedure, the party asking for affirmance of a lower-court decision (see **petitioner**).

Reversal: A court's decision to reverse the ruling of a lower court.

Solicitor General: The Justice Department lawyer who represents the United States in cases before the Supreme Court.

Stare decisis: A Latin term for "let the decision stand"; the judicial doctrine that precedent established in earlier cases should be followed in a present case.

State action: An action taken by an official or agency of government.

Strict scrutiny test: The judicial doctrine that laws will be held unconstitutional if they infringe on "fundamental rights" protected by the Constitution or discriminate against members of minority groups, unless governments can show a "compelling state interest" to justify the law.

Subpoena: A judicial order that a person appear in court or produce a document or other evidence.

Substantive due process: The judicial doctrine that the "liberty" interests protected by the due process clause include rights that cannot be infringed by legislation and are subject to judicial review.

Vacate: A judicial order to rescind the ruling of a lower court.

Venue: The geographic jurisdiction in which a case is heard.

Warrant: A judicial order for an arrest or for a search and seizure of evidence.

Writ: A judicial order commanding a person to perform or refrain from performing an act.

Biographical Notes

Note: These biographies are in chronological order of service on the Supreme Court.

Jay, John (1745–1829). First chief justice; nominated by President Washington. Jay served from 1790 to 1795; he resigned to run for governor of New York. He had been a delegate to the Continental Congress and chief justice of New York, as well as an envoy to England, negotiating the Jay Treaty. The most important decision during his tenure was *Chisholm v. Georgia* in 1793.

Rutledge, John (1739–1800). Second chief justice; nominated by President Washington. Rutledge served as associate justice from 1790 to 1791, when he resigned to become chief justice of South Carolina. He served a recess appointment as chief justice of the Supreme Court in 1795, but the Senate rejected his confirmation because of his criticism of the Jay Treaty.

Ellsworth, Oliver (1745–1807). Third chief justice; nominated by President Washington. He served from 1796 to 1800, resigning to return to politics in Connecticut. During his tenure, Ellsworth spent much time abroad as an envoy to France. He had been a delegate to the Continental Congress and the Constitutional Convention and a U.S. senator from Connecticut.

Marshall, John (1755–1835). Fourth chief justice; nominated by President John Adams. He served from 1801 until his death in 1835. Marshall had been a Virginia state legislator, U.S. envoy to France, a U.S. representative from Virginia, and secretary of state under Adams. Marshall led the Court with a forceful personality and shaped it into an influential branch of government. His most important opinions include *Marbury v. Madison* (1803), *McCulloch v. Maryland* (1819), *Dartmouth College v. Woodward* (1819), and *Gibbons v. Ogden* (1824).

Taney, Roger (1777–1864). Fifth chief justice; nominated by President Andrew Jackson. He served from 1836 until his death in 1864. Taney had been a Maryland legislator and attorney general and secretary of the treasury under Jackson. He was a fervent defender of states' rights and slavery. Taney's most important opinions include *Charles River Bridge Co. v. Warren Bridge Co.* (1837) and *Dred*

Scott v. Sandford (1857), in which he declared that no black person could be a citizen.

Chase, Salmon (1808–1873). Sixth chief justice; nominated by President Lincoln. He served from 1864 until his death in 1873. Chase had been governor of Ohio, a U.S. senator, and secretary of the treasury under Lincoln. He was allied with the Radical Republicans in Congress and was a firm opponent of slavery. His most important opinions include *Ex parte McCardle* (1868) and *Hepburn v. Griswold* (1869).

Bradley, Joseph (1813–1892). Associate justice; nominated by President Grant. He served from 1870 until his death in 1892. As a justice, Bradley served on the commission that examined the disputed electoral votes in the 1876 presidential election; he cast the deciding vote to elect President Rutherford Hayes. His most important opinions include the Slaughterhouse Cases (dissent, 1884), *Bradwell v. Illinois* (concurrence, 1872), and the Civil Rights Cases (1883).

Waite, Morrison (1816–1888). Seventh chief justice; nominated by President Grant. He served from 1874 until his death in 1888. Waite had been a corporate lawyer and an Ohio state legislator. He was widely considered a weak chief justice, and he had little sympathy for blacks. His most important opinions include *Cruikshank v. United States* (1876), *United States v. Reese* (1876), and *Munn v. Illinois* (1876).

Harlan, John Marshall (1833–1911). Associate justice; nominated by President Hayes. He served from 1877 until his death in 1911. Harlan had been Kentucky's attorney general and an unsuccessful candidate for U.S. Congress and governor. He became known for his strong dissents in civil rights cases, arguing that blacks deserved equal rights under the Fourteenth Amendment. His most important opinions include the Civil Rights Cases (dissent, 1883), *Plessy v. Ferguson* (dissent, 1896), and *Hurtado v. California* (dissent, 1884).

Fuller, Melville (1833–1910). Eighth chief justice; nominated by President Cleveland. He served from 1888 until his death in 1910. Fuller had been a corporate lawyer and an Illinois state legislator. He led the Court during one of its most conservative periods and was a firm supporter of corporate interests. His most important opinions include *Pollock v. Farmers' Loan and Trust Co.* (1895), *United States v. E.C. Knight Co.* (1895), and *Loewe v. Lawlor* (1898).

White, Edward D. (1845–1921). Ninth chief justice; nominated by President Taft. He had been named associate justice by President Cleveland in 1894 and became chief justice in 1910, serving in that post until his death in 1921. White had been a Confederate soldier and served as a Louisiana state legislator, state supreme court justice, and U.S. senator. His most important opinion was *Standard Oil Co. v. United States* (1911).

Holmes, Oliver Wendell, Jr. (1841–1933). Associate justice; nominated by President Taft. Holmes served from 1902 until his retirement in 1932. He was one of the most influential justices in the Court's history and the greatest writer on the Court. He served in the Union army during the Civil War and was a Harvard law professor and chief justice of Massachusetts. His most important opinions include *Lochner v. New York* (dissent, 1905), *Schenck v. United States* (1919), *Abrams v. United States* (dissent, 1919), and *Buck v. Bell* (1927).

Brandeis, Louis D. (1856–1941). Associate justice; nominated by President Wilson. He served from 1916 until his retirement in 1939. Brandeis was the first Jewish justice and had been known as the "people's lawyer" for representing women and consumers. He argued the case of *Muller v. Oregon* in 1908, introducing the famous "Brandeis brief." Brandeis also advocated the right to privacy in an influential law review article in 1890. He was a foe of "bigness" in business and government. His most important opinions include *Whitney v. California* (concurrence, 1927), *Olmstead v. United States* (dissent, 1928), and *New State Ice Co. v. Liebmann* (dissent, 1932).

Taft, William Howard (1857–1930). Tenth chief justice; nominated by President Harding. He served from 1921 until his retirement in 1930. Taft was a former Republican president, from 1909 to 1913, and had been an Ohio state judge, U.S. solicitor general, governor of the Philippines, and secretary of war. Taft was a staunch conservative and supported business interests; he also firmly led the Court. His most important opinions include *Truax v. Corrigan* (1922), *Stafford v. Wallace* (1922), and *Adkins v. Children's Hospital* (dissent, 1923).

Hughes, Charles Evans (1862–1948). Eleventh chief justice; nominated by President Hoover. Hughes also served as associate justice from 1910 until he resigned in 1916 to run for president as a Republican; he lost to Woodrow Wilson. Hughes was a forceful leader on the Court and played a key role in the Constitutional Revolution of 1937, in which the Court abandoned the substantive due process doctrine in economic regulation. His most important opinions include *Home Building & Loan v. Blaisdell* (1934), *West Coast Hotel v. Parrish* (1937), and *NLRB v. Jones & Laughlin Steel Co.* (1937).

Black, Hugo (1886–1971). Associate justice; nominated by President Franklin Roosevelt. He served from 1937 until his retirement in 1971. Black had been an Alabama state judge and U.S. senator. He was a firm supporter of Roosevelt's New Deal programs in the Senate; his youthful membership in the Ku Klux Klan did not block his confirmation. Black was a First Amendment absolutist on the Court, strongly supporting free speech and separation of church and state. His most important opinions include *Betts v. Brady* (dissent, 1942), *Everson v. Ewing Township* (1947), *McCollum v. Board of Education* (1948), *Engel v. Vitale* (1962), *Griswold v. Connecticut* (dissent, 1965), and *Tinker v. Des Moines* (dissent, 1969).

Frankfurter, Felix (1882–1965). Associate justice; nominated by President Franklin Roosevelt. He served from 1939 until his retirement in 1962. Frankfurter had been a Harvard law professor and close advisor to Roosevelt. He became a champion of judicial restraint on the Court but strongly supported civil rights; he played a leading role in shaping the Court's unanimous decision in *Brown v. Board of Education* (1954). His most important opinions include *Minersville School District v. Gobitis* (1940) and *West Virginia Board of Education v. Barnette* (dissent, 1943).

Douglas, William O. (1898–1980). Associate justice; nominated by President Franklin Roosevelt. He served from 1939 until his retirement in 1975. Douglas had been a Columbia and Yale law professor and chair of the Securities and Exchange Commission. He was a firm liberal and supported civil rights and free speech. His important opinions include *Skinner v. Oklahoma* (1942), *Roth v. United States* (dissent, 1957), and *Griswold v. Connecticut* (1965).

Stone, Harlan Fiske (1872–1946). Twelfth chief justice; nominated by President Franklin Roosevelt. He served as associate justice from 1925 until 1941, when he replaced Charles Evans Hughes as chief justice, serving until his death in 1946. He had been Columbia law school dean and U.S. attorney general. Stone became a leader of the Court's liberal bloc and fashioned the strict scrutiny doctrine in 1938. His most important opinions include *United States v. Carolene Products Co.* (1938), *Minersville School District v. Gobitis* (dissent, 1940), and *Hirabayashi v. United States* (1943).

Vinson, Frederick (1890–1953). Thirteenth chief justice; nominated by President Truman. He served from 1946 until his death in 1953. Vinson had been a U.S. representative, a federal appeals judge, and secretary of the treasury. He was a political crony of President Truman and was a weak leader on the Court. His important opinions include *Sweatt v. Painter* (1948), *Shelley v. Kraemer* (1948), and *Dennis v. United States* (1951).

Warren, Earl (1891–1974). Fourteenth chief justice; nominated by President Eisenhower. He served from 1953 until his retirement in 1969. Warren had been attorney general and governor of California. He was a firm leader of the Court and shaped it into a liberal body during his tenure. The Warren Court expanded constitutional rights for racial minorities, dissenters, and criminal defendants. His most important opinions include *Brown v. Board of Education* (1954 and 1955), *Reynolds v. Sims* (1964), and *Miranda v. Arizona* (1966).

Brennan, William J., Jr. (1906–1997). Associate justice; nominated by President Eisenhower. He served from 1956 until his retirement in 1990. Brennan had been a New Jersey supreme court justice. He became the intellectual leader of the Warren Court and protected its landmark decisions from reversal in later years. Brennan was a firm liberal, who based his judicial philosophy on the principle of human dignity. His most important opinions include *Baker v. Carr* (1962), *New York Times v. Sullivan* (1964), and *Texas v. Johnson* (1989).

Marshall, Thurgood (1908–1993). Associate justice; nominated by President Lyndon Johnson. He served from 1967 until his retirement in 1991. Marshall was the first black justice on the Court. He headed the NAACP legal staff from 1938 until 1961 and argued many landmark civil rights cases before the Court. He was a firm liberal and a consistent opponent of capital punishment. His most important opinions include *Stanley v. Georgia* (1969), *Furman v. Georgia* (concurrence, 1972), and *San Antonio School District v. Rodriguez* (1973).

Burger, Warren Earl (1907–1995). Fifteenth chief justice; nominated by President Nixon. He served from 1969 until his retirement in 1986. Burger had been a federal appeals judge. Nixon chose him as a conservative, "law and order" judge. Burger was a strong judicial administrator but a weak leader on the Court. His most important opinions include *Swann v. Charlotte-Mecklenburg School District* (1971), *Milliken v. Bradley* (1974), and *Nixon v. United States* (1974).

Rehnquist, William (1924–). Sixteenth chief justice; nominated by President Reagan. He was an associate justice, nominated by President Nixon, from 1972 until he became chief justice in 1986. Rehnquist was a law clerk to Justice Robert Jackson; was later in private practice in Phoenix, Arizona; and served in the Justice Department during the Nixon administration. He has articulated a strong conservative political and judicial philosophy and is a firm opponent of abortion. His Senate confirmation was opposed by liberal Democrats, who considered him too conservative. His most important judicial opinions include *Roe v. Wade* (dissent, 1973), *Texas v. Johnson* (dissent, 1989), and *Planned Parenthood v. Casey* (dissent, 1992).

Justices of the Supreme Court

Name	Position	Years of Service
Jay, John	Chief Justice	1789–1795
Wilson, James	Associate Justice	1789–1798
Rutledge, John	Associate Justice	1790–1791
Iredell, James	Associate Justice	1790–1799
Blair, John	Associate Justice	1790–1795
Cushing, William	Associate Justice	1790–1810
Johnson, Thomas	Associate Justice	1792–1793
Paterson, William	Associate Justice	1793–1806
Rutledge, John	Chief Justice	1795
Chase, Samuel	Associate Justice	1796–1811
Ellsworth, Oliver	Chief Justice	1796–1800
Washington, Bushrod	Associate Justice	1799–1829
Moore, Alfred	Associate Justice	1800–1804
Marshall, John	Chief Justice	1801–1835
Johnson, William	Associate Justice	1804–1834
Todd, Thomas	Associate Justice	1807–1826
Livingston, Henry Brockholst	Associate Justice	1807–1823
Duvall, Gabriel	Associate Justice	1811–1835
Story, Joseph	Associate Justice	1812–1845
Thompson, Smith	Associate Justice	1823–1843
Trimble, Robert	Associate Justice	1826–1828
McLean, John	Associate Justice	1830–1861
Baldwin, Henry	Associate Justice	1830–1844
Wayne, James Moore	Associate Justice	1835–1867
Taney, Roger Brooke	Chief Justice	1836–1864
Barbour, Philip Pendleton	Associate Justice	1836–1841
Catron, John	Associate Justice	1837–1865
McKinley, John	Associate Justice	1838–1852
Daniel, Peter Vivian	Associate Justice	1842–1860
Woodbury, Levi	Associate Justice	1845–1851

 ©2003 The Teaching Company Limited Partnership

Name	Position	Years of Service
Nelson, Samuel	Associate Justice	1845–1872
Grier, Robert Cooper	Associate Justice	1846–1870
Curtis, Benjamin Robbins	Associate Justice	1851–1857
Campbell, John Archibald	Associate Justice	1853–1861
Clifford, Nathan	Associate Justice	1858–1881
Davis, David	Associate Justice	1862–1877
Swayne, Noah Haynes	Associate Justice	1862–1881
Miller, Samuel Freeman	Associate Justice	1862–1890
Field, Stephen Johnson	Associate Justice	1863–1897
Chase, Salmon Portland	Chief Justice	1864–1873
Strong, William	Associate Justice	1870–1880
Bradley, Joseph P.	Associate Justice	1870–1892
Hunt, Ward	Associate Justice	1873–1882
Waite, Morrison Remick	Chief Justice	1874–1888
Harlan, John Marshall	Associate Justice	1877–1911
Woods, William Burnham	Associate Justice	1881–1887
Matthews, Stanley	Associate Justice	1881–1889
Blatchford, Samuel	Associate Justice	1882–1893
Gray, Horace	Associate Justice	1882–1902
Lamar, Lucius Quintus C.	Associate Justice	1888–1893
Fuller, Melville Weston	Chief Justice	1888–1910
Brewer, David Josiah	Associate Justice	1890–1910
Brown, Henry Billings	Associate Justice	1891–1906
Shiras, George, Jr.	Associate Justice	1892–1903
Jackson, Howell Edmunds	Associate Justice	1893–1895
White, Edward Douglass	Associate Justice	1894–1910*
Peckham, Rufus Wheeler	Associate Justice	1896–1909
McKenna, Joseph	Associate Justice	1898–1925
Holmes, Oliver Wendell	Associate Justice	1902–1932
Day, William Rufus	Associate Justice	1903–1922
Moody, William Henry	Associate Justice	1906–1910
White, Edward Douglass	Chief Justice	1910–1921
Lurton, Horace Harmon	Associate Justice	1910–1914

Name	Position	Years of Service
Hughes, Charles Evans	Associate Justice	1910–1916
Lamar, Joseph Rucker	Associate Justice	1911–1916
Van Devanter, Willis	Associate Justice	1911–1937
Pitney, Mahlon	Associate Justice	1912–1922
McReynolds, James Clark	Associate Justice	1914–1941
Brandeis, Louis Dembitz	Associate Justice	1916–1939
Clarke, John Hessin	Associate Justice	1916–1922
Taft, William Howard	Chief Justice	1921–1930
Sutherland, George	Associate Justice	1922–1938
Sanford, Edward Terry	Associate Justice	1923–1930
Butler, Pierce	Associate Justice	1923–1939
Stone, Harlan Fiske	Associate Justice	1925–1941*
Hughes, Charles Evans	Chief Justice	1930–1941
Roberts, Owen Josephus	Associate Justice	1930–1945
Cardozo, Benjamin Nathan	Associate Justice	1932–1938
Black, Hugo Lafayette	Associate Justice	1937–1971
Reed, Stanley Forman	Associate Justice	1938–1957
Douglas, William Orville	Associate Justice	1939–1975
Frankfurter, Felix	Associate Justice	1939–1962
Murphy, Frank	Associate Justice	1940–1949
Jackson, Robert Houghwout	Associate Justice	1941–1954
Stone, Harlan Fiske	Chief Justice	1941–1946
Byrnes, James Francis	Associate Justice	1941–1942
Rutledge, Wiley Blount	Associate Justice	1943–1949
Burton, Harold Hitz	Associate Justice	1945–1958
Vinson, Fred Moore	Chief Justice	1946–1953
Clark, Tom Campbell	Associate Justice	1949–1967
Minton, Sherman	Associate Justice	1949–1956
Warren, Earl	Chief Justice	1953–1969
Harlan, John Marshall	Associate Justice	1955–1971
Brennan, William J., Jr.	Associate Justice	1956–1990
Whittaker, Charles Evans	Associate Justice	1957–1962
Stewart, Potter	Associate Justice	1958–1981

 ©2003 The Teaching Company Limited Partnership

Name	Position	Years of Service
White, Byron Raymond	Associate Justice	1962–1993
Goldberg, Arthur Joseph	Associate Justice	1962–1965
Fortas, Abe	Associate Justice	1965–1969
Marshall, Thurgood	Associate Justice	1967–1991
Burger, Warren Earl	Chief Justice	1969–1986
Blackmun, Harry A.	Associate Justice	1970–1994
Powell, Lewis F., Jr.	Associate Justice	1972–1987
Rehnquist, William H.	Associate Justice	1972–1986*
Stevens, John Paul	Associate Justice	1975–
O'Connor, Sandra Day	Associate Justice	1981–
Rehnquist, William H.	Chief Justice	1986–
Scalia, Antonin	Associate Justice	1986–
Kennedy, Anthony M.	Associate Justice	1988–
Souter, David H.	Associate Justice	1990–
Thomas, Clarence	Associate Justice	1991–
Ginsburg, Ruth Bader	Associate Justice	1993–
Breyer, Stephen G.	Associate Justice	1994–

* Elevated

Bibliography

Alley, Robert S., *Without a Prayer: Religious Expression in Public Schools*. Amherst, NY: Prometheus Books, 1996. Written from a journalistic perspective, this book covers the Court's major school prayer cases from the 1960s through the 1990s.

Alsop, Joseph, and Turner Catledge, *The 168 Days*. New York: DaCapo Press, 1973. Two noted journalists turned out a hot-from-the-headlines and highly readable account of President Franklin Roosevelt's famous "court-packing" plan.

Atkins, Susan, and Brenda Hoggett, *Women and the Law*. New York: Blackwell, 1984. This book covers the cases involving women's rights through the early 1980s, with a focus on legal issues. It provides little context of the feminist movement from which the cases emerged.

Baker, Liva, *Miranda: Crime, Law, and Politics*. New York: Atheneum, 1983. This book recounts the *Miranda* case, the Court's ruling that criminal defendants must be warned by police of their rights to remain silent and consult a lawyer, and the political response to that decision.

Baxter, Maurice G., *The Steamboat Monopoly: Gibbons v. Ogden*. New York: Knopf, 1972. This book offers a brief but cogent account of the Court's first major ruling in a landmark case that established broad federal powers over interstate commerce.

Belknap, Michal R., *Cold War Political Justice: The Smith Act, the Communist Party, and American Civil Liberties*. Westport, CT: Greenwood Press, 1977. A detailed historical account of the prosecutions of Communist Party leaders in the 1940s and 1950s.

Blue, Frederick J., *Salmon P. Chase: A Life in Politics*. Kent, OH: Kent State University Press, 1987. A solid biography of the sixth chief justice, who served from 1864 to 1873, with a focus on Chase's political career before he joined the Court.

Cleary, Edward J., *Beyond the Burning Cross: The First Amendment and the Landmark R.A.V. Case*. New York: Random House, 1994. An even-handed account of the cross-burning case in St. Paul, Minnesota, by the defendant's lawyer, who argued the case before the Supreme Court.

Clinton, Robert L., *Marbury v. Madison and Judicial Review*. Lawrence: University Press of Kansas, 1989. This book provides a brief but insightful discussion of the *Marbury* decision in 1803 and the doctrine of judicial review of legislation.

Craig, Barbara H., and David M. O'Brien, *Abortion and American Politics*. New York: Chatha House, 1993. This book provides a good account and analysis of the political factors that surround the abortion issue, although it is now somewhat dated.

Dionne, E.J., and William Kristol, eds., *Bush v. Gore: The Court Cases and the Commentary*. Washington, DC: The Brookings Institution, 2001. Edited by two journalists, one liberal and the other conservative, this book includes essays on both sides of the political and judicial conflicts over the 2000 presidential election.

Dreyfuss, Joel, and Charles Lawrence III, *The Bakke Case: The Politics of Inequality*. New York: Harcourt Brace Jovanovich, 1979. A good recounting of the *Bakke* case, which dealt with affirmative action in medical school admissions; the book is sympathetic to the school's position.

Dunne, Gerald T., *Hugo Black and the Judicial Revolution*. New York: Simon & Schuster, 1977. This biography of Justice Black, who served from 1937 to 1971, closely examines his opinions in First Amendment cases.

Eisler, Kim Isaac, *A Justice for All: William J. Brennan, Jr., and the Decisions That Transformed America*. New York, Simon & Schuster, 1992. There is not yet a solid biography of Justice Brennan, who served from 1956 to 1990; this book is both admiring and thin in detail.

Eskridge, Jr., William, *Gaylaw: Challenging the Apartheid of the Closet*. Cambridge: Harvard University Press, 2002. This book, by a Yale law professor who is also a gay rights advocate, provides an up-to-date and well-written account of cases in this area.

Fehrenbacher, Don, *Slavery, Law, and Politics: The Dred Scott Case in Historical Perspective*. New York: Oxford University Press, 1981. This book is a readable abridgment of Fehrenbacher's massive and magisterial book, *The Dred Scott Case*, published in 1978.

Fine, Sidney, *Laissez Faire and the General-Welfare State*. Ann Arbor: University of Michigan Press, 1956. A fine historical account of 19th-century political and legal debates over conflicting views of government's role in regulating the economy.

Foner, Eric, *Reconstruction: America's Unfinished Revolution, 1867–1877*. New York: Oxford University Press, 1988. This lengthy book is the best historical account of the Reconstruction period, with a wealth of detail and perceptive analysis of this crucial period in American history.

Freyer, Tony, *The Little Rock Crisis*. Westport, CT: Greenwood Press, 1984. The primary focus of this book is on the legal battles over school integration in Little Rock, Arkansas, which led to an important Supreme Court decision in 1958 in *Cooper v. Aaron*.

Garrow, David, *Liberty and Sexuality: The Right to Privacy and the Making of Roe v. Wade*. New York: Macmillan, 1994. Based on numerous interviews and the papers of groups on both sides of the abortion debate, this is the best account of the cases that preceded and followed the *Roe* decision in 1973.

Goldman, Robert M., *Reconstruction and Black Suffrage: Losing the Vote in Reese and Cruikshank*. Lawrence: University of Kansas Press, 2001. This brief account of the Court's rulings in two Reconstruction-era cases that involved black voting rights is short on historical context, but provides a good analysis of the decisions and their impact.

Goldstein, Robert J., *Flag Burning and Free Speech: The Case of Texas v. Johnson*. Lawrence: University Press of Kansas, 2000. A brief but well-written account of the Texas flag-burning case, which explores the legal background and political context of this issue.

Greenberg, Jack, *Crusaders in the Courts*. New York: Basic Books, 1994. A fascinating insider's memoir of civil rights cases from the 1950s to the 1980s, by the lawyer who succeeded Thurgood Marshall as general counsel of the NAACP Legal Defense and Education Fund.

Highsaw, Robert B., *Edward Douglass White: Defender of the Conservative Faith*. Baton Rouge: Louisiana State University Press, 1981. A largely sympathetic biography of the chief justice who served from 1910 to 1921, after 16 years as an associate justice.

Hyman, Harold M., *A More Perfect Union: The Impact of the Civil War and Reconstruction on the Constitution*. New York: Houghton

Mifflin, 1975. A noted historian of the Reconstruction era offers a detailed account and analysis of the Court's rulings on cases that dealt with blacks and the Civil War amendments.

Irons, Peter, *A People's History of the Supreme Court.* New York: Viking, 1999. A comprehensive account of the Court's major decisions from its founding through 1992, with a focus on the social and political context of the cases and the people who began them.

————, *Brennan Vs. Rehnquist: The Battle for the Constitution.* New York: Knopf, 1994. Based on opinions written in some 100 cases by Justices Brennan and Rehnquist, this book explores their different approaches to the Constitution.

————, *Jim Crow's Children: The Broken Promise of the Brown Decision.* New York: Viking, 2002. An account of the legal struggle over segregated education from 1849 to the present, with a focus on the Court's role in the "resegregation" of American schools and the continuing impact of Jim Crow education on African Americans.

————, *Justice Delayed: The Record of the Japanese American Internment Cases.* Wesleyan, CT: Wesleyan University Press, 1989. This book includes the Supreme Court opinions in the wartime internment cases, and the petitions and decisions in the reopening and reversal of these cases in the 1980s.

————, *Justice at War: The Story of the Japanese American Internment Cases.* New York: Oxford University Press, 1983. This book examines the cases that arose from the mass internment of Japanese Americans during World War II and factors that affected the Court's decisions upholding the internment, including the government's suppression of evidence.

————, *The Courage of Their Convictions: Sixteen Americans Who Fought Their Way to the Supreme Court.* New York: Free Press, 1989. This book includes essays about 16 important cases decided by the Court between 1940 and 1986 and fascinating first-person accounts by the people—from Lillian Gobitis to Michael Hardwick—who initiated these cases.

————, *The New Deal Lawyers*. Princeton: Princeton University Press, 1982. This account of the cases that tested New Deal laws during the first term of President Franklin Roosevelt focuses on the differing litigation strategies of government lawyers who brought these cases to the Court.

Jacobs, Clyde, *The Eleventh Amendment and Sovereign Immunity*. Westport, CT: Greenwood, 1972. Based on the Court's decision in *Chisholm v. Georgia* in 1793, this book recounts the political reaction to that ruling and its later reversal by the Eleventh Amendment.

Johnson, John W., *The Struggle for Student Rights: Tinker v. Des Moines and the 1960s*. Lawrence: University Press of Kansas, 1997. An excellent account of the case that upheld the right of public school students to wear black armbands to protest the Vietnam War.

Kens, Paul, *Lochner v. New York: Economic Regulation on Trial*. Lawrence: University Press of Kansas, 1998. This book offers a brief account of the Court's ruling in the landmark *Lochner* case of 1905, striking down a state maximum-hours law for bakers.

King, Willard L. *Melville Weston Fuller: Chief Justice of the United States, 1888–1910*. New York: Macmillan, 1950. A solid but dry biography of the eighth chief justice, with little attention to the political and social factors that affected the Court's decisions during Fuller's tenure.

Kluger, Richard, *Simple Justice: The History of Brown v. Board of Education*. New York: Knopf, 1976. This is a massive and exhaustive recounting of the five school segregation cases decided as *Brown v. Board of Education* in 1954, based on dozens of interviews with participants in the cases; this book is indispensable for understanding the *Brown* case.

Kutler, Stanley I., *Privilege and Creative Destruction: The Charles River Bridge Case*. Philadelphia: Lippincott, 1971. A relatively brief but insightful account of the case decided in 1837 that upheld a state legislature's power to undo a state-chartered monopoly.

————, *The Wars of Watergate*. New York: Knopf, 1990. This book provides an exhaustive account of the Watergate affair, including the Court's decision in 1974 to uphold a lower-court order that President Nixon turn over the "smoking gun" tape recordings.

Leuchtenberg, William E., *The Supreme Court Reborn: The Constitutional Revolution in the Age of Roosevelt*. New York:

Oxford University Press, 1995. A noted historian of the Roosevelt era argues in this book that the "Constitutional Revolution" of 1937 was less a judicial reaction to FDR's electoral victory in 1936 than a rethinking of constitutional doctrine.

Lewis, Anthony, *Gideon's Trumpet*. New York: Random House, 1964. This short and readable book tells the story of Clarence Earl Gideon, whose hand-written petition from prison resulted in a landmark decision on the right to counsel in all criminal cases.

Lewis, Walker, *Without Fear or Favor: A Biography of Chief Justice Roger Brooke Taney*. Boston: Houghton Mifflin, 1965. This biography of Taney, who served from 1836 to 1864, is largely admiring and does not subject his 1857 opinion in the *Dred Scott* case to critical analysis.

Lofgren, Charles, *The Plessy Case: A Legal-Historical Interpretation*. New York: Oxford University Press, 1987. This book offers a fairly dry and legalistic account of the Court's 1896 decision in *Plessy v. Ferguson*, upholding Jim Crow laws and the separate but equal doctrine.

Madison, James, *Notes of Debates in the Federal Convention of 1787*. Adrienne Koch, ed. Athens: Ohio University Press, 1966. Madison took detailed notes of the debates at the Constitutional Convention between May and September of 1787; this is an invaluable resource and an important historical document.

Magrath, C. Peter, *Morrison Waite: The Triumph of Character*. New York: Macmillan, 1963. This biography of the seventh chief justice, who served from 1874 to 1878, presents an admiring view of a man who showed little support for the rights of black Americans.

Mason, Alpheus T., *Brandeis: A Free Man's Life*. New York: Viking, 1946. This first biography of Justice Louis Brandeis, by a noted historian, provides much detail on his legal career and judicial opinions, but lacks a larger context of his role as a critic of "bigness" in American business and government.

————, *Harlan Fiske Stone: Pillar of the Law*. New York: Viking, 1956. This is an excellent biography of an important justice, who served as chief from 1940 to 1946 and who originated the strict scrutiny test to protect minorities and dissenters.

————, *William Howard Taft: Chief Justice*. New York: Simon & Schuster, 1964. This biography of the only man to serve as president and chief justice is less detailed and insightful than Mason's biography of Stone, perhaps reflecting the author's sympathies.

Mee, Charles L., *The Genius of the People*. New York: Harper & Row, 1987. A good popular account of the Constitutional Convention of 1787, with more attention to the delegates' personalities than their debates over contentious issues.

Murphy, Bruce A., *Wild Bill: The Legend and Life of William O. Douglas*. New York: Random House, 2003. An exhaustive and readable biography of the iconoclastic and liberal justice who served between 1939 and 1975.

Nelson, William E., *Marbury v. Madison: The Origins and Legacy of Judicial Review*. Lawrence: University Press of Kansas, 2000. A brief and excellent account of the landmark decision in 1803 in which Chief Justice John Marshall forcefully asserted the Court's power to strike down congressional statutes.

Novick, Sheldon, *Honorable Justice*. Boston: Little Brown, 1989. This biography of Justice Oliver Wendell Holmes focuses almost exclusively on his judicial career, and provides little insight into his personality and philosophy.

O'Brien, David, *Storm Center: The Supreme Court in American Politics*. New York: Norton, 4th ed., 1996. More of a textbook than a popular study of the Court, this book includes a wealth of detail on the Court's operations and the political context of its decisions.

Paul, Arnold M., *Conservative Crisis and the Rule of Law*. New York: Peter Smith, 1990. This is a short but very insightful discussion of laissez-faire jurisprudence in the late 19th and early 20th century.

Peters, Shawn F., *Judging Jehovah's Witnesses: Religious Persecution and the Dawn of the Rights Revolution*. Lawrence: University Press of Kansas, 2001. A brief and gripping account of the cases that involved Jehovah's Witnesses in the 1930s and 1940s, including the *Cantwell*, *Gobitis*, and *Barnette* cases.

©2003 The Teaching Company Limited Partnership

Peters, William, *A More Perfect Union*. New York: Crown Publishers, 1987. Much like the book by Charles Mee, this recounting of the Constitutional Convention of 1787 is readable but offers little analysis of the process by which the Constitution was drafted.

Polenberg, Richard, *Fighting Faiths: The Abrams Case, the Supreme Court, and Free Speech*. New York Viking, 1987. An excellent historical account of an important free speech case, decided in 1919, in which the Court upheld the convictions of Russian immigrants for criticizing American military intervention in that country's civil war.

Rehnquist, William H., *Grand Inquests: The Historic Impeachments of Justice Samuel Chase and President Andrew Johnson*. New York: William Morrow, 1992. Chief Justice Rehnquist sheds his judicial robe to write as an historian about the impeachments of Justice Chase and President Johnson; he relies largely on published sources in recounting these episodes.

Savage, David, *Turning Right: The Making of the Rehnquist Court*. New York: John Wiley, 1992. This book, by a *Los Angeles Times* reporter who covered the Court, offers a readable—and largely critical—account of the Court's rightward turn under Chief Justice Rehnquist.

Schwartz, Bernard, *A History of the Supreme Court*. New York: Oxford University Press, 1993. This book recounts the Court's decisions in landmark cases from a narrow perspective, staying largely inside the Court's chambers and focusing on internal debates over opinions.

———, *Super Chief*. New York: Oxford University Press, 1983. This lengthy account of the Court under Chief Justice Earl Warren details the back-and-forth circulation of draft opinions before decisions are announced, with little attention to the political and social context of the cases.

———, *Swann's Way: The School Busing Case and the Supreme Court*. New York: Oxford University Press, 1986. This account of the Court's 1971 decision upholding school busing to remedy segregation focuses more on the Court's internal deliberations than on the volatile politics of the busing issue.

Schwartz, Herman, ed., *The Burger Years: Rights and Wrongs in the Supreme Court, 1969–1986*. New York: Viking, 1987. This collection of 15 essays by lawyers and journalists covers the major cases decided under Chief Justice Warren Burger; most authors are highly critical of Burger and the Court's rulings.

Smith, Craig R., *To Form a More Perfect Union: The Ratification of the Constitution and the Bill of Rights, 1787-1791*. Lanham, MD: University Press of America, 1993. This is a somewhat dry but useful account of the ratification debates over the Constitution and Bill of Rights.

Starr, Kenneth W., *First among Equals: The Supreme Court in American Life*. New York, Warner Books, 2002. Written by a former law clerk to Chief Justice Burger who later served as U.S. solicitor general and Whitewater special counsel, this readable book examines the major decisions of the Rehnquist Court from a conservative perspective.

Strum, Philippa, *Brandeis: Justice for the People*. Cambridge: Harvard University Press, 1984. This admiring biography of Justice Louis Brandeis, who served from 1916 to 1939, focuses on his career as a reformist lawyer and his judicial opinions supporting individual rights.

Sunstein, Cass R., *Democracy and the Problem of Free Speech*. New York: Free Press, 1993. A noted and prolific University of Chicago law professor argues that the First Amendment was designed primarily to protect "political" speech from government regulation.

Sunstein, Cass R., and Richard A. Epstein, eds., *The Vote: Bush, Gore, and the Supreme Court*. Chicago: University of Chicago Press, 2001. Two noted law professors, one liberal and the other conservative, have edited a good collection of essays on the legal issues raised by the 2000 presidential election.

Tushnet, Mark, *The NAACP's Legal Strategy against Segregated Education, 1925–1950*. Chapel Hill: University of North Carolina Press, 1987. Written by a former law clerk to Justice Thurgood Marshall, this book recounts the legal assault on Jim Crow schooling before the *Brown* decision.

Ungar, Sanford J., *The Papers and the Papers*. New York: Columbia University Press, 1972. A journalist's account of the *Pentagon Papers* case, in which the Court refused in 1971 to block newspapers from publishing excerpts of a secret government history of the Vietnam War.

Urofsky, Melvin I., *A March of Liberty: A Constitutional History of the United States*. New York: Knopf, 1988. A lengthy book that discusses hundreds of Supreme Court decisions and provides useful background on their political and social context.

———, *Felix Frankfurter: Judicial Restraint and Individual Liberties*. Boston: Twayne Publishing, 1992. The most readable biography of Justice Frankfurter, who served from 1939 to 1962 and whose judicial philosophy had contradictory elements.

———, *The Supreme Court Justices: A Biographical Dictionary*. New York: Garland Publishing, 1994. A useful collection of short essays on every Supreme Court justice from John Jay through Ruth Bader Ginsburg, who joined the Court in 1993.

White, G. Edward, *Earl Warren: A Public Life*. New York: Oxford University Press, 1982. This book provides an excellent account of Warren's life and career before he became Chief Justice in 1953, but it only skims the surface of his role on the Court and his judicial opinions.

Wiecek, William M., *The Sources of Antislavery Constitutionalism in America, 1760–1848*. Ithaca: Cornell University Press, 1977. This book examines the debates over the constitutionality of slavery and looks at the opposing views of the role of blacks as members of the body politic.

Williams, Juan, *Thurgood Marshall: American Revolutionary*. New York: Times Books, 1998. This book, by an African American journalist who knew Justice Marshall well, offers a good portrait of his career but does not make use of the Marshall papers in the Library of Congress.

Woodward, Bob, and Scott Armstrong, *The Brethren: Inside the Supreme Court*. New York: Simon & Schuster, 1979. Written by two *Washington Post* reporters, this book provides an inside-the-Court look at the debates over cases decided during the first decade of Chief Justice Burger's tenure, with a focus on conflicts between the justices.

©2003 The Teaching Company Limited Partnership